FAMILIES AND THE MENTAL HEALTH SYSTEM FOR CHILDREN AND ADOLESCENTS

CHILDREN'S MENTAL HEALTH SERVICES

Series Editor
LEONARD BICKMAN,
Peabody College, Vanderbilt University, Nashville

Series Associate Editor
DEBRA J. ROG,
Vanderbilt University, Washington, DC

The mental health needs of children have concerned policymakers and professionals for nearly a century. These concerns have intensified in recent years with increasing documentation on the magnitude of the problem and the extent to which children's mental health needs continue to be unmet. Sage's **Children's Mental Health Services Series** is aimed at addressing this need for systematic scholarly analysis of children's mental health needs and the policies and programs that serve them. Through involvement in constructing policy to system development to evaluation design, the esteemed authors of these volumes represent pioneers in the development of systems of care. It is our hope that these contributions will provide a rich basis for thought, discussion, and action.

In this series:

1. Children's Mental Health Services: Research, Policy, and Evaluation
   edited by Leonard Bickman and Debra J. Rog

2. Families and the Mental Health System for Children and Adolescents: Policy, Services, and Research
   edited by Craig Anne Heflinger and Carol T. Nixon

FAMILIES AND THE MENTAL HEALTH SYSTEM FOR CHILDREN AND ADOLESCENTS

Policy, Services, and Research

Craig Anne Heflinger and Carol T. Nixon
Editors

CMHS Children's Mental Health Services, Volume 2

SAGE Publications
International Educational and Professional Publisher
Thousand Oaks London New Delhi

For information address:

SAGE Publications, Inc.
2455 Teller Road
Thousand Oaks, California 91320
E-mail: order@sagepub.com

SAGE Publications Ltd.
6 Bonhill Street
London EC2A 4PU
United Kingdom

SAGE Publications India Pvt. Ltd.
M-32 Market
Greater Kailash I
New Delhi 110 048 India

Printed in the United States of America

Library of Congress Cataloging-in-Publication Data

Main entry under title:

Families and the mental health system for children and adolescents: Policy, services, and research / editors, Craig Anne Heflinger, Carol T. Nixon.
p. cm. — (Children's mental health services; v. 2)
Includes bibliographical references and index.
ISBN 0-7619-0267-8 (acid-free paper). — ISBN 0-7619-0268-6 (pbk.: acid-free paper)
1. Child mental health services. 2. Teenagers—Mental health services. 3. Family—Mental health services. I. Heflinger, Craig Anne. II. Nixon, Carol T. III. Series.
RJ499.F36 1996
362.2'0835—dc20 95-50162

96 97 98 99 10 9 8 7 6 5 4 3 2 1

This book is printed on acid-free paper.

Sage Production Editor: Diana E. Axelsen
Sage Typesetter: Joe Cribben

Contents

Preface vii

1. Family Issues in Health Care Reform 1
Sheila A. Pires
Beth A. Stroul

2. Family-Centered Services for Children With Emotional, Behavioral, and Mental Disorders 18
Richard W. Hunter
Barbara J. Friesen

3. A Family-Focused Model of Prevention 41
George W. Albee
Silvia Sara Canetto

4. Implementing Community Mental Health Programs: Lessons Learned From the Mental Health Initiative for Urban Children 63
Mary C. Telesford

5. Families of Children and Adolescents With Serious Emotional Disturbance: Innovations in Theory, Research, and Practice 75
Diane T. Marsh

6. Family Empowerment: A Conceptual Model for Promoting Parent-Professional Partnership 96
Craig Anne Heflinger
Leonard Bickman

7. Family Research Methods: Issues and Strategies 117
Joan M. Patterson

8. The Colorado Family Assessment: A Computer-Based Procedure for Multilevel Family Evaluation 145
Bernard L. Bloom

9. The Cultural Competence Model: Implications for Child and Family Mental Health Services 165
James L. Mason
Marva P. Benjamin
Sarah A. Lewis

10. Alternate Paths to Family Status and Implications for Mental Health Service Delivery and Policy: Adoptive and Foster Families 191
Ellen E. Pinderhughes

11. Mental Health Services for Rural Children, Youth, and Their Families 217
Carolyn E. Cutrona
Marcy B. J. Halvorson
Daniel W. Russell

Index 239

About the Editors 251

About the Contributors 253

Preface

A major issue confronting the mental health service system for children and adolescents is the role of the family. The family plays both direct and indirect roles in the formal mental health services sector, from determining whether and when the child enters treatment to providing the context within which all therapeutic gains are played out. Attention to the needs of families is a growing policy concern, and policymakers and advocates alike are placing more emphasis on formalizing the role of the family in the social policy arena. This volume describes a myriad of policy, research, and practice issues related to families of children with serious emotional disorders.

In Chapter 1, Sheila Pires and Beth Stroul discuss principles to guide health care reform and implementation challenges related to children with mental health and behavioral problems and their families. The uniqueness of the child population within the context of the family demands special attention as policymakers, researchers, and professionals examine alternative approaches to health care.

The next three chapters review services for families that go beyond the traditional mental health service approach that focuses almost solely on the individual child with the problem. Richard Hunter and Barbara Friesen (Chapter 2) describe characteristics, examples, and service strategies for family-centered service delivery. Family-focused therapeutic services, parent educational services, family support, and service coordination are among the recommended strategies. George Albee and Silvia Sara Canetto (Chapter 3) highlight the role that society can play in strengthening the family and preventing child and adolescent emotional disorders. They propose a public health model of primary prevention that emphasizes working with high-risk families and environmental forces that negatively affect family life. Mary Telesford (Chapter 4) describes the Mental Health Initiative for Urban Children, funded by the Annie E. Casey Foundation and started by the Federation of Families for Children's Mental Health. In developing and implementing the broad-based community programs, the initiative aims at recognizing and building on community and individual strengths and using a comprehensive outreach strategy.

Chapters 5 and 6 continue the discussion on family-focused practice by examining theoretical underpinnings to enhance intervention and research in this area. Diane Marsh (Chapter 5) describes a competence paradigm focusing on family strengths that emphasizes the ecological and systems perspective. Craig Anne Heflinger and Leonard Bickman (Chapter 6) review the supports for and barriers inhibiting parent-professional partnership and propose a conceptual model for promoting and evaluating family empowerment.

The next two chapters focus on research issues. Joan Patterson (Chapter 7) discusses the importance of definitional clarity, theoretically grounded research, and rigorous design. Bernard Bloom (Chapter 8) reviews the complexity of assessing family functioning and describes a computer-based approach that allows multiple levels of measurement.

Chapter 9 through 11 continue the focus on service, policy, and research issues related to families and the mental health system for children and adolescents by examining specific topics. James Mason, Marva Benjamin, and Sarah Lewis (Chapter 9) discuss the barriers that currently exist to culturally sensitive and competent service delivery. They present an approach for professional and organizational change. Ellen Pinderhughes (Chapter 10) highlights the needs of families who have taken an alternative path to family status, specifically through adoption and fostering. Carolyn Cutrona, Marcy Halvorson, and Daniel Russell (Chapter 11) review the difficulties that children and families in rural areas have had in accessing appropriate services and provide examples of overcoming barriers.

Several themes run throughout this volume. First is the recognition of the importance of families and the need to improve practice, research, and policy approaches to child and adolescent mental health service delivery. Second, a focus on family strengths is combined with a recognition of the complexity and diversity of families. Third, recommendations for improving actions at the face-to-face level of service delivery are accompanied by a call for system reform at the societal and policy level. Finally, to meet the diverse needs of children, youth, and their families more appropriately, a broad array of services is called for.

This volume is dedicated to families: those with whom we work, those who participate in our research, and specifically, those with whom we live. We hope that these chapters provide helpful information and support to those who work to improve services to and the quality of life of children and adolescents with emotional and behavioral problems and their families.

—CRAIG ANNE HEFLINGER
—CAROL T. NIXON

Family Issues in Health Care Reform

SHEILA A. PIRES
BETH A. STROUL

The most recent epidemiological estimates suggest that approximately 14% to 20% of all children from birth to age 18 have some type of emotional disorder, and about 3% to 5% of all children have a serious disorder (Brandenburg, Friedman, & Silver, 1990; Costello, Burns, Angold, & Leaf, 1993). Although these estimates may reflect the need for mental health services, current use levels are significantly lower, with only approximately 2% of all children currently using mental health services (Burns, 1991). It is estimated that 70% to 90% of children with severe disorders are not receiving mental health services (Costello et al., 1993; MECA, 1993).

Low use rates for children and adolescents are attributable to several factors, including denial that problems exist, the stigma attached to emotional disorders that discourages families from seeking treatment for their children, lack of early identification and intervention efforts for emotional disorders, scarcity and inappropriateness of services, and lack of adequate insurance coverage coupled with the inability to pay for services. Health care reform is an important mechanism for addressing many of these problems.

Whether implemented at state or national levels, health care reform presents an opportunity to restructure insurance coverage for mental health disorders, increase the availability and appropriateness of services, promote early identification, reduce the stigma of mental illness, and reduce financial risk to families. To fulfill this promise, a number of issues must be considered, including the uniqueness of the child population, the need to view children in a family context, and barriers that families traditionally have encountered in obtaining services for their children who have emotional problems. Further, principles must be considered that address important policy goals for health care reform. Finally, regardless of the specific plan for health care reform that is adopted, implementation challenges are inevitable and should be anticipated. This chapter discusses issues to consider in health care reform, principles for health care reform, and implementation challenges—all of which are critical to effective service delivery to children and adolescents with emotional disorders and their families.

Issues to Consider in Health Care Reform

Uniqueness of the Population and Family Context

Children with emotional disorders are a diverse group that differs from adult populations in several important ways (Frank & Dewa, 1991). Recognition of these distinctions is a fundamental consideration in health care reform.

Children as a group span a broad developmental range and present with highly variable problems, from infants with attachment disorders to adolescents with comorbid emotional and substance abuse disorders. Their service needs are complex and change rapidly relative to the needs of adult populations (Lynch, 1991). Often, children with emotional disorders are involved in multiple service delivery systems, such as the education, child welfare, and juvenile justice systems. Such children not only require support services from these agencies, as do adults from other systems, but also have unique legal relationships with these systems.

Most important, children must be served in the context of their families. Parents (perhaps both natural and foster parents), siblings, and often extended family members play key roles in the lives of children. The needs and wishes of families must be an integral consideration throughout the planning and delivery of services for children with emotional disorders. Historically, the health care system has not adequately accounted for either the unique characteristics of the child and adolescent population or the concerns of families. (See Hunter & Friesen, Chapter 2 in this volume, for discussion of family-centered services.)

Problems With Current Insurance Benefit Structures

Traditional insurance benefit structures are particularly remiss in their failure to take into account the complexity and variability of the population of children with emotional disorders and their families (Lynch, 1991). Typically limited to acute care coverage for inpatient hospitalization and brief office-based psychotherapy, today's benefit structures result in an overreliance on costly inpatient care (Frank & Dewa, 1991). This poses problems not only for families who cannot afford the cost of care and/or who do not want to see their children hospitalized when a less restrictive alternative would suffice but for the larger society as well.

Excessive and inappropriate hospitalization of children and adolescents has been the major factor in driving up the total cost of mental health care in the last decade (Frank, Salkever, & Sharfstein, 1991; Knitzer, 1988). Typical benefit structures have encouraged the development of excess inpatient capacity in many areas of the country, while at the same time discouraging the development of alternative home- and community-based service options by failing to cover them (Knitzer, 1988). For families, traditional benefit design has meant a lack of home and community treatment options and often inappropriate treatment for their children (Lynch, 1991).

An important lesson learned from current benefit design is that limiting the array of covered services does not equate to limiting costs. By the same token, limiting the array of covered services also fails to encourage use of the most effective treatment modalities.

Research on treatment efficacy shows that the largest proportion of resources are allocated to service settings, namely, inpatient and residential treatment, for which there is the least evidence of effectiveness on the basis of controlled trials (Burns & Friedman, 1990).

Exclusionary Coverage and High Consumer Cost Sharing

In addition to the tendency of traditional insurance to limit the types of services that are covered to hospitalization and office-based psychotherapy, the insurance industry typically also excludes from coverage individuals who have so-called preexisting conditions. Thus, a family with a child who has a previously diagnosed emotional disorder might be unable to obtain coverage. This is problematic both for families without any insurance coverage and for families in which the insured wage earner wishes to change jobs. Switching jobs may mean losing insurance coverage for the family. According to President Clinton's Task Force on Health Care Reform, nearly 20% of Americans lack insurance coverage for mental illness, and more than 100,000 Americans currently lose their insurance coverage every month.

Even when families have mental health coverage, typically they pay more for this coverage out-of-pocket than for physical health care. Mental health benefit design traditionally imposes high cost sharing on the consumer through copayments for the use of some services and high annual out-of-pocket limits (Frank, Goldman, & McGuire, 1992). Higher cost sharing for mental health services in traditional benefit design indirectly reinforces the stigma attached to mental illness. At the same time, it discourages families from seeking treatment. By failing to provide incentives to families to seek early intervention services, traditional benefit design also fails to maximize the chances for successful outcomes.

Cost sharing and benefit limits for mental health services, although historically employed in benefit design to control costs, work against ending incentives to use more restrictive and expensive service components, namely, hospital care. They also fail to protect families from the cost of, and current fragmented response to, catastrophic illness

(Frank et al., 1992). Families of youngsters with serious emotional disorders remain at great financial risk.

Fragmented Delivery System

Limited insurance coverage and traditional benefit design have been major factors in shifting care and costs to public child-serving systems (Frank et al., 1992). The current mental health delivery system is fragmented, two-tiered, and two-class (Arons, Frank, Goldman, McGuire, & Stephens, 1994). Families who are poor, who lack adequate insurance, and whose children have extended treatment needs must turn to the public system.

For children and their families, the public system is, in reality, multiple systems—mental health, child welfare, juvenile justice, education, and health. The education, child welfare, and juvenile justice systems, in particular, bear a disproportionate share of the cost of providing mental health services for children because of their legal mandates to serve children. State data, for example, indicate that these three public systems bear more than 90% of the cost of residential treatment centers for children and adolescents involved in public systems (National Mental Health Association, 1989). Yet none of these systems have designated mental health funding streams, nor are they structured or intended to be health care providers. The child welfare, education, and juvenile justice systems frequently provide the only avenue to mental health services for families who do not have private insurance or who have exhausted their insurance coverage. As a consequence, families often must resort to perverse means to secure mental health treatment for their children, including relinquishing custody to the child welfare system or suing the education system to obtain needed services (Cohen, Harris, Gottlieb, & Best, 1991; Ervin, 1992).

In a national study (Research and Training Center on Family Support and Children's Mental Health, 1989), one out of four parents of children with serious emotional disorders reported having been asked to give up custody of the child to obtain services. Only 29 states had provisions for voluntary placement whereby parents could retain full legal custody of their children. An unsuccessful class action suit was filed on behalf of New York State children challenging a state law requiring parental relinquishment of custody as a condition of admission to residential treatment centers at state expense (Research and Training Center on Family Support and Children's Mental Health, 1989). Recently, several states, including Oregon, Minnesota, and Maine, have enacted legislation to abolish parental relinquishment requirements as a condition to obtain treatment services, but the problem remains widespread (Cohen et al., 1991; Ervin, 1992).

Principles for Children in Health Care Reform

Several goals or principles have special significance for children and adolescents and their families in health care reform. These principles guided the development of the recommendations of the Mental Health and Substance Abuse Working Group of President Clinton's Task Force on Health Care Reform (Plaut & Arons, 1994; Stroul, Pires, Katz-Leavy, & Goldman, 1994). These principles encompass the following:

- Universal coverage
- Elimination of exclusions for preexisting conditions
- Inclusion in the benefit design of a broad array of home- and community-based services, moving beyond the traditional outpatient and inpatient care
- Encouragement of alternatives to hospitalization and service provision in the least restrictive environment appropriate to the needs of the individual
- Provision of organized systems of care for children with serious emotional disorders and their families
- Mechanisms to ensure the appropriate use of services, regardless of the type of health plan, so that consumers receive the appropriate scope, volume, and duration of services commensurate with their needs and the severity of their illness
- Provision of mental health services on the same terms and conditions as other health services, with the same copayments, deductibles, and day or visit limits

Two of the principles are of critical importance for children with emotional disorders and their families—providing coverage for a broad array of services and providing organized systems of care. These fundamental issues are discussed below.

Coverage for a Broad Array of Services

The emphasis on covering a broad array of home- and community-based services and encouraging the use of alternatives to hospitalization in health care reform directly addresses the most pressing problems (from both clinical and economic perspectives) in the current service delivery environment. The mental health coverage proposed by the Mental Health and Substance Abuse Working Group of President Clinton's Task Force on Health Care Reform (Plaut & Arons, 1994; Stroul, Pires, Katz-Leavy, & Goldman, 1994) encompasses a broad range of services:

- Inpatient and residential care that will cover hospital care or 24-hour care in other residential environments such as therapeutic family homes, therapeutic group homes, crisis residential facilities, residential detoxification centers, and residential treatment centers
- Intensive nonresidential services that include a range of services as alternatives to hospitalization—day treatment, partial hospitalization, psychiatric rehabilitation, ambulatory detoxification programs, home-based services, and behavioral aides
- Outpatient care that includes such services as assessment, crisis services, psychotherapy, substance abuse counseling and relapse prevention, medical management, somatic treatments, collateral services, and case management

The inclusion of this expanded range of services in health care reform is perhaps the most significant step forward in mental health coverage for children yet is not well understood. The intensive nonresidential services, in particular, represent state-of-the-art service technologies. These services are increasingly used for children with serious emotional disorders on the basis of the recognition that psychotherapy alone has been ineffective in averting the need for treatment in hospitals and other residential settings and equally ineffective in maximizing level of functioning in the community for children with serious disorders. The intensive nonresidential interventions specified by the working group move beyond the boundaries of traditional, office-based psychotherapy and provide high levels of therapeutic interventions and support, maximizing the use of normalized environments.

To illustrate, day treatment and partial hospitalization programs for children and adolescents provide intensive treatment, education, family involvement, and support while enabling youngsters to remain at home. Provided in a variety of settings, day treatment and partial hospitalization programs generally employ a multifaceted intervention approach (including individual and group counseling, individualized education, family counseling and support, skill building, recreational therapy, and crisis intervention), and program staff work with youngsters for many hours on a daily basis (Isaacs & Goldman, 1985).

Home-based services provide therapists to work with families when a youngster is in imminent danger of out-of-home placement in hospitals or other residential treatment settings. Counselors work intensively with families, sometimes for 10 to 20 hours a week, to help stabilize the crisis, to link the child and family with clinical services and supports, and to strengthen the child's and family's coping skills and capacity to function effectively in the community. The interventions are delivered primarily in the family's home, and the hours of service delivery are flexible to meet the needs of the family. Home-based services are multifaceted and include counseling and skill training. Providers help the family to obtain and coordinate necessary services, resources, and supports. Often, 24-hour crisis intervention is provided (Stroul, 1988).

Behavioral aides can provide the extra supervision, assistance, and support needed by a child at home or in school. These services involve using a trained worker under clinical supervision to assist an individual youngster and the other persons involved in the youngster's care and treatment. Behavioral aides can spend a specified number of hours in the home to assist a child and family during difficult times during the day, they may be assigned to the classroom to support the teacher in managing the youngster's behavior and educational program, and they may assist in the day-to-day implementation of therapeutic programs designed by a youngster's therapist and treatment team. Behavioral aides have proven extremely effective in averting the need for hospitalization or other types of residential placements (Katz-Leavy, Lourie, Stroul, & Zeigler-Dendy, 1992).

One of the residential services that is particularly important for children is therapeutic family homes. This approach involves providing treatment in the homes of trained families within the community. Treatment parents in these homes are seen as the primary therapeutic agents and are specially trained, licensed, and clinically supervised. Clinical, supportive, and case management services are provided to each child, treatment family, and natural family (Stroul, 1989).

Coverage for collateral services (services to family members), allowing for the involvement of families in planning and delivering care to youngsters with emotional disorders, also is essential in health care reform. Similarly, coverage for case management services is critically important for children with serious mental disorders. Case management plays a pivotal role in accessing and coordinating the services needed by youngsters with serious disorders as well as services needed by their families; it also is crucial to the coordination of mental health service delivery with other systems involved in children's care, such as the education and child welfare systems and health care providers.

Thus, the family of a child with an emotional disorder might avoid having to hospitalize their child if the family has access to a day treatment program, home-based services, or behavioral aides. If an out-of-home placement is needed, in many cases, therapeutic family homes or other community-based residential options can substitute for more restrictive and expensive inpatient and residential environments.

These services are not intended to be provided in isolation; they are provided in conjunction with medical management, medication, and psychotherapy when appropriate, as well as hospitalization if needed. They are important components in the continuum of care for children that will become more widely available only if they are covered services in a reformed health care system.

Coverage for a wide range of service options would begin to shift current perverse incentives away from expensive and restrictive treatment environments and encourage the development and use of alternatives. This type of coverage in a reformed health care system would allow families and mental health professionals far greater flexibility in designing appropriate plans of care for children with emotional disorders.

Organized Systems of Care for Children

Another especially critical principle for benefit design in health care reform advanced by the Mental Health and Substance Abuse Working Group is that of ensuring that children and adolescents with serious emotional disorders are served within organized systems of care. This principle reflects both a historical movement and recent promising innovations in service system implementation.

Calls for the development of comprehensive, community-based systems of care for youngsters with mental health disorders date to the Joint Commission on the Mental Health of Children (1969). Numerous studies, task forces, commissions, and reports since then have reiterated that coordinated systems of care providing a range of services are required to serve these children and their families more effectively (President's Commission on Mental Health, 1978; Saxe, Cross, & Silverman, 1986).

Organized systems of care emphasize comprehensive and individualized services that are provided in the least restrictive environment, full participation of families, cultural competence, an organized network of community-based providers, management mechanisms, and coordination across multiple providers and child-serving systems (Stroul & Friedman, 1986). Despite calls for such systems of care, until recently there were few examples of local systems of care principally because of the lack of financial incentives for coordinated care approaches in the delivery system (Stroul, 1993).

During the past decade, a number of federal, state, local, and foundation-supported activities have coalesced and resulted in significant progress toward the development of systems of care. In 1984, the National Institute of Mental Health launched the Child and Adolescent Service System Program (CASSP), which has provided grants and technical assistance to states and communities to assist them in developing community-based systems of care. A number of states have assumed leadership in developing such systems on a demonstration or statewide basis. Further, system building has been enhanced by national foundation initiatives, such as the Robert Wood

Johnson Foundation's Mental Health Services Program for Youth and the Annie E. Casey Foundation's Urban Mental Health Initiative for Children. As a result, many communities now have evolving systems of care that can be described and studied (Stroul, 1993; Stroul, Lourie, Goldman, & Katz-Leavy, 1992).

Emerging data and research on organized systems of care are documenting improvements in clinical and functional outcomes and cost efficiency (Stroul, 1993). Specifically, systems of care are associated with reductions in out-of-home and out-of-community placements (Illback, 1993; Rugs, 1992; Vermont Department of Mental Health and Mental Retardation, 1993); reduced reliance on restrictive service settings, such as hospitals and residential treatment centers (Behar, 1992; Bickman, 1993); functional improvements, such as a reduction in both internalizing problem behaviors (e.g., withdrawal, anxiety, and depression) and externalizing problem behaviors (e.g., aggression; Illback, 1993); improvements in such areas as educational status (Martinez & Smith, 1993; Virginia Department of Mental Health, Mental Retardation, and Substance Abuse Services, 1992) and reduced involvement with the juvenile justice system (Martinez & Smith, 1993; Rugs, 1992); high parent satisfaction ratings (Vermont Department of Mental Health and Mental Retardation, 1993; Virginia Department of Mental Health, Mental Retardation, and Substance Abuse Services, 1992); improved access to services (Behar, 1992; Bickman et al., 1995); and cost savings in comparison with traditional service delivery (Bickman, Heflinger, Pion, & Behar, 1992; Illback, 1993; Vermont Department of Mental Health and Mental Retardation, 1993).

Organized systems of care, especially as developed in the public sector, go beyond private sector managed care concepts, particularly in their emphasis on coordination across public child-serving systems, integration of public and private sector service provision, family involvement, and cultural competence. Without a specific mandate for inclusion of organized systems of care, they may be at risk in a reformed health system.

The Clinton Administration's Health Care Reform Plan

The health care reform legislation proposed by the Clinton administration in 1993, known as the Health Security Act, addressed a number of these principles for mental health service delivery to children and adolescents. First, as a result of its provisions for universal coverage and the elimination of exclusions for preexisting conditions, the legislation expanded coverage for mental health services to those who are currently uninsured and those with minimal or no mental health benefits.

Second, the act significantly expanded the range of services covered from those now covered by the typical private insurance policy. For children, in particular, this represented a major advance in that a far wider array of state-of-the-art approaches would be financed by the health care system. By covering a wider range of service options, the proposed benefit would begin to shift current perverse incentives away from expensive and restrictive treatment environments and encourage the development of alternatives.

Although the Health Security Act of 1993 incorporated a phased approach to mental health coverage and imposed day and visit limits and higher consumer cost sharing than for physical health care during an interim 5-year period, the act also incorporated the mandate that all interim limits and higher copayments be phased out by the year 2001. This is an extremely important mandate, embodying significant policy goals. This mandate would move the traditional system toward a flexible, managed mental health benefit that covers both acute and rehabilitative care. It embraces the goal of parity with physical illnesses for mental health coverage.

The mandate for comprehensive coverage in the Health Security Act of 1993 also embodies the important policy goal of ending the two-tiered, two-class nature of the current mental health delivery system. The legislation included an option for states to demonstrate this comprehensive approach to covering mental health through a pilot program, if they chose to do this earlier than the year 2001. In addition, the act required states to submit a plan to demonstrate how they would integrate public mental health services with the services included in the benefit package. Because most of the comprehensive, organized systems of care developed for children with serious emotional disorders have been under the auspices of public agencies, this provision would help ensure that consideration is given to incorporating systems of care into a new health care delivery system.

The final form of health care reform at the national level remains uncertain, and health care reform efforts at the state level may take many shapes as well. Regardless of the specific plans that emerge from the federal and state-level debates, consideration of these principles will be essential to ensure appropriate service delivery to children with emotional disorders and their families.

Implementation Challenges of Health Care Reform

Health care reform that embodies the principles and goals discussed in this chapter raises a number of implementation challenges that are inevitable in reforming the current system and are important to anticipate. A major challenge is related to the lack of infrastructure to provide the full continuum of services needed by children and adolescents that would be included in a redesigned mental health benefit package. Currently, service and workforce capacity is insufficient, particularly for the home- and community-based services, to meet the challenges of health care reform (Pires, 1992). Investments by both the public and private sectors to increase and develop service capacities, as well as to increase and train the child mental health workforce, will be essential to successfully implement health care reform. It will be particularly important in a reformed health care system that currently available appropriate services be included in provider networks. This is a special challenge in the children's area because mental health service capacity currently is spread across multiple public systems—mental health systems as well as child welfare, education, and juvenile justice systems. In addition, service capacity exists in a host of private, nonprofit agencies, which may provide services under contract to one or more of these public systems, and in the private, for-profit sector, with arrangements ranging from large firms to groups to sole practitioners. Ensuring that the most appropriate services are available, regardless of which sector or system currently "owns" them, will require a new level of collaboration among sectors and systems, as well as advocacy by consumers.

In a similar vein, the role of existing and new organized systems of care for youngsters with severe disorders has yet to be determined in relation to health plans and the way in which youngsters will access such organized systems when necessary. The public and private, for-profit sectors currently do not share a common framework for systems of care. The private sector historically has operated largely from an acute care perspective, providing a less extensive array of services than the public sector and little integration with public systems. For a truly integrated health care system, the two sectors will need to move to a closer shared understanding of the components and philosophy of organized systems of care for children.

Another significant challenge for a reformed system will be to guard against underserving those with serious disorders, particularly in managed care environments, which provide an incentive for favorable risk selection, that is, they are biased toward serving healthier populations because they are less costly to serve (Arons et al., 1994). Risk adjustment mechanisms compose one important means to deter underserving. In risk adjustment, health plans would receive additional payments for providing services to populations whose care is more costly, such as children with serious emotional disorders. There is limited experience with risk adjustment in the mental health arena, however; some degree of experimentation will be inevitable in health care reform in this area.

Quality assurance and monitoring mechanisms, coupled with consumer education and advocacy, also are essential to ensure that all children receive appropriate services. Families whose children have emotional disorders need to be actively engaged in the design, implementation, monitoring, and evaluation of health care reform initiatives.

Finally, the future of Medicaid in a reformed health care system will have profound implications for mental health service delivery to children and adolescents because Medicaid represents a major source of current funding for such services. States currently are especially reliant on Medicaid to help fund rehabilitative and extended care services. Constraints on Medicaid, in the absence of a comprehensive mental health benefit, could jeopardize services for children, especially for those with serious disorders. If a comprehensive benefit is mandated, Medicaid financing, along with state and local match dollars, must shift to an integrated system. This shift will require careful planning to ensure an adequate resource base for an integrated system (Arons et al., 1994).

Conclusion

Implementation of health care reform that embodies the principles and goals described here, although posing enormous challenges to all sectors and systems, public and private, also holds great promise for children with emotional disorders and their families. It provides opportunity to create coverage for catastrophic illness, to integrate the currently fragmented delivery system and make service delivery more efficient, to generate home- and community-based alternatives to restrictive and costly placements, and to create greater opportunity for families and providers to ensure appropriate care for children than the current system and traditional benefit designs allow.

References

Arons, B., Frank, R., Goldman, H., McGuire, T., & Stephens, S. (1994, Spring). Mental health and substance abuse coverage under health reform. *Health Affairs*, 192-205.

Behar, L. (1992). *Fort Bragg child and adolescent mental health demonstration project.* Raleigh: North Carolina Division of Mental Health, Developmental Disabilities, and Substance Abuse Services.

Bickman, L., Guthrie, P. R., Foster, E. M., Lambert, W., Summerfielt, W. T., Breda, C. S., & Heflinger, C. A. (1995). *Evaluation managed mental health services: The Fort Bragg Experiment.* New York, NY: Plenum.

Bickman, L., Heflinger, C. A., Pion, G., & Behar, L. (1992). Evaluation planning for an innovative children's mental health system. *Clinical Psychology Review, 12*(8), 853-865.

Brandenburg, N., Friedman, R., & Silver, S. (1990). The epidemiology of childhood psychiatric disorders: Prevalence findings from recent studies. *Journal of the American Academy of Child and Adolescent Psychiatry, 29*, 76-83.

Burns, B. (1991). Mental health service use by adolescents in the 1970s and 1980s. *Journal of the American Academy of Child and Adolescent Psychiatry, 30*, 144-150.

Burns, B., & Friedman, R. (1990). Examining the research base for child mental health services and policy. *Journal of Mental Health Administration, 17*, 87-98.

Cohen, R., Harris, R., Gottlieb, S., & Best, A. (1991). States' use of transfer of custody as a requirement for providing services to emotionally disturbed children. *Hospital and Community Psychiatry, 42*(5), 526-532.

Costello, E., Burns, B., Angold, A., & Leaf, P. (1993). How can epidemiology improve mental health services for children and adolescents? *Journal of the American Academy of Child and Adolescent Psychiatry, 32*(6), 1106-1117.

Ervin, C. (1992). Parents forced to surrender custody of children with neurobiological disorders. In E. Peschel, C. Howe, & J. Howe (Eds.), *Neurobiological disorders in children and adolescents* (New Directions for Mental Health Services, Vol. 54). San Francisco: Jossey-Bass.

Frank, R., & Dewa, C. (1991). Towards a research agenda on the economics of mental health care for children and adolescents. In A. Algarin & R. Friedman (Eds.), *A system of care for children's mental health: Expanding the research base: 4th annual research conference proceedings* (pp. 191-197). Tampa: University of South Florida, Florida Mental Health Institute, Research and Training Center for Children's Mental Health.

Frank, R., Goldman, H., McGuire, T. (1992, Fall). A model mental health benefit in private health insurance. *Health Affairs*, 98-117.

Frank, R., Salkever, D., & Sharfstein, S. (1991, Summer). A new look at rising mental health insurance costs. *Health Affairs*, 116-123.

Health Security Act, H.R. 3600, S. 1757, 103d Cong., 1st Sess. (1993).

Illback, R. (1993). *Evaluation of the Kentucky impact program for children and youth with severe emotional disturbances.* Frankfort, KY: Department for Mental Health and Mental Retardation, Division of Mental Health, Children and Youth Services Branch.

Isaacs, M., & Goldman, S. (1985). *Profiles of residential and day treatment programs for seriously emotionally disturbed youth.* Washington, DC: Georgetown University Child Development Center, National Technical Assistance Center for Children's Mental Health.

Joint Commission on the Mental Health of Children. (1969). *Crisis in child mental health.* New York: Harper & Row.

Katz-Leavy, J., Lourie, I., Stroul, B., & Zeigler-Dendy, C. (1992). *Individualized services in a system of care.* Washington, DC: Georgetown University Child Development Center, National Technical Assistance Center for Children's Mental Health.

Knitzer, J. (1988). Policy perspectives on the problem. In J. Looney (Ed.), *Chronic mental illness in children and adolescents.* Washington, DC: American Psychiatric Press.

Lynch, F. (1991). Providing family based services for children and adolescents with mental health problems: The potential of private health insurance. In A. Algarin & R. Friedman (Eds.), *A system of care for children's mental health: Expanding the research base: 4th annual research conference proceedings* (pp. 199-206). Tampa: University of South Florida, Florida Mental Health Institute, Research and Training Center for Children's Mental Health.

Martinez, M., & Smith, L. (1993). *The Family Mosaic Project: Report submitted to the Washington Business Group on Health.* San Francisco: Family Mosaic Project.

MECA. (1993). *Methodological epidemiological catchment area study: Preliminary findings.* Unpublished data, National Institute of Mental Health, Rockville, MD.

National Mental Health Association. (1989). *Report of the Invisible Children Project.* Washington, DC: Author.

Pires, S. (1992). *Staffing systems of care for children and families.* Columbia, SC: Southern Human Resource Development Consortium for Mental Health.

Plaut, T., & Arons, B. (1994). President Clinton's proposal for health care reform: Key provisions and issues. *Hospital and Community Psychiatry, 45*(9), 871-876.

President's Commission on Mental Health. (1978). *Report of the sub-task panel on infants, children and adolescents.* Washington, DC: Government Printing Office.

Research and Training Center on Family Support and Children's Mental Health. (1989, Summer). Barriers to accessing services: Relinquishing legal custody as a means of obtaining services for children with serious emotional disabilities. *Focal Point, 4*(2), 1-9. (Newsletter available from Portland State University, Regional Research Institute for Human Services, Portland, OR.)

Rugs, D. (1992). *Mountain State Network Project.* Unpublished report, University of South Florida at Tampa, Florida Mental Health Institute, Department of Child and Family Studies.

Saxe, L., Cross, T., & Silverman, N. (1986). *Children's mental health: Problems and services.* Washington, DC: Congress of the United States, Office of Technology Assessment.

Stroul, B. (1988). *Series on community-based services for children and adolescents who are severely emotionally disturbed: Vol. 1. Home-based services.* Washington, DC: Georgetown University Child Development Center, National Technical Assistance Center for Children's Mental Health.

Stroul, B. (1989). *Series on community-based services for children and adolescents who are severely emotionally disturbed: Vol. 3. Therapeutic foster care.* Washington, DC: Georgetown University Child Development Center, National Technical Assistance Center for Children's Mental Health.

Stroul, B. (1993). *Systems of care for children and adolescents with severe emotional disturbances: What are the results?* Washington, DC: Georgetown University Child Development Center, National Technical Assistance Center for Children's Mental Health.

Stroul, B., & Friedman, R. (1986). *A system of care for children and adolescents with severe emotional disturbances* (Rev. ed.). Washington, DC: Georgetown University Child Development Center, National Technical Assistance Center for Children's Mental Health.

Stroul, B., Lourie, I., Goldman, S., & Katz-Leavy, J. (1992). *Profiles of local systems of care for children and adolescents with severe emotional disturbances.* Washington, DC: Georgetown University Child Development Center, National Technical Assistance Center for Children's Mental Health.

Stroul, B., Pires, S., Katz-Leavy, J., & Goldman, S. (1994). Implications of the Health Security Act for mental health services for children and adolescents. *Hospital and Community Psychiatry, 45*(9), 877-882.

Vermont Department of Mental Health and Mental Retardation. (1993). *Vermont New Directions evaluation of children and adolescent services.* Waterbury, VT: Division of Mental Health.

Virginia Department of Mental Health, Mental Retardation, and Substance Abuse Services. (1992). *Demonstration project interim evaluation results.* Richmond, VA: Office of Research and Evaluation.

Family-Centered Services for Children With Emotional, Behavioral, and Mental Disorders

RICHARD W. HUNTER
BARBARA J. FRIESEN

In recent years, a large number of changes have occurred in both the conceptualization of mental health services for children and the development of new technologies and approaches to meet the needs of children with emotional and/or behavioral problems and their families. Significant among these changes have been (a) a shift from an emphasis on institutionalized care of children with mental health needs to the development of community-based services, (b) a change from child-focused treatment to a family-focused system of care and support, and (c) an increased recognition of the positive role families can play in the effective treatment of their children.

The reasons for these dramatic changes in the conception and development of effective mental health services stem from what Bergman (1989) noted to be a growing perception that "public policy has dismally failed children with mental health problems" (p. 1). A multitude of factors have contributed to this perception, including an overreliance on psychiatric hospitalization, residential treatment, and other highly restrictive forms of care; fragmentation and lack of coordination between social service, mental health, education, and other service systems; the inaccessibility and/or lack of community-based programs and treatment; and fiscal and policy barriers that restrict eligibility for services or impede timely and adequate delivery of services (see Pires & Stroul, Chapter 1 of this volume, for a review of these factors).

Considerable effort has been directed toward documenting these needs and developing an agenda of service delivery responses at federal, state, and local levels (e.g., Joint Commission on the Mental Health of Children, 1969; Knitzer, 1982; Knitzer, Steinberg, & Fleisch, 1990; President's Commission on Mental Health, 1978; Saxe, Cross, & Silverman, 1988). Particular emphasis has been placed on the need to develop comprehensive, community-based, family-centered systems of care that provide a wide array of educational, mental health, and social services for children with emotional disorders and their families (Duchnowski, Algarin, Friedman, & Henderson, 1988; Stroul & Friedman, 1986).

The development of family-centered services to address these pressing needs requires professionals to adopt new ways of viewing and working with families. More often than not, these new attitudes and skills conflict with and challenge traditional perspectives and practices. Moreover, they require changes in the way services are organized and funded, personnel are trained, and programs are administered. Perhaps most significantly, family-centered services require a fundamental change in the nature of the relationship between professionals and the families served—from a relationship clearly marked by boundaries such as "therapist" and "client" to a relationship based on partnership and the mutual collaboration of the skills, knowledge, and experiences of each.

Characteristics of Family-Centered Service

In light of changing trends in the care and treatment of children with emotional disorders and new perspectives on the biological and psychosocial factors underlying the genesis of emotional disorders, researchers and practitioners are increasingly recognizing that mental disorders in children have a complex and multifactorial basis requiring a wide variation of service responses. As static notions of etiology and treatment are abandoned, new models of service delivery emphasize the need for a family-centered approach.

Family-centered service refers to the development of services in response to the needs of the entire family, including the child with an emotional disorder (Friesen & Koroloff, 1990). Undergirding the concept of family-centered service, and discussed further below, are three defining principles:

1. Services to children with emotional disorders and their families flow out of an expanded ecological view of the family within the context of the greater community.
2. Services for children with emotional disorders and their families are designed to meet the unique needs of all family members and employ a wide variety of both formal and informal support strategies.
3. Parents and other family members are involved in all aspects of service planning, delivery, and evaluation in partnership with formal service providers and policymakers.

Expanded Ecological View: The Family Context

Recent trends in service delivery have been increasingly influenced by family systems theory (Bronfenbrenner, 1979; Garbarino & Gilliam, 1980). As opposed to child-focused interventions that emphasize individual change within the child, family systems theory has expanded the focus of change efforts to that of the family, often with the goal of strengthening family relationships and interactions.

As Weiss and Jacobs (1988), Koroloff and Friesen (1991), and Kagan and Weissbourd (1994) argued, however, the shift from a child-as-client to a family-system-as-client perspective does not ensure effective treatment. Rather, interventions must take into account the complex interactions and interdependence of the child, family, and greater community. Such interventions recognize not only the importance of internal factors of family interactions but also the interplay of forces outside the immediate family that include relationships with informal social support networks, community agencies, and institutions such as schools, employers, and formal helping systems, as well as the impact of broad societal, social, economic, and political forces on the family.

An expanded ecological perspective implies that change efforts are not only designed for the individual child and family but also take into account changes or modifications needed in other systems and institutions that affect the child and family. Examples of these broader interventions include efforts such as educating relatives, service providers, and the general public on the nature of mental illness to reduce the negative effects of stigma felt by family members and developing flexible policies that allow for the treatment of children in residential care or state institutions without the requirement that parents give up legal custody of the child.

Addressing Family Needs

The past decade has been witness to a rapid growth in the development of various family support and home-based services. Outside the mental health field, as families have increasingly opted to care for their children with serious disabilities at home, there has been growing attention to the services needed by these families. Because these families generally are not perceived as responsible for the cognitive and/or physical disabilities of their children, both they and service providers have focused more on building programs that support families rather than on treating or changing individuals or families as a unit. These efforts recognize the challenges associated with caring for children with disabilities while maintaining a balanced and healthy life for all members.

Additional advances in research and public policy have been evident. Without the stigma and presumed causal responsibility attributed to families dealing with mental health problems, research attention in other fields has focused on issues such as identifying sources of stress in families whose children have disabilities (e.g., Blacher, Nihira, & Meyers, 1987; Quine & Pahl, 1985) and developing and evaluating ways of providing effective support to families (Joyce, Singer, & Isralowitz, 1983; Singer, Irvin, Irvine, Hawkins, & Cooley, 1989; Telleen, Herzog, & Kilbane, 1989). In contrast to an overemphasis on the negative impact of disability on families, recent research attention has turned to identifying factors that account for or increase family strength or resilience (Patterson, 1991), including cognitive coping strategies associated with greater optimism and problem-solving capacity (Turnbull et al., 1993).

For families of children with emotional disorders, family-centered services also incorporate the aims of helping families stay together, find balance in their lives, and provide attention to the needs of all family members. The term *family support* represents both a philosophy and an approach to serving children and families that should be built into all child and family services. Support suggests an expanded set of services, including those that "involve helping families acquire the support they need to cope with the extra stresses that accompany caring for a child with emotional disabilities" (Friesen & Koroloff, 1990, p. 14).

Other definitions of family support appear to distinguish family support services from the more traditional treatment services provided by the mental health system. This is evident, for example, in the definition of family support adopted by the Federation of Families for Children's Mental Health (1992):

> Family support is a constellation of formal and informal services and tangible goods that are defined and determined by families. It is "whatever it takes" for a family to care for and live with a child or adolescent who has an emotional, behavioral or mental disorder. It also includes supports needed to assist families to maintain close involvement with their children who are in out-of-home placement and to help families when their children are ready to return home. (p. 1)

Such a needs-based perspective of family support emphasizes that parents hold the primary and continuing responsibility for the care, treatment, education, and development of their child. Service planning encompasses a range of psychological, social, and material needs identified jointly by family members and service providers. With the exception of children in long-term institutional care, parents of children with emotional disorders are primarily responsible for their child, often receiving only episodic assistance from professionals and formal service systems. Therefore, effective support must give priority to interventions that build on and buttress family strengths in meeting their needs and promoting the family's skills and abilities to obtain and sustain resources for problem solving.

Family Participation in Service Planning and Evaluation

Dunst, Trivette, and Deal (1988) noted that "the focus on family and not professionally identified needs and aspirations as the target of intervention recognizes the family's rightful role in deciding what is most important and in the best interest of the family unit and its members" (p. 8). In a review of home-based family support programs for children with emotional disabilities, Stroul (1988) argued that such programs are based on the belief that parents are in charge of their families and that services are provided "to support, encourage, and assist [families] in the parenting role" (p. 14).

Proponents of family participation in decision making about their needs and the services they receive advance a variety of arguments ranging from statements about consumers' rights and democratic participation (e.g., Katan & Prager, 1986; Knoll & Bedford, 1989) to conceptions that focus on better outcomes for children, families, and society (Anglin, 1985-1986; Katan & Prager, 1986; Ooms, 1990). Educational policy (P.L. 94-142, the Education of All Handicapped Children Act of 1975, and P.L. 101-476, the Individuals With Disabilities Education Act of 1990, or IDEA) mandates parental involvement in planning for special education services. It also addresses early intervention services for preschool children with disabilities and builds in a number of additional requirements for family participation and review. Thus, policy advances in fields outside mental health have already shifted attention from the question of whether family participation is a good idea to investigation about how best to implement it (Bailey, Buysse, Smith, & Elam, 1992; see also Heflinger & Bickman, Chapter 6 in this volume).

The primacy of family members in all aspects of care is both explicit and implicit within a family-centered perspective, shifting the role of parents and other family members from the traditional position of patient or client to one of valued ally and partner. Such a partnership recognizes that both family members and professionals possess critical information on the nature and course of the child's disorder and needs; that family members and professionals share the mutual goal of helping the child to cope, adapt, and move into adulthood with skills and supports that promote independence and responsibility; and that collaboration will promote development of services that are appropriate to the unique needs of each family and child (Vosler-Hunter, 1989).

Putting Family-Centered Service Into Practice

Recent advances in mental health services, stimulated in large part by the 1980s initiatives of the Child and Adolescent Service System Program (CASSP), are beginning to translate concepts of family-centered care and family support into practice. Prominent among these advances are attempts to develop a comprehensive system of care to serve children with emotional disorders and their families, with a particular emphasis on the concept of individualized care (Stroul & Friedman, 1986).

Stroul and Friedman (1986) provided a framework for a comprehensive service system that emphasizes individualized planning and service delivery; integrated, community-based and least-restrictive treatment options; and involvement of families in decision making. In describing the system's philosophy, Pires (1990) noted that the model emphasized several core values, namely, that the system must be child centered, family focused, and community based. A number of other authors also have addressed the challenge of delivering appropriate services to children and their families. Hill (1989), for example, outlined goals to the National Governor's Association that emphasized individualization, comprehensiveness, coordination, flexible funding, and increased support for research, training, and advocacy. In a similar vein, the Education and Human Services Consortium identified several essential elements of comprehensive service delivery, including access to a wide array of services, emphasis on appropriate and flexible services, focus on the whole family, and agency efforts to empower families within an atmosphere of mutual respect (Melaville & Blank, 1991).

Stroul and Friedman (1986) defined "a comprehensive spectrum of mental health and other necessary services which are organized into a coordinated network to meet the multiple and changing needs of severely emotionally disturbed children and adolescents" (p. 3). Their framework includes several dimensions of service deemed essential to a comprehensive system of care, including mental health, social, and educational services; health services; vocational and recreational services; and operational services such as advocacy and mutual support services. In contrast to traditional approaches that impose agency boundaries for each of these services, their model is functionally specific in that each of the service dimensions must be addressed through coordination and collaboration to provide a comprehensive system as dictated by the needs of the family and child, rather than by the needs of programs and service providers.

Burchard and Clarke (1990) have elaborated on the notion of individualized care in which services are "unconditional, flexible, child and family-focused, and inter-agency coordinated" (p. 48). They asserted that although Stroul and Friedman's continuum of component care programs is necessary for providing needed resources, an individualized care approach will improve services for children who will continue to fall through the cracks of a component-based system.

Central to the notion of individualized care is the concept of wraparound services in which all needed resources follow the child and family until services are no longer required. Services are conceptualized as unconditional, least restrictive, flexible in time and configuration, and coordinated through an interdisciplinary team that includes all service providers, parents, and, when appropriate, the child. As suggested by Burchard and Clarke (1990), providing individualized, flexible, family-centered services will require a shift in the way traditional mental health services have been conceptualized.

A family-centered perspective places the family at the center of the conceptual universe in which family needs are identified first, and then current service delivery options are examined to see what place they may have in a comprehensive service plan for the family. A family-centered service approach involves the following questions: (a) What are the unique needs of this child and family? (focus on family-defined needs); (b) What are the strengths and resources of this family, including informal supports? (focus on strengths, not deficits); (c) What role do formal services have in addressing the needs of families? (broad conception of possible interventions); (d) What are the preferences of the family with regard to the type, timing, and location of services? (focus on family choice); and (e) How can a system be designed to be flexible and responsive to the changing needs of families? (focus on flexibility and individualized services).

Service Strategies for a Family-Centered System

During the last decade, service options that are available for adaptation to particular community and family circumstances have greatly expanded. Four major categories of services for families may be identified according to their differing goals: (a) family-focused therapeutic services, (b) educational services, (c) family support services, and (d) case management/service coordination.

Family-Focused Therapeutic Services

Family-focused therapeutic services are designed to change some aspect of family functioning. In family therapy, the entire family meets with one or more therapists to work toward goals such as improved communication; better problem-solving skills; greater clarity and agreement with regard to roles, responsibilities, and authority; and increased expressions of support (Atwood, 1992). Family therapy approaches are notable for expanding the earlier focus on only the child or on only mother-child interactions. Family therapy also allows for attention to the impact of a child's difficult behavior on the family through an examination of the effect of each member's behavior on others and on overall family functioning. These services can be beneficial for families, but Johnson (1986) warned that they also may be associated with unanticipated negative consequences, such as a focus limited to family dynamics at the exclusion of other issues such as physical or neurobiological conditions that should be addressed.

Family therapy concepts also provide part of the foundation for home-based services that feature brief intensive services, usually in the family's home, designed to avert out-of-home placement for a child or adolescent (Nelson, Landsman, & Deutelbaum, 1990). Developed in the child welfare field as family-preservation services, programs such as Homebuilders (Fraser & Haapala, 1987-1988) and other home-based approaches usually involve one or more service providers who meet with all family members in their own homes, sometimes daily, for as long as needed during periods of crisis. The home-based staff employ a variety of interventions such as crisis management; conflict resolution; and instruction in family communication, problem solving, and parenting skills. These therapeutic interventions are often combined with the provision of concrete services such as transportation, food, clothing, respite, and homemake services. In a study of in-home services based on the Homebuilders approach, Fraser and Haapala found that concrete services combined with therapeutic techniques had more positive outcomes than therapeutic intervention alone.

Therapeutic foster care, although involving out-of-home placement for the child, may also involve services for the child's family. Therapeutic foster care usually involves specially selected and trained foster parents who participate in regular support and problem-solving meetings with other therapeutic foster parents, have access to respite care, and obtain other professional support. In the North Idaho CASSP Rural System of Care (National Institute of Mental Health, 1991), a central responsibility of therapeutic foster parents is to work closely with the child's family so that parents are involved in the child's service planning, participate fully in decision making regarding the child's education and treatment, and are central to implementing plans for the child's return to home and community.

Educational Services

Educational services are designed to improve the information base from which families make decisions and initiate actions (see also Marsh, Chapter 5 in this volume). For example, efforts can include instruction designed to improve parenting skills (Singer et al., 1989), to increase family members' knowledge about the nature of childhood emotional disorders and related services, and to train family members to become more effective advocates for their own children (Kelker, 1987), and similar efforts to empower parents to promote improved parent-professional partnerships (see Heflinger & Bickman, Chapter 6 in this volume). Training also may focus on helping parents and other family members learn how to participate more effectively on boards, advisory groups, and other decision-making bodies (Vosler-Hunter & Hanson, 1992).

Family Support Services

Family support services are designed to assist families in meeting the special demands associated with caring for a child with an emotional disorder. These services can encompass virtually any intervention that might be needed by a family to ease the caretaking load and provide the best possible environment for the child as well as for all other family members. Family self-help, support, and advocacy groups and organizations provide information and mutual support, as well as concrete services and case and class advocacy (Fine & Borden, 1989). In a study involving low-income mothers enrolled in a family support program, Telleen et al. (1989) compared a mothers' self-help discussion group with a parent education group. After 3 months of program participation, mothers in both groups felt less social isolation and parenting stress than mothers in a control group. The few studies of parent support groups that specifically focus on families whose children have emotional disorders suggest that these families find these groups supportive and rewarding (Rowe, 1991). Koroloff and Friesen (1991) found that participants in parent groups were more likely to identify relationships with other parents as a major source of emotional support and to identify a need for and to use more services than parents who were not group members.

Respite care is another service that is widely offered in other fields but is less commonly available to families whose children have mental health problems (Butler & Friesen, 1988a, 1988b; U.S. General Accounting Office, 1990). Children with serious emotional disorders, especially those with difficult behaviors, often require special child care services and supervision that are difficult to locate. Consequently, many families become socially isolated, and family activities such as eating out and taking vacations may present immense difficulties. The benefits of respite care for families who have a child with a disability include positive outcomes for brothers and sisters (Powell & Ogle, 1986) and reduction in family isolation (Wikler, Hanusa, & Stoycheff, 1986). Joyce et al. (1983) reported that respite care had positive impact on family relations, social activities, emotional and physical strains on parents, and plans for institutional care among families whose children had severe developmental disabilities.

Other family support services may include concrete services such as transportation, food, home maintenance services, and cash assistance. For example, to test the benefits of service flexibility and to encourage families to care for their children with developmental and emotional disabilities at home, the Illinois Department of Mental Health provided "no strings" cash assistance to families who agreed to spend their grants to enhance the family's capacity to keep their child at home (Goerge & Osuch, 1992).

In addition to studies of specific family support services, a few researchers also have examined the effects of clusters of services. In a study focused on families whose children had severe developmental disabilities, Singer et al. (1989) compared regular family support services consisting of respite care and case management with intensive family support services consisting of additional classes in stress and behavior management and volunteer assistance in providing activities for the children. Mothers who participated in the intensive program showed significant improvement on measures of depression and anxiety. Further, these gains were maintained at a 1-year follow-up.

A few programs combine therapeutic, educational, and family support services into more comprehensive support programs. For example, Armstrong and Evans (1992) described one such program in children's mental health. As part of a research demonstration program, therapeutic foster care is being compared with Family-Centered Intensive Case Management, a program designed to provide intensive services in homes and communities. This program provides an array of services including intensive case management, access to respite care, family support groups and other family support services, the services of a paid family advocate, and recreational activities.

Case Management/Service Coordination

Case management/service coordination involves service mechanisms focused on improving access to and coordination of services. As Vosler-Hunter (1989) suggested, the preponderance of service coordination for children and adults with psychiatric disabilities is provided by their own families. Although the need for formal service coordination is likely to fluctuate with the changing needs of families, those families whose children have complex needs that cross a number of service systems often need formal case management. This may include assisting with planning services, gaining access to resources, communicating with multiple service providers, and monitoring the quality and appropriateness of services.

Case management services vary greatly in scope, ranging from what Ross (1980) called the *minimal model,* involving basic services of outreach, assessment, case planning, and referral to service providers, to an expanded *comprehensive model,* offering basic services plus client advocacy, direct casework, working with natural support systems, resource development, monitoring quality, public education, and crisis intervention. In the children's mental health field, services also vary widely according to whether they include a clinical or therapeutic function and whether the case manager is expected to develop new resources. Resource development as an expectation for case managers may be unique to children's mental health, reflecting the underdeveloped state of many service systems.

During the next several years, case management services are likely to expand for children with emotional disorders. Public Law 99-660's mandate (State Mental Health Services Comprehensive Plan, 1986) that case management services be provided to children with serious mental health problems is likely to have an impact on the development and availability of a variety of service coordination functions. As services expand and local systems of care are developed, case management is likely to be seen increasingly as an essential mechanism for ensuring service continuity and quality.

Implications of a Family-Centered Approach

It is important to reiterate that the degree to which programs or services are family centered must be assessed on a program-by-program basis; family-centered services are "in the eye of the beholder" and are family/consumer driven. Thus, no program or service can be declared family centered without examining the program's philosophy, goals, and operation. Many programs that have *family-centered* or *family-based* in their titles do not operationalize the principles of family participation and choice, flexibility, and comprehensiveness. Services that appear to be similar may vary greatly along these dimensions. For example, two parent training programs may have similar content but may differ greatly in intent and effect. The training developed and offered by professionals actually may be perceived by these families as critical, blaming, and perhaps coercive. The same training package offered after joint planning and the mutual identification of needs and goals may be viewed more positively. The identity of the trainers (professionals, parents, or joint trainers) also may have an effect on how such services are perceived by parents.

In addition, the following implications for program planning, policy, and research rely heavily on concepts that are untested or on a research base that has been developed mostly in fields other than children's mental health. These recommendations, therefore, should be treated as research questions that can be subjected to empirical examination and testing.

Practice and Program Issues

Meeting the goal of providing family-centered services calls for several practice and program reforms. These include (a) expanding current assessment approaches to maximize the principles of comprehensiveness, individualization, and addressing the needs of the entire family; (b) making available a wider range of services; (c) developing new skills and attitudes of professional staff; and (d) promoting program and service flexibility.

Assessment Approaches. The principle of comprehensiveness in assessment expands the focus from the mental health problems and treatment needs of the child and family to include a full range of health, educational, recreational, social, and other needs so that a plan can be prepared that addresses all aspects of the child's and family's life. The principle of individualized services calls for assessment approaches that take into account the needs and preferences of families and that are culturally appropriate. Fortunately, a number of resources that address culturally appropriate assessment and diagnosis of children are available (Gibbs & Huang, 1989; Jones, 1988; Powell, 1983), as well as a growing literature on family assessment that takes culture into account (McGoldrick, Pearce, & Giordano,

1982; Vargas & Koss-Chioino, 1992). Considering the needs of all family members in implementing services and support also should be emphasized in an expanded approach to assessment.

Range of Services. Conducting comprehensive assessments will represent a significant change for many agencies. A major issue created by this approach is who or what agency has responsibility for meeting the identified needs. It is not reasonable to suggest that an individual agency should address directly all of the service needs identified; in a family-centered system, individual workers, agencies, and the network of relevant service organizations must collectively assume responsibility to ensure that each family receives assistance in developing and implementing a comprehensive plan, with agreed-on mechanisms to assign responsibility and ensure accountability.

Clearly, an expanded range of services is necessary to address the comprehensive needs of children and families. Although no state or community has fully implemented the concept of family-centered care, a number of strategies can be identified to increase the ability to provide comprehensive family services. One option is to expand the services offered by individual agencies, for example, to provide a wider range of family support services, as in the previously mentioned Family-Centered Intensive Case Management program described by Armstrong and Evans (1992). This strategy requires new resources, or a reallocation of resources from specialized to more general services, and is unlikely to achieve widespread adoption among specialized mental health organizations. Another approach to expanding services available to children and families is through interagency agreements that create a network for planning and service delivery (Yelton & Miller, 1991). Interagency collaboration is essential for service coordination. Some savings may be realized through reducing duplication and streamlining services, but this strategy also requires increased funding for services. Agencies have come together to create flexible pools of funding through which needed services may be purchased and, in some cases, may actually expand the funds available for services by attracting increased federal participation through Medicaid. Pooled funding is a strategy adopted by a number of projects supported by the Robert Wood Johnson Child and Youth Mental Health Program (Beachler, 1990). The provision of cash grants or vouchers so that families can purchase an individualized package of needed services is a strategy that has much logical appeal because of the flexibility and choice it offers. This approach has been implemented in Illinois on a demonstration basis (Goerge & Osuch, 1992), where it was found that successful implementation was highly contingent on the availability of needed services and their accessibility to families.

Training and Human Resource Issues. Implementing family-centered services requires new skills for existing staff as well as enhanced preprofessional education. Moving to a family-centered system will require support for existing staff as they implement the general principles of family-centered care and learn how to enter into partnerships with families. Practitioners will need to integrate existing skills with new service delivery strategies, for example, combining existing family therapy skills with a variety of other approaches in a home-based services program. A general decision that agencies face is whether existing staff will be encouraged to learn more skills, that is, to move from a specialized to a more generalized model of service delivery, or whether they should add staff with a variety of specialized skills to create a more comprehensive service delivery capacity within the organization or network of organizations.

Changes in professional training programs are needed to support the goal of family-centered care. In addition to expanded assessment skills, other essential content that is not generally a part of professional training programs includes parent-professional collaboration and skills in interprofessional and interagency practice (Friesen, 1989; Friesen & Schultze, 1992).

Moreover, program administrators can provide considerable organizational support for the provision of family-centered care through the review of policies and programs that reflect the principles of family-centered care, the provision of incentives for staff to learn new skills and adopt new roles, and the adoption of personnel evaluation and program monitoring systems that support the goals of family-centered service. (For an expanded discussion of the administrative implications of family-centered service, see Friesen & Koroloff, 1990.)

Service and Program Flexibility. This is perhaps the most crucial and difficult change to achieve because creating program flexibility so that services can be tailored to the needs of children and families requires a pool of funds that is not committed to particular programs or service strategies. In a climate of scarce resources, this usually means shifting resources from existing commitments. The interagency pooled funding strategies discussed earlier represent one approach to creating flexible funds. Another strategy that many states have employed is to return treatment dollars from out-of-state residential programs to in-state community-based alternatives by returning children to their communities for treatment (Burchard & Clarke, 1990).

Implications for Research

Because many of the ideas about family-centered service exist as goals and principles but are not yet widely implemented, establishing a research agenda in this area poses many challenges. These challenges include decisions pertaining to what constitutes reasonable and acceptable outcomes as well as a host of other measurement issues. How to study attitudes, practices, and services that may be only partially in place, along with the more general question of where to begin, constitutes puzzles to be solved. In addition, research in this area is characterized by the general problems faced in service system research: how to conduct high-quality research in a climate of rapid change and uncertainty, how to carve out meaningful studies from the interrelated whole, and how to maximize the usefulness of related studies (see also the chapters by Marsh and Patterson, Chapters 5 and 7 in this volume).

Choosing Relevant and Acceptable Dependent Variables. Because all variables defined as outcomes of interest reflect value positions, establishing a research agenda related to family-centered service will require the identification of mutually acceptable outcomes, that is, which variables can be agreed to as goals in and of themselves, as well as which must be tied to other valued outcomes. Three major constituencies—policymakers, service providers, and family members—have ideas about what the goals of children's mental health services should be. In most instances, the outcomes to which each group gives priority are not in conflict but rather reflect different ideas about what is and what should be important. For example, if the full participation of parents in decision making about their child's treatment is not widely accepted as important, research attention is likely to focus on examining the relationships between such participation and other variables of interest such as positive changes in child functioning, maintenance of change through time, or increased family member compliance with the treatment regimen. If the participation of parents in decision making is a generally accepted value by all stakeholders (as in special education, for which parent participation is mandated by law), research attention can shift from whether parental participation is a good idea to questions of how to effectively implement and support such participation.

Studying a Partially Implemented Concept. Attempting to conduct research about ideas that have not been translated into practice presents the researcher with many problems to solve. First, there are likely to be little relevant literature, little or no prior research, and, thus, a lack of well-developed measures that address the concepts of interest. Fortunately, considerable conceptual work and research addressing core concepts of family-centered care have been conducted in fields such as developmental disabilities and chronic illness in children. Although care must be taken in extrapolating from research findings in other fields, studies addressing family-professional collaboration, parent participation in decision making, and family support services suggest promising avenues of research.

Initial steps for research include the need to conduct studies that document families' expressed needs and preferences, examine the variation in "family-centeredness" among existing services and organizations, and begin to define and develop measures of relevant constructs. Unfortunately, traditional research funding has not been available for exploratory-descriptive work, thus discouraging researchers from moving into uncharted territory. In recent years, a small amount of necessary developmental research has been supported by some federal agencies and private foundations.

Research demonstration projects that provide funds to develop interventions as well as to conduct research hold much appeal because they allow experimental or quasi-experimental designs. These projects are difficult to implement, however, especially where programs must be built from the ground up. When programs must be developed and stabilized during the same period that data about the intervention(s) in question are collected, the research process often is compromised by a variety of complications associated with implementing innovations in the field. For this reason, it is important that research demonstration projects include a period to implement and document the service delivery approach before beginning collection of data that are used to evaluate the program. Such projects should be funded for sufficient time to measure long-term as well as short-term effects of the intervention(s).

Despite the challenges posed by research in the area of family-centered services, it is an exciting area of investigation. Results of relevant studies are likely to be rapidly and widely used as advances in family-centered services and research efforts are disseminated within the community of families, service providers, planners, and researchers who are working to improve services for children with emotional, behavioral, and mental disorders and their families.

Conclusion

The full development of a family-centered approach to serving children with emotional, behavioral, and mental disorders and their families, although enjoying considerable political currency, poses significant challenges to service providers, policymakers, and researchers. Innovative service approaches that are attuned to individual family needs and desires require providers to develop new skills related to collaborative assessment, problem solving, and mutual goal setting with families. Such practices may be in conflict with traditional training approaches that have viewed families as "clients" as opposed to active and equal partners in the change process. Similarly, in the policy-making and program development arena, the inclusion of families fundamentally changes traditional decision-making processes, requiring a more open and inclusive approach that recognizes family members as having legitimate seats at the boardroom table. Finally, the development of empirical evidence to evaluate the effectiveness of family-centered services challenges researchers to ask new questions, fashion meaningful designs, and measure complex individual and system-related outcomes. Taken as a whole, the emergence of family-centered services offers new opportunities for families and professionals to join in partnership to address these challenges and significantly improve services to children with emotional, behavioral, and mental disorders.

References

Anglin, J. P. (1985-1986). Developing education and support groups for parents of children in residential care. *Residential Group Care and Treatment, 3*(2), 15-27.

Armstrong, M. I., & Evans, M. E. (1992). Three intensive community-based programs for children and youth with serious emotional disturbance and their families. *Journal of Child and Family Studies, 1*(1), 61-74.

Atwood, J. D. (Ed.). (1992). *Family therapy.* Chicago: Nelson-Hall.

Bailey, D. B., Buysse, V., Smith, T., & Elam, J. (1992). The effects and perceptions of family involvement in program decisions about family-centered practices. *Evaluation and Program Planning, 15,* 23-32.

Beachler, M. (1990). The Robert Wood Johnson mental health services program for youth. *Journal of Mental Health Administration, 17*(1), 115-121.

Bergman, G. T. (1989). Mental health policy developments in the child mental health field. *State Health Reports on Mental Health, Alcoholism, & Drug Abuse, 44,* 1-15.

Blacher, J., Nihira, K., & Meyers, C. E. (1987). Characteristics of home environments of families with mentally retarded children: Comparison across levels of retardation. *American Journal of Mental Deficiency, 91,* 313-320.

Bronfenbrenner, U. (1979). *The ecology of human development.* Cambridge, MA: Harvard University Press.

Burchard, J. D., & Clarke, R. T. (1990). The role of individualized care in a service delivery system for children and adolescents with severely maladjusted behavior. *Journal of Mental Health Administration, 7*(1), 48-60.

Butler, T. E., & Friesen, B. J. (1988a). *Respite care: A monograph.* Portland, OR: Portland State University, Research and Training Center on Family Support and Children's Mental Health.

Butler, T. E., & Friesen, B. J. (1988b). *Respite care: An annotated bibliography.* Portland, OR: Portland State University, Research and Training Center on Family Support and Children's Mental Health.

Duchnowski, A., Algarin, A., Friedman, R., & Henderson, E. (1988). *Mental health and education: Partners in serving emotionally disturbed youth.* Tampa: University of South Florida, Florida Mental Health Institute, Research and Training Center for Children's Mental Health.

Dunst, C. J., Trivette, C. M., & Deal, A. G. (1988). *Enabling and empowering families.* Cambridge, MA: Brookline.

Education of All Handicapped Children Act of 1975, Pub. L. No. 94-142, 20 U.S.C. § 1400 et seq., 89 Stat. 773-796 (1977).

Federation of Families for Children's Mental Health. (1992). *Family support statement.* Alexandria, VA: Author.

Fine, G., & Borden, J. R. (1989). Parents Involved Network: Support and advocacy training for parents. In R. Friedman, A. Duchnowski, & A. Henderson (Eds.), *Advocacy for children with serious mental health problems* (pp. 68-78). Chicago: Charles C Thomas.

Fraser, M., & Haapala, D. (1987-1988). Home-based family treatment: A quantitative-qualitative assessment. *Journal of Applied Social Sciences, 12,* 1-23.

Friesen, B. J. (1989). Child mental health training in schools of social work: A national survey. In L. Abramczyck (Ed.), *Social work education for working with seriously emotionally disturbed children and adolescents* (pp. 62-84). Columbia: University of South Carolina School of Social Work, National Association of Deans and Directors of Schools of Social Work.

Friesen, B. J., & Koroloff, N. M. (1990). Family-centered services: Implications for mental health administration and research. *Journal of Mental Health Administration, 17*(1), 13-25.

Friesen, B. J., & Schultze, K. H. (1992). *Parent-professional collaboration content in professional education programs: A research report.* Portland, OR: Portland State University, Research and Training Center on Family Support and Children's Mental Health.

Garbarino, J., & Gilliam, G. (1980). *Understanding abusive families.* Lexington, MA: D. C. Heath.

Gibbs, J. T., & Huang, L. N. (1989). *Children of color: Psychological interventions with minority youth.* San Francisco: Jossey-Bass.

Goerge, R. M., & Osuch, R. (1992). The effect of cash assistance on families of children with severe emotional disturbance or developmental disabilities: An evaluation of the family assistance program in Illinois. In K. Kutash, C. J. Liberton, A. Algarin, & R. M. Friedman (Eds.), *A system of care for children's mental health: Expanding the research base: 5th annual research conference proceedings* (pp. 323-335). Tampa: University of South Florida, Research and Training Center for Children's Mental Health.

Hill, A. S. (1989). *Children with serious emotional disturbance: Bridging the gap between what we know and what we can do.* Washington, DC: National Governor's Association.

Individuals With Disabilities Education Act of 1990 (IDEA), Pub. L. No. 101-476, 20 U.S.C. § 1400 et seq., 104 (Pt. 2) Stat. 1103-1151.

Johnson, H. C. (1986). Emerging concerns in family therapy. *Social Work, 31*(4), 299-306.

Joint Commission on the Mental Health of Children. (1969). *Crisis in child mental health: Challenge for the 1970s.* New York: Harper & Row.

Jones, R. (Ed.). (1988). *Psychoeducational assessment of minority group children: A casebook.* Berkeley, CA: Cobb & Henry.

Joyce, K., Singer, M., & Isralowitz, R. (1983). Impact of respite care on parents' perceptions of quality of life. *Mental Retardation, 21,* 153-156.

Kagan, S. L., & Weissbourd, B. (1994). *Putting families first: America's family support movement and the challenge of change.* San Francisco: Jossey-Bass.

Katan, J., & Prager, E. (1986). Consumer and worker participation in agency-level decision-making: Some considerations of their linkages. *Administration in Social Work, 10,* 79-88.

Kelker, K. A. (1987). *Taking charge: A handbook for parents whose children have emotional handicaps.* Portland, OR: Portland State University, Research and Training Center on Family Support and Children's Mental Health.

Knitzer, J. (1982). *Unclaimed children: The failure of public responsibility to children and adolescents in need of mental health services.* Washington, DC: Children's Defense Fund.

Knitzer, J., Steinberg, Z., & Fleisch, B. (1990). *At the schoolhouse door: An examination of programs and policies for children with behavioral and emotional disorders.* New York: Bank Street College of Education.

Knoll, J., & Bedford, S. (1989). Respite services: A national survey of parents' experience. *Exceptional Parent, 19*(4), 34-43.

Koroloff, N. M., & Friesen, B. J. (1991). Support groups for parents of children with emotional disorders: A comparison of members and non-members. *Community Mental Health Journal, 27*, 265-279.

McGoldrick, M., Pearce, J. K., & Giordano, J. (Eds.). (1982). *Ethnicity and family therapy.* New York: Guilford.

Melaville, A. I., & Blank, M. J. (1991). *What it takes: Structuring interagency partnerships to connect children and families with comprehensive services.* Washington, DC: Education and Human Services Consortium.

National Institute of Mental Health. (1991). *Project summary updates: NIMH child and adolescent research and demonstration grants.* Washington, DC: National Institute of Mental Health, Division of Applied and Services Research, Child and Family Support Branch.

Nelson, K. E., Landsman, M. J., & Deutelbaum, W. (1990). Three models of family-centered placement prevention services. *Child Welfare, 69*(1), 3-21.

Ooms, T. (1990). *Implementation of P.L. 99-457 parent/professional partnership in early intervention: Background briefing report and meeting highlights.* Washington, DC: American Association of Marriage and Family Therapists, Family Impact Seminar.

Patterson, J. M. (1991). Family resilience to the challenge of a child's disability. *Pediatric Annals, 20*(9), 491-499.

Pires, S. A. (1990). *Sizing components of care: An approach to determining the size and cost of service components in a system of care for children and adolescents with serious emotional disturbances.* Washington, DC: Georgetown University Child Development Center, CASSP Technical Assistance Center.

Powell, G. J. (Ed.). (1983). *The psychosocial development of minority group children.* New York: Brunner/Mazel.

Powell, T. H., & Ogle, P. A. (1986). Brothers and sisters: Addressing unique needs through respite care services. In C. Salisbury & J. Intagliata (Eds.), *Respite care: Support for persons with developmental disabilities and their families* (pp. 29-50). Baltimore: Paul H. Brookes.

President's Commission on Mental Health. (1978). *Report to the president of the President's Commission on Mental Health* (Vol. 1). Washington, DC: Government Printing Office.

Quine, L., & Pahl, J. (1985). Examining the cause of stress in families with severely mentally handicapped children. *British Journal of Social Work, 15*, 501-517.

Ross, H. (1980). *Proceedings of the conference on the evaluation of case management programs.* Los Angeles: Volunteers for Services to Older Persons.

Rowe, K. (1991). *Study of groups for parents of children with serious emotional disorders in Virginia.* Richmond, VA: Department of Mental Health, Mental Retardation and Substance Abuse Services.

Saxe, L., Cross, T., & Silverman, N. (1988). Children's mental health: The gap between what we know and what we do. *American Psychologist, 43*(10), 800-807.

Singer, G. H. S., Irvin, L. K., Irvine, B., Hawkins, N., & Cooley, E. (1989). Evaluation of community-based support services for families of persons with developmental disabilities. *Journal of the Association for Persons With Severe Handicaps, 14*, 312-323.

State Mental Health Services Comprehensive Plan, Pub. L. No. 99-660, 42 U.S.C. § 300 et seq., 100 Stat. 3794-3797 (1986).

Stroul, B. (1988). *Series on community-based services for children and adolescents who are severely emotionally disturbed: Vol. 1. Home-based services.* Washington, DC: Georgetown University Child Development Center, CASSP Technical Assistance Center.

Stroul, B., & Friedman, R. (1986). *A system of care for severely emotionally disturbed children and youth.* Washington, DC: Georgetown University Child Development Center, CASSP Technical Assistance Center.

Telleen, S., Herzog, A., & Kilbane, T. L. (1989). Impact of a family support program on mother's social support and parenting stress. *American Journal of Orthopsychiatry, 59,* 410-419.

Turnbull, A. P., Patterson, J. M., Behr, S. K., Murphy, D. L., Marquis, J. G., & Blue-Banning, M. J. (1993). *Cognitive coping, families, and disability.* Baltimore: Paul H. Brookes.

U.S. General Accounting Office. (1990). *Respite care: An overview of federal, selected state, and private programs* (GAO/HRD-90-125). Washington, DC: Government Printing Office.

Vargas, L. A., & Koss-Chioino, J. D. (Eds.). (1992). *Working with culture: Psychotherapeutic interventions with ethnic minority children and adolescents.* San Francisco: Jossey-Bass.

Vosler-Hunter, R. W. (1989). *Changing roles, changing relationships: Parent-professional collaboration on behalf of children with emotional disabilities.* Portland, OR: Portland State University, Research and Training Center on Family Support and Children's Mental Health.

Vosler-Hunter, R., & Hanson, S. (1992). Parents as policy makers: Challenges for collaboration. *Focal Point: The Bulletin of the Research and Training Center on Family Support and Children's Mental Health, 6*(1), 1-5. (Available from Portland State University, Research and Training Center on Family Support and Children's Mental Health, Portland, OR)

Weiss, H. B., & Jacobs, F. H. (Eds.). (1988). Evaluating family programs for the mentally ill. *Hospital and Community Psychiatry, 34*(10), 925-938.

Wikler, L. M., Hanusa, D., & Stoycheff, J. (1986). Home-based respite care, the child with developmental disabilities, and family stress: Some theoretical and practical aspects of process evaluation. In C. Salisbury & J. Intagliata (Eds.), *Respite care: Support for persons with developmental disabilities and their families* (pp. 243-262). Baltimore: Paul H. Brookes.

Yelton, S., & Miller, J. (1991). *The child welfare/children's mental health partnership: A collaborative agenda for strengthening families.* Tampa: University of South Florida, Florida Mental Health Institute, National Association of Public Child Welfare Administrators and State Mental Health Representatives for Children and Youth.

A Family-Focused Model of Prevention

GEORGE W. ALBEE
SILVIA SARA CANETTO

Many of the chapters in this volume focus on the role that the family can play in therapeutic interventions with children and adolescents. This chapter is concerned with the role that society can play in strengthening the family and preventing child and adolescent emotional disorders. In the field of public health, it is understood clearly that individual treatment, however successful, does little or nothing to reduce the number of future new cases (the incidence) of any particular disorder. Although therapeutic intervention is humane, desirable, and rewarding to the individuals involved, both therapists and clients, it does not significantly affect incidence (Albee, 1982).

The only way to reduce significantly the incidence of mental and emotional disorders is through primary prevention. The successful reduction or elimination of many of the great plagues that have afflicted humankind has come about as a result of successful prevention efforts, rather than as a consequence of successful individual

AUTHORS' NOTE: Some of the material in this chapter appeared in a slightly different form in an article titled "What Is Normal Family: Common Assumptions and Current Evidence" in the *Journal of Primary Prevention*, Vol. 17, No. 1, 1996.

treatment. The field of public health has seen the elimination of such diseases as smallpox and plague as well as the steady reduction in incidence of diseases such as polio and other childhood conditions that once claimed the lives of a great many young people. Some of these childhood diseases continue to take their toll among poor children, especially those in the developing world. Annual reports of the United Nations Children's Fund (UNICEF; see Grant, 1988, 1989) found that 12 to 14 million children around the world die each year as a consequence of preventable conditions. Children die from lack of immunization, from contaminated drinking water, and because of malnutrition. Also, a great many children in the United States die unnecessarily as a result of lack of prenatal maternal care, lack of immunization against childhood diseases, malnutrition, family violence, and environmental hazards. Accidents are the greatest cause of child mortality (Hamburg, 1990). Infant mortality is clearly associated with poverty (Mirowsky & Ross, 1989). The darker the skins of groups of people, the more likely they are to live in close proximity to toxic dumps and other serious environmental hazards (Anderson, 1988; Bullard, 1990; Lambrecht, 1991). There also is evidence that when children live with adults who are poor, unemployed, or socially isolated, they are more likely to suffer from emotional and behavioral disorders (Bond & Joffe, 1982).

In this chapter, we argue that primary prevention efforts should focus on high-risk families and on environmental forces that negatively affect the family. Therapy with individual children and/or individual families, although admirable and humane, will do little or nothing to reduce the incidence of family problems in the society (Albee, 1990a). Only effective prevention offers hope for the future reduction of the family distress that adversely affects children.

The Family in North American Psychology

Family-focused efforts involving primary prevention of child and adolescent problems must begin with a clarification of what constitutes a family (see also Patterson, Chapter 7 in this volume). Such clarification will require an exploration of prevalent definitions of family and the adequacy of these definitions for current family demographics. Family-focused prevention also requires articulating a philosophy of what is normal family functioning on the basis of reliable empirical data. Therefore, this section will focus on the following questions: (a) How has the "family" been defined in North American psychology? (b) What do these prevalent definitions omit and what distortions do they foster? and (c) What are the implications of such prevailing definitions of family for prevention efforts?

Prevalent Definitions

The formal academic study of the family is a comparatively recent phenomenon in North American psychology, a consequence perhaps of psychology's historical identity as a discipline dedicated to the study of *individual* functioning. In addition, psychology has devoted more attention to developing techniques for family change ("family therapy") than to promoting dialogue on normal family functioning. Therefore, psychological definitions of the family and normal family functioning have to be inferred from the literature on family problems and therapy. Another source of definitions are texts of individual human development, which, however, often reflect the biases of middle-class text writers.

The prevalent conceptualization of the normal family is often synonymous with the nuclear family. More specifically, the normal family often is considered equivalent to a first-marriage conjugal couple with biological children in which the wife is solely in charge of child and domestic responsibilities, and the husband is the breadwinner. For example, a survey of undergraduate adolescent psychology textbooks from the late 1950s to the present (Canetto, 1992) revealed that most authors assume that the normal family comprises "two parents, their children, and no one else" (Cole & Hall, 1970, p. 398). Such family structure is often described as normal in the sense of average, as well as normal in the sense of well-functioning. For example, when families other than nuclear-patriarchal (such as dual career, single-parent, blended, adoptive, and parental-relatives with children families) are mentioned, it is in sections devoted to variations from the normal family or in sections focusing on deviance.

Problems and Limitations of Prevalent Definitions

The main problem of prevailing definitions of the normal family in North American psychological texts is that the definitions are inaccurate. Inaccuracies characterize what is assumed to be the most common type of family, as well as what is considered as the most healthy type of family. Concerning the question of the normal family as average, the nuclear "traditional" family is far from the most common type of family unit. According to a review of the literature by Coontz (1992), households containing a "breadwinner father, a full-time homemaker mother, and dependent children" (p. 23) represented less than 10% of American families. (See Pinderhughes, Chapter 10 in this volume, for a discussion of alternative routes to family status.)

Traditional nuclear families being a minority is not a new phenomenon. By 1977, traditional nuclear families represented only 16% of families in the United States (Thorne, 1982). In fact, according to Coontz (1992), the "Leave It to Beaver" nuclear traditional family is a historical fluke, "an invention of the 1950s" (p. 6). "Like most visions of a 'golden age,' the 'traditional family' . . . is an ahistorical amalgam of structures, values and behavior that never coexisted in the same time and place" (p. 9), except in television shows.

Not only are the gender arrangements of the traditional nuclear family historically untraditional, but also they are class- and race-specific. The ideal of full-time motherhood, even if desired, was never an option for the majority of working-class women, especially women of color. Men in working-class families "rarely earned a 'family wage,' and women had to combine income earning activities with child care and domestic labor" (Glenn, 1987, p. 359). Historically, women of color were not deemed to be "truly women" (p. 360). For them, job responsibilities took precedence over motherhood. Furthermore, even in the 1950s, homemaking was not always freely chosen. Many women were forced out of the jobs they had been asked to fill during World War II (Coontz, 1992).

Concerning the question of what constitutes a normal healthy family, there is no evidence that the nuclear traditional family is the best functioning and most rewarding family unit of all. First of all, men disproportionately benefit from, and are more satisfied with, traditional family arrangements than women (Coontz, 1992; Glenn, 1987). The benefits men accrue range from economic to psychological. For example, according to Curtis (1986), "Men can receive from their wives a market value of housework that is greater than their own incomes, yet housework is only a portion of what a wife contributes in order to have partial claim on that income" (p. 179). Men also "claim a greater share of resources, irrespective of who brings them into the household" (Glenn, 1987, p. 367). For example, in times of shortage, men consume more and better food than women, whereas in times of surplus, men control discretionary spending. Furthermore, married men enjoy better mental health than married women; in fact, gender differences in mental health are greater among the married (Clearly & Mechanic, 1983). Homemakers have been found to report more psychological symptoms than employed women (see Baruch, Biener, & Barnett, 1987, for a review). In sum, a traditional nuclear family sometimes is achieved at enormous physical and psychological costs to the wife, "who is expected to subordinate her needs and aspirations to those of both her husband and her children" (Coontz, 1992, p. 36).

Second, maternal unemployment is detrimental to women's well-being, just as paternal unemployment is detrimental to men's (Baruch et al., 1987). For example, lack of employment is a risk factor for depression in women. Furthermore, maternal employment, like paternal employment, can have a positive effect on mother-child interactions and child adjustment (see Phares, 1992, for a review). This is not to say that mothers find it easy to combine the demands of work and parenting. In fact, according to a review of the literature by Coontz (1992), many mothers would "trade a day's pay for an extra day off" (p. 19). Mothers also reported, however, that they "would miss their work if they did manage to take time off" (p. 19). Contrary to popular belief, married mothers were not more stressed by their jobs than were employed fathers, but rather they were more likely to carry the greatest proportion of domestic and child responsibilities (Baruch et al., 1987; Glenn, 1987).

Implications for Research, Clinical Intervention, Prevention, and Social Policy

Labeling the patriarchal nuclear family normal, average, and healthy has problematic consequences for research, clinical intervention, and preventive social policy. Setting the patriarchal family as both the standard and the ideal has prevented a frank analysis of its problems, including the recognition that home is not a haven (Coontz, 1992; Glenn, 1987); that full-time parenting is highly stressful (Baruch et al., 1987); that women are more likely to be victims of violence by family members than by strangers (Hare-Mustin, 1987); and that fathers' insufficient commitment to parental responsibility may harm children (Phares, 1992).

Conversely, defining the patriarchal family as the norm has rendered invisible or pathologized all other family forms. Mental health clinicians may attribute all problematic behaviors of children of lesbian couples to the parental couple's sexual orientation, despite the lack of evidence that growing up in a lesbian household per se puts a child at risk for psychological disorders (Falk, 1989). The idealization of the nuclear patriarchal household also may lead to misguided preventive social policies. For example, in response to the poverty of African American single-mother households, some may advocate programs encouraging these mothers to marry instead of programs addressing the racist and sexist economic barriers preventing African American women from making a "family" salary.

What does all this mean for prevention? It means that before considering the appropriate family role in prevention, we must become conscious of the field's biased definition of the "normal family." We recognize that prejudice is common against some family structures. In addition, prevailing definitions of the normal-as-well-functioning family presume the subordination and exploitation of women. Our call to preventionists is to examine critically the assumptions about normal family functioning. In a sense, we cannot plan just preventive programs for "the family" without confronting the injustice that women—employed and unemployed—carry total responsibility for domestic maintenance and child care. Nor can we advocate for more equal representation for women in the labor market and political institutions without addressing the gender hierarchy and inequities within the family.

Public Health Methods

The primary prevention of mental and emotional disorders uses methodologies similar to those that are common to the field of public health. These methods include (a) identifying the *noxious agents* responsible for the problems and taking steps to reduce or eliminate them, (b) taking steps to strengthen the *resistance of the host* to the noxious agents, and (c) *preventing transmission* of the noxious agents to the host (Albee, 1990b).

Research has already revealed many of the noxious agents responsible for mental and emotional disorders in children and adolescents (Bond & Joffe, 1982). These include physical and organic pathogens, parental stress, social discrimination, and economic exploitation. There also are known ways to strengthen the resistance of the host. For example, successful resistance to psychological disorders can be enhanced through building social competencies and parenting abilities and additional skills training such as vocational and sex education (Albee, 1982). Also clear are the importance of ensuring self-esteem and the power of support groups and networks in helping children and adolescents resist noxious agents. Finally, psychological interventions with high-risk groups can prevent transmission of such baleful experiences as child physical and sexual abuse.

The rapidly growing literature reviewing successful primary prevention programs for families (see Bond & Wagner, 1988) encourages more widespread training in and funding for prevention. Ironically, most advanced-level training programs for mental health professionals offer scant coverage of the field of primary prevention. Current mainstream clinical training in social work and psychology emphasizes one-to-one therapeutic interventions. The financial and the status rewards of independent one-to-one therapy are powerful motivators. Opposition to prevention comes largely from those who prefer the social status quo and who argue that it is not the business of mental health workers to be involved in social change (Henderson, 1975; Lamb & Zusman, 1981; Torrey, 1991). Despite the major contributions of public health prevention initiatives to the improvements in people's physical health (including the elimination or reduction of disease and improvements in life expectancy), it is still individual medical treatment that gets all the public visibility, media exposure, and financial support. In the United States, persons of means are often willing to pay almost anything for treatment that may cure their individual disease and improve their individual physical health, their psychological functioning, and their life expectancy. The same persons may not be as willing to pay increased taxes for primary prevention programs that protect or improve the general level of mental health and that will prevent or reduce stress-related disorders in the population. If expenditures for physical and mental health are a zero-sum game, then increasing expenditures for prevention takes away funding for treatment. This in fact has been the source of arguments against funding mental health programs focused on prevention.

Eventually, we hope, the value of prevention programs will be recognized because of the accumulating evidence that prevention programs actually reduce the incidence of children's mental health disorders. There are reasons to be optimistic about the future of primary prevention. First, public health-style interventions are fairly simple and straightforward. Second, the evidence is accumulating and becoming more and more compelling that prevention programs actually reduce incidence (Albee, Bond, & Monsey, 1992; Bond & Wagner, 1988; Joffe, 1982). Third, recognition is greater that investing exclusively in treating psychopathology may be futile (Albee, 1990a). It is not that psychotherapeutic interventions do not help but rather that the large number of problem families cannot be reached by the minuscule number of therapists.

Micro and Macro Approaches to Prevention

De Lone (1979, 1982) developed an interesting contrast between what he refers to as micro approaches and macro approaches to the prevention of disturbed child development. The micro approach emphasizes the discovery of "at-risk groups" and then provides these groups with specific targeted interventions. Examples include such efforts as infant health care, home visiting, parent education, and early childhood socialization programs. These programs are applied by the selected professionals who have been carefully and extensively trained to administer the programs for the targeted group. de Lone prefers the alternative macro approach that aims at changing the broad distribution of income and wealth. One of the basic elements of such a macro program is the insurance that conditions such as full employment and economic development, especially beneficial to members of low-income groups, are the focus of change. These interventions include affirmative action programs, minimum income support systems, and other efforts aimed at achieving greater equality of at-risk groups. De Lone (1982) stated, "In current rhetoric, the foundation of a 'family policy' is viewed as economic support" (p. 495). The strategy for the macro approach involves changes in taxation and in the regulatory agencies rather than a reliance on human services bureaucracies. The goal is less to help strengthen individual victims and more to empower those who are disenfranchised. De Lone argued that targeted and specific micro interventions are often time limited, marginal, sporadic, and fleeting. More powerful interventions involve designing an income tax system that gives every family a minimum income and that redistributes income to achieve this goal. At the core of his argument is the view that economic security and high self-esteem in the parents (that comes from being freed from being welfare recipients) will lead to improved child care.

Macro programs nearly always involve the passage of laws requiring changes in behavior and redistribution of resources. One of the advantages of laws is that laws have a permanence that is lacking in micro programs. Although laws are sometimes repealed or changed, the process is much more difficult than simply a decision to stop funding a micro prevention program. Laws raising the minimum wage, requiring vaccinations for entrance to school, guaranteeing women's right to choose whether to go through a pregnancy, and forbidding social and economic exploitation and sexual harassment may be controversial, but if such laws are enforced, they can have wide-ranging preventive consequences.

Social Justice

Primary prevention perspectives often come to the conclusion that the most sensible and parsimonious way to improve the health and well-being of individuals and families is to bring about social and political changes leading to a rebalancing of power and opportunities for disadvantaged groups such as women, ethnic minority groups, and persons who are poor (Joffe & Albee, 1981). The long-range goal is a just society in which every individual and every family have an opportunity to maximize their prospects. Such a society stresses "justice as fairness."

One of the most careful and extensive expositions of the justice-as-fairness perspective was articulated by a major American philosopher, John Rawls (1971). He stated three principles:

> 1. Each person is to have an equal right to the most extensive total system of equal basic liberties compatible with a similar system of liberty for all.
> 2. Social and economic opportunities are to be arranged so they are both (a) of the greatest benefit to the least advantaged, and (b) attached to offices and positions open to all under conditions of fair equality of opportunity.
> 3. All social primary goods—liberty and opportunities, income and wealth, and the bases of self-respect—are to be distributed equally unless an unequal distribution of any or all of these goods is to the advantage of the least favored. (pp. 302-303)

In a conference sponsored by the Rosalynn Carter Institute for Human Development (Nottingham & Nottingham, 1990), Rawls's formulations were applied to the issue of family care. Participants argued that Rawls's recommendations were grounded in contract theory that emphasizes people's rights and pays less attention to people's needs. Focusing on needs alone, however, also has limitations (de Lone, 1982). The most important limitations of programs that focus on specific needs or micro programs is that they do not deal with "the cause of the causes" (Joffe, 1988). The problem with such targeted and specific interventions is that they are nearly always time limited. A home visitor program, for example, although demonstrably helpful, is in constant danger of termination as a result of changing budget priorities. Innumerable examples of micro programs are based on time-limited funding so that when the program support ends, the families who would have benefited from its continuance fall back into the same situation of unmet needs that existed before the program began.

If the underlying cause of the causes of stress results from poverty and powerlessness, then only a macro program will be effective. A macro program guaranteeing full employment or instituting a negative income tax that provides funds to the poor while taxing progressively more advantaged groups would come closer to dealing with the ultimate cause.

Such questions raise major issues about the importance of social and political action as primary prevention. Leading figures in psychiatry seriously question whether it is appropriate for mental health professionals to get involved in social and political problems (Henderson, 1975; Lamb & Zusman, 1981). But if the data suggest social contributions to psychopathology, then prevention strategies must involve intervention at the level of social variables.

A Little Epidemiology

The past two or three decades have seen a resurgence of biological explanations of child and adolescent emotional disorders (Lamb & Zusman, 1981). Organized groups of parents have joined forces with organically oriented psychiatrists to argue that mental disorders are the result of organic and biological diseases. Social learning explanations of mental disorders are rejected by some. By looking at these trends from a historical perspective, one could have predicted the present popularity of biological explanations on the basis that prior social learning explanations of mental disorders were too simplistic. Now, however, evidence from many sources supports a social learning model of mental disorder. Some of the social learning factors for which evidence is strong include family violence, poverty, and substance abuse. In addition, unmet health needs and genetic and prenatal risks are sources of stress on children and families.

Family Violence. A study of a sample of more than 2,000 two-parent American families in 1985 (Gilles & Straus, 1988) found a strikingly high level of violence by husband against wife (16%) in a given year. Violence against children was also common. Nearly 100% of young children experienced some violence during the year, with 14% being victims of severe violence (with a high risk of injury). The same report noted that violence against teenagers occurred in 34% of American families, with 6% of teenagers suffering severe violence. Violence by children against siblings and against parents occurred in 53% and

18% of the sample, respectively. The figures for teenagers were 64% and 36%. Violence was found to be more frequent in poor families. Such association of poverty and violence was explained by the stresses of economic disadvantage.

Poverty. The number of children living in poverty in the United States has continued to be high, estimated at 21% (Annie E. Casey Foundation, 1995). This figure is particularly striking given that the total number of young children has been decreasing. Working-class and ethnic minority status increases the risk for poverty. Nearly half of African American children and more than one third of children of Latin American descent are poor. Children born in poverty suffer increased levels of prematurity, low birth weight, malnutrition, and resulting mental retardation. Children have replaced elderly persons as the poorest age group.

Many responsible voices add to the chorus intoning the high risk of being poor. David Hamburg (1990), president of the Carnegie Corporation of New York, wrote about the importance of "A Decent Start: Promoting Healthy Child Development in the First Three Years of Life." Hamburg cited many problems associated with poverty. Poor women with little formal education tend to be the heaviest smokers, alcohol users, and cocaine abusers. Women at the lowest socioeconomic levels need better medical care, increased social support, better information about nutrition, and access to day care. They need medical care for their own health and the health of their children. Hamburg pointed out that fewer than half of poor and ethnic minority children under age 4 are fully immunized against preventable infections. They are at greater risk for injuries, which is the leading cause of death and disability among children, and for any stress. Hamburg called for comprehensive child development programs for economically disadvantaged children and stressed the positive consequences of home visiting programs to help with more effective child rearing in disadvantaged families.

Substance Abuse. Infants of mothers addicted to alcohol have high rates of physical and mental abnormalities (for detailed statistics on statements in this section, see U.S. Department of Health and Human Services, 1991). The most severe consequence of maternal alcohol addiction is fetal alcohol syndrome. Mothers who smoke cigarettes heavily during pregnancy tend to have infants with lower birth weight. Children born with low weight often have a range of visual-motor coordination difficulties together with more serious later social and learning problems. The incidence of fetal and infant death is also more common among children of smoking mothers. Even more serious problems are associated with maternal use of narcotics with addiction to heroin and methadone during pregnancy.

Unmet Health Needs. Somehow one becomes insensitive to the recitation of statistics that document the problems of children in society, especially the numbers who are at high risk for later mental, emotional, and learning problems. Still, any serious prevention program must examine the epidemiology of child and adolescent problems. Zigler and Finn (1982) provided a detailed summary of the unmet needs of children. The United States ranked 16th in both the incidence of infant mortality and the death of mothers in childbirth at the time of the International Year of the Child in 1979. The U.S. morbidity statistics have worsened since then. Both rates are associated with the degree of poverty, ethnic minority status, and the region of the country. The lack of prenatal care due to poverty takes a serious toll. Although the number of pregnant teenage girls has reached epidemic proportions, it is the lack of prenatal care that is largely responsible for infant mortality and prematurity. Zigler and Finn cited a Danish study that demonstrated that teenage mothers who had proper prenatal care had the fewest complications in childbirth of any age group. Poor childhood health is also associated with lack of medical care. In the United States, half the children age 15 or younger and 90% of those under age 5 have never visited a dentist. Federal health care dollars are not spent on children. Few of the children living in poverty get proper inoculations.

More than half a million children are in foster care, often permanently, throughout their childhood (Zigler & Finn, 1982). A low proportion of children placed in foster care ever return to their families. Children placed in public institutions (correctional settings, jails, and homes for children who are mentally retarded and/or disabled) are at extremely high risk for institution abuse (physical and sexual). For many of the children in these public systems, health care is absent or minimal, whereas health needs are great (Chernoff, Combs-Orme, Risley-Curtiss, & Heisler, 1994; Combs-Orme, Kager, & Chernoff, 1991).

Genetic and Prenatal Risks. Joffe (1982) completed a detailed study of genetic and prenatal factors leading to adverse outcomes in children. After a major review of these risk factors and their prevention, he discussed the cause of the causes and pointed out that major global causes often include low socioeconomic status, poor maternal education, and the low standard of living more likely to occur in disadvantaged ethnic groups. Joffe goes on,

> An interesting question arises, however. Because the broad demographic variables seem to encompass something closer to ultimate causes, and because we seem to be better able to design prevention programs when we deal with causes of causes, why do we choose a middle ground? Why do we ask: What is there about poverty that produces increases in birth defects, prematurity, perinatal death, instead of designing programs to prevent poverty? Why do we ask, what is it about powerlessness that produces breakdown, misery, and violence, instead of trying to redistribute power? (p. 148)

What is the point of citing genetic, prenatal, and early childhood disadvantage when our concern is with families and their relationship with the mental health system? The answer seems obvious. If poor and powerless families, and their children, are at significantly higher risk for later physical and mental disability, then efforts at prevention and at competence building will eventually reduce the need for therapeutic interventions. And again, as stated earlier, only successful efforts at prevention will eventually reduce the incidence of mental and emotional disorders.

Other Sources of Stress on Children and Families. Corporal punishment in the schools is permitted, and, as Zigler and Finn (1982) asked, "If the highest court in the United States condones physical abuse of children, how are we to expect parents to reject this form of discipline?" (p. 447). In addition, the need for child care has increased with the increase in the number of women in the labor force working outside the home and the continuing minimal participation of fathers in child rearing (Phares, 1992). Nearly 2 million children ages 7 to 13 come home to an empty house or apartment (Zigler & Finn, 1982). These latchkey children are truly neglected during several critical hours of the day because the quality and quantity of available child care are generally poor. There are no enforced uniform standards for child care centers. Children spend a great amount of time each day watching television or "hanging out" in malls or on street corners. A major consequence is the steadily declining level of competence in reading, mathematics, writing, and other academic subjects. With the decrease in the number of extended families and the continuing increase in the number of single-parent families living in poverty, it is clear that society must find ways of providing support for both the parent(s) and children.

Zigler and Finn (1982) suggested the development of referral information centers in every community to make families aware of day care, food stamps, and legal and health services. They emphasized the importance of expanding home visitor programs with individuals who can develop a close, trusting relationship with the individual family. They suggested the need for improvements in foster care and dramatic improvements in schools and school services. Their other recommendations included education, reduction or elimination of corporal punishment in the schools, publicly supported child care outside the home, and improvements in the training of child care professionals. Although parental leave policies in many European nations include 6 to 12 months of maternity or paternity leave with pay to provide all the benefits of a healthy start between child and parent(s), the United States is only beginning to implement parental leave policies, which are generally met with strenuous opposition from conservative business groups.

Zigler and Finn's (1982) major survey of needs and solutions was written more than a decade ago. But all of these problems still exist, and few of the recommended solutions have been carried out. Programs proposed at the federal level to support parenting, day care, child care, and child health care have been vetoed by a succession of conservative administrations. Poor children and families have little political clout, whereas dramatic improvements in the support programs for older persons reflect the political power of organized groups that vote. Although social security helps support older persons, there is no comparable social security for a majority of families and children at risk. A negative income tax, paid to those who are poor from higher taxes on affluent persons, would do far more than the sparsely available family therapy in dealing with current injustices that are the real causes of the emotional problems of children and adolescents.

Taking a Primary Prevention Approach

A Model for Primary Prevention

Most primary prevention programs developed by mental health professionals are micro programs aimed at strengthening competence, self-esteem, and social support (host resistance). A few programs target noxious agent reduction, but these are more likely to call for political and social change and are more difficult to achieve.

Reviewing a large number of effective prevention programs, Albee (1982) developed a formula using six areas of intervention that reduced incidence. Three of these (in the numerator) were aimed at reducing noxious agents, and three (in the denominator) involved efforts at increasing the resistance of the host. The model is similar to the methods of public health described earlier. The scheme covered most of the wide range of existing prevention programs (Albee, Joffe, & Dusenbury, 1988) and focused largely on specific discrete prevention programs. The formula is as follows:

$$\text{Reduction of incidence} = \frac{\text{Organic factors} + \text{Stress} + \text{Exploitation}}{\text{Social competence} + \text{Self-esteem} + \text{Support networks}}$$

For each of the six categories in the formula, given below is an example of a micro program followed by an example of a macro program.

Organic Factors. An example of a micro program focusing on organic factors is providing information to future parents about the dangers of smoking and heavy alcohol consumption during pregnancy and urging reduced use. A macro program addressing organic factors is legislation of a sharp increase in the taxes on alcohol and cigarettes, thereby reducing use.

Stress. Offering support groups for the children of alcoholic or psychotic parents may relieve some of the stresses associated with this painful family experience. Legislation that makes it possible for parents to be employed with good compensation may improve the parents' morale and provide the financial resources that benefit the children's well-being by reducing the stress associated with involuntary unemployment.

Exploitation. Home-based educational programs modeling child care skills is an effective micro program for the reduction of abuse. On the other hand, a law prohibiting the physical punishment of children, as in Sweden, has much wider macro effects.

Social Competence. Offering a course to selected kindergarten children on interpersonal problem-solving skills may enhance their social competence. But a law requiring sex education in all the schools would reach a far larger number of children and could be effective in the prevention of unplanned pregnancies and the transmission of the AIDS virus.

Self-Esteem. A school program promoting appreciation of cultural and racial differences may help to diminish the ethnic and racial discrimination and thus enhance the well-being of ethnic minority children in that school. But laws requiring affirmative action in hiring and forbidding sexual harassment, hate crimes, and child abuse are likely to have a much wider impact on the well-being of disadvantaged and discriminated-against groups.

Support Networks. A community-based foster grandparent program in which helping hands reach out to provide emotional support for children at risk has value, but social assistance programs provide support for millions of at-risk families.

A great many specific primary prevention programs are applicable to families. Most of the programs reported to "work" are micro programs (Bond & Wagner, 1988). Family-focused prevention programs supporting families through normative transitions include employer-supported child care, home-based programs for families of newborns, skills training for family relationship enhancement, cognitive training approaches to young children, programs helping the accommodation to widowhood, and programs offering support groups for caregivers of memory-impaired older persons. Programs that support families through nonnormative transitions include support for divorcing families, programs aimed at family power redistribution to reduce family violence, and programs to help families with children with chronic illness. One limitation of these micro interventions is that they often depend on temporary funding from outside sources and are sometimes short-lived.

The argument is not whether macro programs are better than micro programs. Clearly both are needed and useful. But a focus exclusively on micro programs is not the answer when, in the last analysis, the causes of a great many problems affecting children, adolescents, and families are macro factors, such as economic and social disadvantage.

A Worldwide Problem

Understandably, most of the chapters in this volume are oriented toward families, children, and adolescents in the United States. But it is worth noting that similar and even more serious problems of family poverty and children's misery exist in many other parts of the world (Albee, 1990b). A recent Vermont Conference volume (Albee et al., 1992) examined the need for improving children's lives around the world. Forty-eight authors, writing 29 chapters, discussed prevention programs in Germany, Ghana, Poland, India, Mexico, Pakistan, New Zealand, the Netherlands, the former Soviet Union, Thailand, and Canada. The basic problems for children are often reflections of excessive population growth in developing countries (in which nearly a third of the population is under the age of 15) as well as problems resulting from mass migration, rapid urbanization, and poverty. In some ways, these crises make the problems in the United States seem small by comparison. The problems of children and adolescents in other countries teach us a great deal about the social origins of psychopathology, as demonstrated by the following two examples. A chapter by Dytrych (1992) using data from Prague demonstrated the long-term negative effects on children that followed the refusal by government authorities of requests for abortion of unwanted pregnancies. Another chapter (Abbott, 1992) demonstrated the increase in aggressiveness in children as a result of watching television violence. Other chapters clearly illustrate economic and social problems in developing countries and their social consequences that operate negatively on children. Because individual therapy is not available in the developing countries, primary prevention is the only strategy that could be considered.

The Best Prevention

The Commission on the Prevention of Mental/Emotional Disorders of the National Mental Health Association (1986) sought testimony from a wide range of experts in the fields of genetics, family planning, infancy and early childhood experience, adolescence, marital relationships, nutrition, and aging. The commission's goal was to develop a monograph that might stimulate programs designed to reduce the incidence of mental and emotional disabilities across the life span. One afternoon, as the members of the commission were discussing the testimony they had heard from experts that morning, one of the members asked, "If we had just one prevention program we could put into place, and knew that it would succeed, which one would that be?" This question led to a couple of hours of discussion. Finally, members of the commission agreed on an answer. They would choose a program that would ensure that every baby born would be a healthy, full-term infant who was welcomed into the world by parents (a parent) who were financially secure, who had decided in advance that they (she) wanted the child, and who had planned for the child's conception and birth. Members of the commission agreed that such a child would have a significantly better chance of growing up to be both physically and emotionally healthy. If every child arrived under these conditions, the rate of mental and emotional problems in the next generation would be reduced significantly. There would also be a gradual reduction in overpopulation.

Various members of the commission began adding footnotes. Child spacing is important. It would be wonderful if the child were breast-fed by a physically and emotionally nourished mother. The mother (and father) should not be a smoker or a heavy user of alcohol or other drugs before or during pregnancy and subsequent to the arrival of the child. The mother would have had adequate prenatal health care including a diet sufficient in protein, calcium, iodine, iron, and other essential nutrients. For mothers who were at high risk, amniocentesis would have been available with an opportunity to decide about the termination of the pregnancy if the fetus was found to be damaged. The child would be born into a society that made both female and male children equally welcomed. The parent(s) would enjoy economic security and be engaged in meaningful work. The child would have access to good day care, good schools, and good social support systems.

In reality, unfortunately, there are many exceptions and barriers to these ideal arrangements. But many groups even oppose striving to achieve the ideal conditions that are described. Opposition to family planning, to contraception, and to providing the economic and social supports for parents are widespread and well known (see Joffe & Albee, 1981).

Conclusion

Children and adolescents are influenced strongly, positively or negatively, by their family situation. Families, in turn, are influenced strongly, positively or negatively, by economic and social opportunities and cultural climate. Where poverty, powerlessness, unemployment, racism, sexism, and homophobia prevail, so will children's vulnerability to physical and mental disorders. If society commits itself to finding ways of reducing stress on the family and to providing economic and social opportunities to parents, it will at the same time increase the likelihood that children's well-being will improve. Such commitments require a focus on economic policies and programs that are based on social justice.

References

Abbott, M. W. (1992). Television violence: A proactive prevention campaign. In G. W. Albee, L. A. Bond, & T. C. Monsey (Eds.), *Improving children's lives: Global perspectives on prevention* (pp. 263-278). Newbury Park, CA: Sage.

Albee, G. W. (1982). Preventing psychopathology and promoting human potential. *American Psychologist, 37,* 1043-1050.

Albee, G. W. (1990a). The futility of psychotherapy. *Journal of Mind and Behavior, 11,* 369-384.

Albee, G. W. (1990b). Suffer the little children. *Journal of Primary Prevention, 11*(2), 69-82.

Albee, G. W., Bond, L. A., & Monsey, T. C. (Eds.). (1992). *Improving children's lives: Global perspectives on prevention.* Newbury Park, CA: Sage.

Albee, G. W., Joffe, J. M., & Dusenbury, L. (Eds.). (1988). *Prevention, powerlessness, and politics: Readings on social change.* Newbury Park, CA: Sage.

Anderson, H. (1988, November 7). The global poison trade: How toxic waste is dumped on the Third World. *Newsweek, 112,* 66.

Annie E. Casey Foundation. (1995). *Kids Count data book: State profiles of child well-being.* Baltimore: Author.

Baruch, G. K., Biener, L., & Barnett, R. C. (1987). Women and gender in research on work and family stress. *American Psychologist, 42,* 130-136.

Bond, L. A., & Joffe, J. M. (Eds.). (1982). *Facilitating infant and early childhood development.* Hanover, NH: University Press of New England.

Bond, L. A., & Wagner, B. M. (Eds.). (1988). *Families in transition: Primary prevention programs that work.* Newbury Park, CA: Sage.

Bullard, R. D. (1990). Ecological inequities and the New South: Black communities under siege. *Journal of Ethnic Studies, 17,* 101-115.

Canetto, S. S. (1992, August). *The family mystique in American psychology.* Paper presented at the 100th meeting of the American Psychological Association, Washington, DC.

Chernoff, R. G., Combs-Orme, T., Risley-Curtiss, C., & Heisler, A. H. (1994). Assessing the health status of children entering foster care. *Pediatrics, 93,* 594-601.

Clearly, P. D., & Mechanic, D. (1983). Sex differences in psychological distress among married people. *Journal of Health and Social Behavior, 24,* 111-121.

Cole, L., & Hall, I. N. (1970). *Psychology of adolescence.* New York: Holt, Rinehart, & Winston.

Combs-Orme, T., Kager, V., & Chernoff, R. (1991). Utilization of health care by foster children: Application of a theoretical framework. *Children and Youth Services Review, 13,* 113-129.

Commission on the Prevention of Mental/Emotional Disorders. (1986). *Report of the commission.* Alexandria, VA: National Mental Health Association.

Coontz, S. (1992). *The way we never were: American families and the nostalgia trap.* New York: Basic Books.

Curtis, R. (1986). Household and family in theory on inequality. *American Sociological Review, 51,* 168-183.

de Lone, R. H. (1979). *Small futures: Children, inequality, and the limits of liberal reform.* New York: Harcourt Brace Jovanovich.

de Lone, R. H. (1982). Early childhood development as a policy goal: An overview of choices. In L. A. Bond & J. M. Joffe (Eds.), *Facilitating infant and early childhood development* (pp. 485-502). Hanover, NH: University Press of New England.

Dytrych, Z. (1992). *Children born from unwanted pregnancies: Prevention of psychological subdeprivation.* In G. W. Albee, L. A. Bond, & T. C. Monsey (Eds.), *Improving children's lives: Global perspectives on prevention* (pp. 97-106). Newbury Park, CA: Sage.

Falk, P. J. (1989). Lesbian mothers: Psychosocial assumptions in family law. *American Psychologist, 44,* 941-947.

Gilles, R. J., & Strauss, M. A. (1988). *Intimate violence.* New York: Simon & Schuster.

Glenn, E. N. (1987). Gender and the family. In B. B. Hess & M. M. Ferree (Eds.), *Analyzing gender* (pp. 348-380). Newbury Park, CA: Sage.

Grant, J. P. (1988). *The state of the world's children* [UNICEF annual report]. New York: Oxford University Press.

Grant, J. P. (1989). *The state of the world's children.* [UNICEF annual report]. New York: Oxford University Press.

Hamburg, D. (1990). A decent start: Promoting healthy child development in the first three years of life. President's essay reprinted from the 1990 *Annual Report* (pp. 3-16). New York: Carnegie Corporation.

Hare-Mustin, R. T. (1987). The problem of gender in family therapy theory. *Family Process, 26,* 15-27.

Henderson, J. (1975). Object relations and the new social psychiatry: The illusion of primary prevention. *Bulletin of the Menninger Clinic, 39,* 233-245.

Joffe, J. M. (1982). Approaches to prevention of adverse developmental consequences of genetic and prenatal factors. In L. A. Bond & J. M. Joffe (Eds.), *Facilitating infant and early childhood development* (pp. 121-158). Hanover, NH: University Press of New England.

Joffe, J. M. (1988). The cause of the causes. In G. W. Albee, J. M. Joffe, & L. Dusenbury (Eds.), *Prevention, powerlessness, and politics: Readings on social change.* Newbury Park, CA: Sage.

Joffe, J. M., & Albee, G. W. (Eds.). (1981). *Prevention through political action and social change.* Hanover, NH: University Press of New England.

Lamb, H. R., & Zusman, J. (1981). A new look at primary prevention. *Hospital and Community Psychiatry, 32,* 843-848.

Lambrecht, B. (1991, November 17). The American Indians' hunting grounds are now dumping grounds. *St. Louis Post-Dispatch,* pp. 1A, 10A, 11A.

Mirowsky, J., & Ross, C. E. (1989). *Social causes of psychological distress.* New York: Aldine de Gruyter.

Nottingham, J., & Nottingham, J. (Eds.). (1990). *The professional family caregiver: Dilemmas, rewards and new directions* [Inaugural conference papers, Rosalynn Carter Institute for Human Development]. Americus: Georgia Southwestern College.

Phares, V. (1992). Where's poppa? The relative lack of attention to the role of fathers in child and adolescent psychopathology. *American Psychologist, 47,* 656-664.

Rawls, J. (1971). *A theory of justice.* Cambridge, MA: Harvard University Press.

Thorne, B. (1982). Feminist rethinking of the family: An overview. In B. Thorne & M. Yalom (Eds.), *Rethinking the family: Some feminist questions* (pp. 1-24). New York: Longman.

Torrey, E. F. (1991, January). The guru of prevention calls for social change. *APA Monitor,* p. 28.

U.S. Department of Health and Human Services, Public Health Service. (1991). *Healthy people 2000: National health promotion and disease prevention objectives: Full report with commentary.* Washington, DC: Government Printing Office.

Zigler, E., & Finn, M. (1982). A vision of child care in the 1980s. In L. A. Bond & J. M. Joffe (Eds.), *Facilitating infant and early childhood development* (pp. 443-465). Hanover, NH: University Press of New England.

Implementing Community Mental Health Programs

Lessons Learned From the Mental Health Initiative for Urban Children

MARY C. TELESFORD

The Mental Health Initiative for Urban Children was funded by the Annie E. Casey Foundation in October 1992. Its goal is to improve the life chances of children and youth in urban areas. The initiative views mental health in broad terms, including concern for the healthy development of all children in the target neighborhoods, support for families to help them nurture and care for their children, and development of a pro-family system of care for children with severe emotional or behavioral problems. Thus, the long-range vision of the initiative is the development of a reconfigured continuum of prevention, early intervention, and intensive services, experienced by the family as a seamless network of services and supports. The initiative is operating in four urban communities—Boston, Massachusetts; Miami, Florida; Richmond, Virginia; and Houston, Texas. These communities have an overwhelming preponderance of community and personal poverty, illicit drug activity, alcoholism, lower-income families, high school dropouts, and unwed and teenage mothers. Many households are headed by minority, single females with limited education and job skills, dependent on public assistance to maintain their families. In addition, high rates of violent crime permeate the whole environment, making it unsafe and particularly homicidal for African American and Latino/Hispanic men. Furthermore, because of the environment in which these families live, they have learned to be distrustful and suspicious of "another program designed to help them." They have seen programs come and go, but their neighborhoods and families continue to face the same and escalating problems. Combating this suspicion and lack of trust is a major concern when developing and implementing community mental health programs and outreach strategies to get parents involved.

This initiative uses two approaches to develop and implement these community programs. First, community and individual strengths are recognized. Second, a comprehensive outreach strategy is used.

Using Strengths in Building a System of Care

Some people look at a glass of water and say it is half empty. Looking at the same glass of water, others declare it half full. When observing the Casey Mental Health Initiative sites, some persons choose to focus on the deficits. Approaching the development of a system of care on the basis of deficits or a deficit model is a big mistake. A deficit model fosters a system for, and not with, those who will have to use it and increases the likelihood of the system inappropriately addressing the needs of a community. Conversely, developing a system of care on a strength-based model facilitates the involvement of those who will be using the services, thereby enhancing the appropriateness of the system for community residents. Thus, a strength-based model promotes a pro-family system of care and encourages family preservation and well-being (see also Hunter & Friesen, Chapter 2, and Marsh, Chapter 5, in this volume).

To build on the existing strengths of the communities and individuals, mental health programs encouraging reformed systems of care should include the following considerations to appropriately respond to the needs of children, adolescents, and their families in the community in which the program is implemented:

- Build capacity in the neighborhood by better supporting and building liaisons among community-based organizations, especially around service delivery practices.
- Identify individuals of strength to enhance their leadership skills and educational pursuits and to assist them in their desire to attain meaningful employment so they can maintain their families outside the public assistance system.

Strengths in Communities

These communities have several strengths. They provide—in some cases, informally—support, education, and guidance to community residents.

Churches. In many of the sites, churches provide not only religious training and spiritual uplift but also food and clothing banks, soup kitchens, day care centers for elderly persons, child care services for working mothers, recreational programs, and a safe haven for homeless families, individuals, and children. Preachers and elders in the church are often community leaders and can provide the history of a community, as well as basic assessments of needs, wants, and fears of residents. Churches represent organized constituency bases in many of these communities.

Community-Based Organizations. Nested throughout the neighborhoods, community-based organizations (CBOs) provide various direct services to residents. These services include substance abuse clinics and counseling, parenting skills education, tutoring, and various training from literacy to employment preparedness. These organizations are funded both privately and publicly. Many of them serve as beacons of hope for the most unserved and underserved community residents. These organizations regularly hire local community members; because of the CBOs' close proximity to and long history with community residents, they strive to provide culturally and linguistically appropriate services.

Schools. Schools are the optimal setting for assessing the well-being of children. Often, it is at school that the problems of a child or a child's home life are noticed, particularly if the child is coming to school unkempt, hungry, sleepy, withdrawn, or noncommunicative or has recurring absences. These and other problems can result in poor behavior and poor classroom performance. Those schools in the Casey Initiative sites that provide strengths are those that have developed the trust of parents and have strong parent-family input bonds and parent-teacher-administrator relationships. The schools for some of these communities house other activities, especially recreational activities, that are sorely lacking in the community as a whole. Schools are also sites for adult education and parenting classes, especially targeting teenage mothers. Some schools also serve as clothing and food distribution centers.

Individual Strengths

As previously mentioned, these communities are overwhelmingly composed of households headed by women. Many of these women live in public housing communities and rely on public assistance to maintain their families. Many had their secondary education interrupted by starting their families as teenagers. Despite these hardships, some of these women exhibit personal strengths that are to be commended and encouraged in similarly situated women who are not coping as well. These "women of strength" have some of the following common characteristics.

Spiritual Base. Whether they are affiliated with churches or mosques, those women for whom spirituality plays an important role in their lives seem to be able to meet the challenges of maintaining themselves and their families. This spirituality sustains their optimism and keeps them striving.

Strong Support Systems. A strong support system affords many of the women an extra pair of hands for child care or a shoulder to cry on when situations get tough. This support network may include biological relatives but, most likely, comprises an extended family network including friends and neighbors.

Value of Education. Education is highly valued. Realizing the dire consequences in not obtaining or delaying their own education, these women insist that their children do well in school. They have come to understand that education is the ticket out of poverty not only for their children but for themselves as they strive to obtain their own high school diplomas, GEDs, or additional job training.

Employment Possibilities. Along with valuing education is a concomitant desire to gain a job. These women want not just any position but one that leads to a career opportunity that will offer a wage or salary sufficient to cover all living expenses including child care, food, housing, and health insurance.

Involvement in the Community. Involvement in community activities provides the women an opportunity to give back to the community and helps to raise self-esteem. They are involved in school and church activities. Many of their homes become safe havens for neighborhood children. Some of the women are part of an informal neighborhood watch, assisting police in addressing the violence and illegal drug activity rampant in their communities.

Sobriety. Sobriety plays a part in enhancing coping skills for the women as they maintain themselves and families. This is no surprise, because a clear mind obviously is better than one clouded by substance abuse. Despite the prevalence of drug and alcohol abuse in these communities, most of the women have never had a problem with drug or alcohol abuse. For those women who are recovering from such addictions, their ability to achieve and sustain abstinence means they too can successfully maintain themselves and families. A driving incentive for drug-abusing parents to get help is the desire to take care of their children. The dilemma, however, is that overcoming their substance abuse may involve hospitalization for an extended time, forcing questions of child care and custody. Many substance-abusing parents do not want to relinquish their children to the foster care system for fear their children will be lost or abused. Simply admitting a substance abuse problem also carries the overriding concern of losing custody of children. Involvement in designing foster care arrangements while retaining some control of their children's eventual setting seems to ameliorate this fear. These arrangements can include placing children with biological family members or in the parents' extended family networks. This allows the parents to address their substance abuse issues in earnest while their children remain in a familiar and caring environment. The unification of the family on rehabilitation is most successful when parents continue to follow up their recovery through either Alcoholics Anonymous or Narcotics Anonymous.

The Outreach Strategy

Although recognizing that each neighborhood is different geographically, culturally, and linguistically, a "generic" outreach strategy to reach families in the mental health initiative sites should include the following elements:

- Identification of community leaders
- Appropriate logistical planning for meetings
- Presentation of an initiative that is "family friendly"
- Intensive follow-up with support group development and parent involvement, leading to empowerment

Identification of Community Leaders

Each community has natural leaders. Many times, these community leaders are not particularly well educated or worldly in knowing much about that which is beyond their communities. Nevertheless, they are trusted and well-known in their respective communities and, therefore, once their support for the program is obtained, are valuable in encouraging others in the community to participate in an initiative. These natural leaders can be found in various places including churches, schools, resident councils of public housing projects, Head Start and day care programs, senior citizen centers, teen programs (especially those that address the needs of teenage parents), and the homes of Good Samaritans, those moms who watch others' children in addition to their own or who participate in community crime watch patrols.

Appropriate Logistical Planning for Meetings

Respecting Geographical Boundaries. Community leaders should be consulted to identify geographical boundaries that the community residents respect. In many of the Casey Mental Health Initiative sites, community residents recognize definitive neighborhoods to which they give their allegiance and support. Any other area, even just a block away, is not of concern even though it is within the designated initiative site. For instance, many of the sites have more than one public housing complex, and each of these complexes views itself as a neighborhood and wishes to address only the concerns of that particular housing complex. There are also areas that are not part of public housing complexes in which residents address only the concerns of these areas.

Meeting Site Selection. Once the geographical boundaries have been discerned, thereby giving an indication of how many first meetings need to be held, a meeting site should be selected within each of the areas. When choosing the meeting site, consideration should be given to its accessibility either by public transportation or on foot because many of the families may not own or have access to a car. In public housing complexes, usually a hall or recreation center can be acquired free of charge by residents. Other good meeting sites include schools and churches that are viewed as sensitive to the community. If the residents, for whatever reason, feel that the site is not a friendly place, they will not attend a meeting there.

Meeting Time and Date. In many of these neighborhoods, safety is a big issue, and many parents are fearful of being robbed or mugged, especially after dark. For many of the families, especially in public housing complexes, the best time of day is between 4:30 and 7:00 p.m.

Meetings scheduled between the 2nd and the 15th of the month (except on Sundays, because of church activities) usually result in the best turnouts. Those on public assistance tend to have more money, be in better spirits, and be more receptive to something new during the first half of the month. Toward the end of the month, when food stamps begin to run out and money is tighter, parents are worried about holding on until the first of the month and, understandably, are not in a frame of mind to hear about "something new." Some communities schedule their meetings as part of some other common festivity in the community such as an annual picnic or community festival.

Publicizing the Meeting. The meeting needs to be publicized in places that families frequent because many of the families do not have telephones or have mail or newspapers delivered to their homes. Community leaders are helpful in identifying these places. Some of the best ways to reach families include the following:

- Fliers posted in laundromats, places that cash checks (not banks), clinics, schools, churches, grocery stores, public transportation stops, and day care centers
- Announcements made by community leaders at PTA meetings, church meetings, Head Start meetings, and resident council meetings
- Public service announcements on local radio and television stations
- Word of mouth

The aforementioned ways of reaching families do not preclude the more conventional ways of reaching some families. Mailing lists and telephone numbers supplied by schools, churches, day care centers, and other organizations within the community are also effective tools for reaching families who have telephones and regular mail delivery.

Incentives. It is important to provide and publicize the availability of child care and food at the meeting, as well as transportation to and from the meeting, if necessary. In addition, meetings should have a festive air, including music, balloons, and door prizes.

Presentation of a Family-Friendly Initiative

The first meeting to discuss a program should be presided over by a community leader. Program presentations should include a description of the initiative by an individual from the funding agency or by a state representative. The description should be just the facts—not too technical and with a strong emphasis on *how it will help the families and what they can expect.* The issue of mental health should be described in the broadest of terms to include mental well-being, at-risk children, and prevention to lessen anxiety that might discourage program participation. The director of the project or parent coordinator can address some of the specific concerns exhibited by the community that the initiative could target for reform.

The value of family input to this type of initiative should be emphasized, and assistance in the development of family and advocacy support groups to get families involved in a hands-on way should be provided. It is critical in the implementation of any program that families understand that they are a valued part of the initiative. Through the support networks and their collective voice, families can help to implement and, moreover, sustain system reform that is responsive to their needs.

Intensive Follow-Up

It is important to follow up the first meeting with another meeting relatively quickly, within the next month. The purpose of the second meeting is to organize the parents' efforts to fulfill two basic roles. The first role is to support and organize activities to deliver relief to parents who are experiencing problems with public services such as child welfare, housing, employment, mental or physical health, transportation, and education. The second role is to involve parents in the collaborative process. These two roles will shape and guide the activities that parents will engage in during the course of the Casey Mental Health Initiative.

Support Group Development

As stated above, one of the main roles for parents in the Casey Initiative is to support activities to deliver relief to parents who are experiencing problems with public services. Support group development facilitates this process.

At the follow-up meeting, parents discuss working together to make the community better through the guidance of a facilitator. The group can select priorities for the group as a whole, or smaller work groups can be formed to address the issues. For example, if the education support group wants to understand the individual education plan process that affects many of the families whose children are being screened for special education, the project staff would be responsible to schedule training to assist parents in understanding what this process is and how to negotiate it. After the training, parents will have the tools and skills necessary to work in an informed manner and in the best interest of their children. In addition to taking part in issue-specific training, parents could participate in advocacy and other training deemed necessary to facilitate the empowerment process.

Support group development, coupled with training that leads to success in addressing families' immediate problems, motivates parents to stay involved in the project and to experience an empowering process, individually and collectively, that can be sustained. Moreover, support group activity increases the potential for system reform by identifying issues and gaps in service delivery that need to be addressed through the program. The support groups are also a direct line to the community and, therefore, serve as a current barometer of community concerns and activity.

Parent Involvement in the Collaborative Process

The second role for parents in an initiative is parent involvement in the collaborative process. Historically, parents, especially poor minority parents on public assistance, were viewed by professionals as part of the children's problems. They were never seen as partners in addressing the needs and concerns that directly affected their families. Professionals *assessed* families, *talked* to families, and *arranged* their lives for them. Many parents accepted the professionals' roles as caretakers and caregivers, trusting their fate to those who, because of education and title, knew what was best—or at least what was available—for their families. It is clear that this relationship between parents and professionals has not worked in the best interest of the families.

One way that the Casey Initiative promotes parent and professional collaboration is through the participation of both groups on neighboring governing boards. Parents bring family and community history that is equally valuable as professional expertise in effecting systems change and reform. Trainers can aid in the collaborative process, which may not be the smoothest at all times, particularly at the beginning.

The Role of Parents in the Context of the Empowerment Process

Understanding support group development and parent-professional collaboration in the context of the empowerment process for parents is critical to sustaining parent involvement in the initiative. As mentioned earlier, many of the parents in the mental health initiative sites suffer from low self-esteem and self-worth. These feelings result from being on the lower rung of the socioeconomic ladder, living in the "worst part of town," and relying on many public systems that are, at best, mediocre and often poor. These conditions of life are often internalized, and many parents do not feel that they are "the masters of their fates." They feel that they are at the mercy of something or someone else—the welfare system, the transportation system, the social worker, the education system, the public housing system—that or who determines how their families' most basic needs of food, shelter, clothing, health care, and education are met. It is a challenge of the empowerment process to get parents to feel good about themselves and to channel the positive energy into action that will improve their lives and the lives of their children (see also Heflinger & Bickman, Chapter 6 in this volume).

It cannot be stressed enough that the empowerment process is one that comes from the inside out, not the outside in. This means that parents have to initiate this process because they feel they can, they have the right to, and they have a means to take control of their lives. Increased control over one's life is directly related to the rise in self-esteem and overall self-concept. In short, the empowerment process means assisting in the realization of power on the basis of positive self-concept; *empowerment cannot be given or granted.*

Professionals will struggle with their need to dominate and lead parents. Parents, amazed and testing their new "empowered attitudes," may still be somewhat intimidated by professionals and, therefore, may not assert themselves or engage in a forthright manner in neighborhood governing board activities. The flip side of the coin is that parents, imbued with their new sense of importance, will be overbearing and demand that professionals only do things their way. Of course, the correct posture for collaboration between parents and professionals is somewhere in between. Striking a happy median is the job of various trainers who will help parents and professionals work together in a collaborative way. As the new governing boards struggle with the collaborative process, it is hoped that the historical polarization of parents and professionals abates and that a true parent-professional partnership is formed to facilitate the systems reform that will serve their respective communities in the most appropriate way.

Conclusion

The experience gained through the Casey Mental Health Initiative demonstrates that programs offering mental health services to children, adolescents, and their families should be designed in a way that is sensitive to the communities and populations for which the programs are intended. Program designers should take advantage of community and individual strengths, rather than focusing solely on their deficits. Moreover, community and population characteristics should guide program implementation, thereby ensuring appropriate service delivery to children and families.

Families of Children and Adolescents With Serious Emotional Disturbance

Innovations in Theory, Research, and Practice

DIANE T. MARSH

Approximately 15% to 19% of children and adolescents suffer from emotional or other problems that warrant mental health treatment (Tuma, 1989), including 12% (7.5 million) who are believed to have a diagnosable mental illness (Institute of Medicine, 1989). There is general agreement that the system has failed to meet the needs of this population. For example, only 20% to 30% of children and adolescents in need are receiving appropriate mental health services (Dougherty, 1988). The knowledge of how to serve this population effectively is not reflected in the allocation of funds or the availability of services (Knitzer, 1988), and the families of these young people often receive little assistance (McElroy, 1987). The price of this failure is incalculable for these children and adolescents, for their families, and for society. As Horowitz and O'Brien (1989) have remarked, "Every child who does not take his or her place as a productive adult diminishes the power of that society's future" (p. 445).

Needed is fundamental change in the way we conceptualize, finance, and provide mental health care for children and adolescents (Inouye, 1988). That change is currently under way. It is manifested both in a transformation of parent-professional relationships and in a restructuring of mental health services for children and adolescents. The new modes of family-professional relationships are reflected in a commitment to "building bridges" between the two groups (Backer & Richardson, 1989); in more favorable attitudes and cognitions (Lefley, 1989); in an emphasis on family empowerment (Collins & Collins, 1990; Heflinger & Bickman, Chapter 6 in this volume); and in the formation of institutional alliances with families that are designed to meet the needs of all family members (Grunebaum & Friedman, 1988; Hunter & Friesen, Chapter 2 in this volume).

Family-professional relationships are increasingly viewed as collaborative partnerships that are designed to build on the expertise of both parties; to respect the needs, desires, concerns, and priorities of families; to enable families to play an active role in decisions that affect them; and to establish mutual goals for treatment and rehabilitation. In a manner consistent with these positive developments, greater emphasis is being placed on the strengths, resources, and adaptive capacities of families, which have often been minimized in the past (e.g., Hatfield & Lefley, 1987), and on the value of parental input regarding their children and the service delivery system (Tarico, Low, Trupin, & Forsyth-Stephens, 1989). There also has been increasing recognition of the adverse consequences of earlier models that incorporated unverified assumptions of family pathogenesis or dysfunction (Friesen & Koroloff, 1990; Lourie & Katz-Leavy, 1991).

Concurrently, many developments have occurred at the level of mental health systems planning. As Tuma (1989) has discussed, a child advocacy system is needed that can coordinate federal, state, and local services in a comprehensive network designed to meet the mental health, physical, and social needs of children and adolescents. The Child and Adolescent Service System Program (CASSP) offers such a comprehensive system of care. Stroul and Friedman (1986) have provided an overview of CASSP that is child centered, with the needs of the child and family dictating the types and mix of services provided, and community based, with the locus of services as well as management and decision-making responsibility resting at the community level. Objectives of the program include the following: (a) access to a comprehensive array of services that can address all of the needs of this population, (b) coordination and integration of services, (c) an individualized service plan, (d) treatment in the least restrictive environment, (e) full participation of families and surrogate families, (f) early identification and intervention, and (g) protection of the rights of children and adolescents and of their families.

The CASSP system of care model consists of seven major dimensions of service: (a) mental health services, (b) social services, (c) educational services, (d) health services, (e) vocational services, (f) recreational services, and (g) operational services designed to facilitate service integration and coordination. Such a unified service system mandates new roles for parents, enhancing the parent-professional collaborative relationship through parents' full membership on interdisciplinary treatment teams and their involvement in service system assessment and planning (Lourie & Katz-Leavy, 1991).

Theory: A Competence Paradigm

Needed also are new conceptual models that can foster constructive developments in theory, in research, and in practice with families of children and adolescents who have serious emotional disturbance. A competence paradigm for clinical practice with families offers a positive alternative to the traditional pathology paradigm that has guided clinical practice in the past. As indicated in Table 5.1, these paradigms differ in (a) their fundamental nature, (b) their view of families, (c) emphasis, (d) the role of professionals, (e) the role of families, (f) the basis of assessment, (g) the goal of intervention, (h) modus operandi, (i) systemic perspective, and (j) services model.

On the other hand, the paradigms are not mutually exclusive because a competence paradigm offers a more comprehensive framework that subsumes a pathology paradigm as a particular instance. For example, a competence paradigm acknowledges the possible presence of pathology, as well as the potential benefits of psychotherapy in empowering individuals or families when such pathology is present. Similarly, an ecological systems framework includes the family system at an intermediate level in a much larger complex that contains many such levels, ranging from the individual to society.

There are many advantages to a competence paradigm for professional practice, which assumes that families are basically competent

Table 5.1 A Paradigm Shift in Professional Practice With Families

	Pathology Paradigm	*Competence Paradigm*
Nature of paradigm	Disease-based medical model	Health-based developmental model
Families Viewed as	Pathologic, pathogenic, or dysfunctional	Potentially competent
Emphasis on	Weaknesses, liabilities, and illness	Strengths, resources, and wellness
Role of professionals	Practitioners	Enabling agents
Role of families	Clients or patients	Collaborators
Assessment based on	Clinical topologies	Competencies and competence deficits
Goal of intervention	Treatment of family pathology	Enablement and empowerment or dysfunction
Modus operandi	Provision of psychotherapy	Enhancement of coping effectiveness
Systemic perspective	Family systems	Ecological systems
Services model	Authoritarian/ medical model	Collaborative/ educational model

SOURCE: Adapted from Marsh (1992c).

and that the role of professionals is to assist them in meeting their own goals (Roberts & Magrab, 1991). As Masterpasqua (1989) has discussed, a competence paradigm receives strong empirical support from many areas of psychology, facilitates the identification and remediation of adaptational competencies, tends to destigmatize psychotherapy through its emphasis on competencies and competence deficits rather than on normality or abnormality, views individual problems as embedded in a sociopsychological matrix, and offers the potential for more precise research regarding therapeutic outcome. Similarly, Maluccio (1981) has specified the benefits of a competence-oriented social work practice that is designed to facilitate the natural adaptive process of clients and to promote their competence in interacting with their environment.

A competence paradigm has been applied to professional practice with families in general (e.g., Beavers & Hampson, 1990; Ponzetti & Long, 1989), as well as with families who have a member with a disability (Dunst, Trivette, & Deal, 1988; Marsh, 1992b) and with families of people who have serious mental illness (Marsh, 1992a). From the perspective of such a paradigm, the objective of professional practice is to empower families in achieving mastery and control over the circumstances of their lives. A competence paradigm also offers an excellent framework for research and professional practice with families of children and adolescents who have serious emotional disturbance.

Research: The ABCX Model

Hill's (1949) ABCX model of family stress provides an example of the competence paradigm applied to research on families (also see Patterson, Chapter 7 in this volume). The general literature concerned with familial stress rarely addresses the catastrophic nature of serious mental health problems for families. Yet the serious mental illness or emotional disturbance of a family member meets all but one of the criteria of catastrophic stressors identified by Figley (1989). For example, serious emotional disturbance is often characterized by little time to prepare, slight previous experience, few sources of guidance, an absence of shared experience with other families, a continuing crisis, lack of control and a sense of helplessness, a sense of loss, disruption and destruction, possible dangerousness, and high emotional impact. Only a single criterion, the presence of medical problems, does not apply to this tragic family event.

As is the case for other catastrophic stressors, such as the serious physical illness or developmental disability of a family member, families undergo a process of adaptation. There is empirical support for the value of the ABCX model in delineating the familial process of adapting to mental retardation (Bristol, 1987; Frey, Greenberg, & Fewell, 1989; Minnes, 1988), as well as to other familial stressors. The model has limitations, however, including the failure to attend to the multiple interdependent levels of the social systems and the need for more precise specification of the central variables (Walker, 1985). Despite these limitations, there is general agreement that the ABCX model has heuristic value for research and important implications for intervention with families (e.g., Orr, Cameron, & Day, 1991).

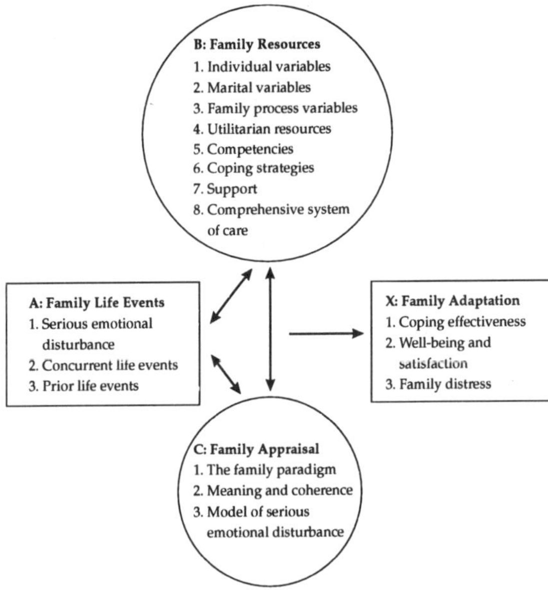

Figure 5.1. Familial Adaptation to Serious Emotional Disturbance: An Application of the ABCX Model

The ABCX model provides a useful framework for research concerned with the familial experience of serious emotional disturbance. This model draws heavily from research concerned with coping and adaptation (e.g., Kessler, Price, & Wortman, 1985; Matheny, Aycock, Pugh, Curlette, & Cannella, 1986); with familial stress (e.g., Figley, 1989); and with the familial experience of developmental disability (Friedrich, Wiltumer, & Cohen, 1985; Wikler, 1986). In general, the ABCX schema includes four components or categories of variables (discussed below): A, the life event; B, the family's resources; C, the family's appraisal of the event; and X, the impact on the family. See Figure 5.1 for an application of the ABCX model.

As applied to serious emotional disturbance, the ABCX model includes a number of variables in each of the four components. The first category, family life events, includes (a) the serious emotional disturbance of a young family member, (b) concurrent life events, and (c) prior life events. The second category, family resources, consists of (a) individual variables (wellness, self-esteem, self-efficacy, beliefs, and commitments); (b) marital variables (status, satisfaction, roles, and consensus); (c) family process variables (boundaries, hierarchical organization, family homeostasis, information processing, differentiation, and emotional climate); (d) utilitarian resources (educational level and family income); (e) competencies (cognitive, behavioral, affective, and social); (f) coping strategies; (g) support (informal support network and formal support network); and (h) a comprehensive system of care. The third category, family appraisal, consists of (a) the family paradigm, (b) meaning and coherence, and (c) the family's model of serious emotional disturbance (interpersonal, biological, and diathesis-stress). The final category, family adaptation, includes (a) coping effectiveness (with the serious emotional disturbance and with other adaptive demands), (b) sense of well-being and satisfaction, and (c) level of family distress. Measures of many of these variables are available.

A: Family Life Events

Family life events consist of those present and past events that are potential stressors for family members. One such event is the serious emotional disturbance of a child or adolescent. There is much evidence of the devastating impact of this event for families (e.g., Marsh, 1992a; McElroy, 1987). As Lefley (1989) has discussed in connection with serious mental illness, families generally experience a subjective burden that includes the experience of a range of negative emotions including stress, worry, anxiety, resentment, guilt, depression, anger, fear, frustration, and bitterness; a powerful sense of loss of the family member they knew prior to the onset of the illness; and the presence of empathic pain, as families share in the distress of their relative over an impoverished life.

Families also experience a substantial objective burden related to caregiving, the symptomatic behavior of the relative, disruptions in family functioning, stigmatization in the larger society, and problems with the mental health system. Indeed, the burden of families has sometimes been increased by a mental health system that is insensitive and unresponsive to their needs (e.g., Collins & Collins, 1990; Friesen & Koroloff, 1990; Knitzer, 1988; Lourie & Katz-Leavy, 1991; McElroy, 1987; Modrcin & Robison, 1991; Tarico et al., 1989). In addition to the life events related to serious emotional disturbance, the overall context of familial stress includes concurrent life events that may increase the family burden, as well as prior events that may have depleted the resources of the family.

B: Family Resources

An extensive literature is concerned with the familial process of coping and adaptation to stress and with the resources that can facilitate that process. For example, Matheny et al. (1986) formulated a comprehensive model that includes a taxonomy of behaviors and resources that are related to coping. Coping behaviors include (a) cognitive restructuring, (b) problem solving, (c) tension reduction, (d) use of social skills, (e) self-disclosure/catharsis, (f) structuring, (g) seeking information, (h) stress monitoring, (i) assertive responses, (j) avoidance/withdrawal, (k) suppression/denial, and (l) self-medication. Coping resources include the following: (a) social support, (b) beliefs/values, (c) confidence/control, (d) wellness, (e) self-esteem, and (f) other behaviors or resources. On the basis of their meta-analysis of research in the area, Matheny and his colleagues cite the relative effectiveness of social skills training, problem solving, cognitive restructuring, and relaxation training.

Considerable literature also deals with family adaptation to stressful events. For example, Figley (1989) identified 11 characteristics of functional family coping: (a) clear acceptance of the stressor, (b) a family-centered locus of problem, (c) solution-oriented problem solving, (d) high tolerance, (e) clear and direct expressions of commitment and affection, (f) open and effective communication, (g) high family cohesion, (h) flexible family roles, (i) efficient use of resources, (j) absence of violence, and (k) infrequency of substance use.

This general literature has been applied productively to the familial experience of developmental disability. Wikler (1986) cited eight potential resources among families of children with disabilities: (a) individual variables; (b) marital variables; (c) family interactional variables; (d) extended family variables; (e) intimate friends; (f) friends and neighbors; (g) community groups, clubs, and workplace acquaintances; and (h) professionals and human services organizations. She identified three levels of family resources including personal supports, the informal support network, and the formal support network. In their work with parents of children with Down syndrome, Damrosch, Lenz, and Perry (1985) developed a Parental Coping Scale that generated the following eight subscales: (a) cognitive restructuring, (b) expression of negative affect, (c) wish-fulfilling fantasy, (d) self-blaming, (e) information seeking, (f) minimization of threat, (g) communication of feelings, and (h) special feelings (e.g., feeling special about parenting a child with Down syndrome).

In addition, valuable literature concerns the familial experience of serious mental illness. Zipple and Spaniol (1987) described four categories of coping responses: problem oriented, emotional, cognitive, and physical. More specifically, there is now evidence for the value of such coping strategies as seeking information about mental illness and its treatment, acquiring skills for coping with the illness and its consequences for the family, joining a support group, seeking outlets outside of the family, and advocating for better services (e.g., Hatfield & Lefley, 1987).

Eight family resources are relevant to coping with the serious emotional disturbance of a child or adolescent. The discussion below summarizes variables that have been examined in research.

Individual Variables. There is general agreement that such personal qualities as wellness (overall physical and mental health), self-esteem (positive feelings about oneself), and self-efficacy (expectations of personal mastery) can enhance coping effectiveness (e.g., Bandura, 1990; Matheny et al., 1986). Other variables that can influence the process of adaptation include beliefs, such as those concerned with religiosity and locus of control, and commitments (e.g., Lazarus & Folkman, 1984).

Marital Variables. Given the central role of parents in coping with the serious emotional disturbance of a child, the nature and quality of their relationship is an important consideration. For example, coping effectiveness is likely to be influenced by separation or divorce, by the level of marital satisfaction, by the degree to which caregiving and other responsibilities are shared, and by the extent of consensus regarding the serious emotional disturbance and its treatment.

Family Process Variables. Many family process variables are relevant to coping with serious emotional disturbance (see Marsh, 1992a). These include the following: (a) boundaries, which can range from permeable to rigid; (b) hierarchical organization, which pertains to the arrangement of family subsystems (parental, marital, sibling, and extrafamilial); (c) family homeostasis, which involves the maintenance of family equilibrium and coherence; (d) information processing, which is concerned with the communication within the family and between the family and the larger ecosystem; (e) differentiation, which focuses on the separation and individuation of family members; and (f) a satisfactory emotional climate in the home. A number of professionals have discussed these and other family process variables (e.g., Steinglass, 1987).

Utilitarian Resources. The utilitarian resources of the family can make a substantial difference in their ability to locate and access appropriate services. These resources include parental level of education and yearly income.

Competencies. Families need a range of competencies for coping with the serious emotional disturbance, with its consequences for the family, and with the mental health system. These competencies fall into four general areas (see Marsh, 1992a): (a) cognitive (e.g., an understanding of serious emotional disturbance and its treatment); (b) behavioral (e.g., behavior management skills); (c) affective (e.g., resolution of the emotional burden); and (d) social (e.g., use of the support network).

Coping Strategies. As discussed above, many coping strategies can assist families in coping with serious emotional disturbance. Cognitive strategies include seeking information, developing realistic expectations, and reframing to focus on personal and family strengths. Behavioral coping strategies include the development of skills such as conflict resolution, assertiveness, behavioral management, and stress management. Emotional strategies include employment of mature defenses and seeking of personal or family counseling when appropriate. Finally, social strategies include seeking informal and formal sources of support, striving to maintain a normal family lifestyle, developing interests and connections outside the family, and moving into advocacy roles.

Support. In light of the family burden that accompanies the serious emotional disturbance of a young family member, an essential resource for families is support from their informal and formal support networks. The informal support network consists of the nuclear family, the extended family, friends and acquaintances, neighbors, coworkers, and other families. The formal support network includes professionals and service providers, social institutions, and the government. Much evidence exists for the value of social support in mitigating the deleterious effects of stress (e.g., Kessler, Price, & Wortman, 1985) and in benefiting families of people with mental illness (e.g., Hatfield & Lefley, 1987).

A Comprehensive System of Care. The availability of an adequate system of care for children and adolescents would significantly improve the lives of their parents, who often find themselves pressed into service to compensate for gaps in the continuum of care and to serve as case managers for their children. As exemplified by the CASSP model, a comprehensive system of care incorporates all of the structural components that constitute a true continuum of care as well as operational or functional interconnections for enhancing service coordination and integration. Such a system of care also must include a strong family support component, including respite care.

Friesen and Koroloff (1990) cited four barriers to the development of a system of family-centered services: (a) an emphasis on the child, rather than the family, as the target of services; (b) a narrow concern with mental health services, rather than the full range of services needed by the child and the family; (c) an overemphasis on formal services that has often ignored the support provided by informal networks; and (d) a failure to make use of the resources and expertise of parents and other family members. They also noted the constructive changes that are currently under way, as well as the new roles for parents as partners of administrators and providers.

C: Family Appraisal

From the perspective of a transactional model of stress, a life event becomes stressful only after it has been appraised as threatening (Singer & Davidson, 1991). Family appraisal involves the collective members' beliefs about the stressor that may or may not make it traumatizing for the family system (Figley, 1989). Many variables can influence the process of appraisal (e.g., Lazarus & Folkman, 1984). As Wikler (1986) has discussed, family members may view a stressor as easy or difficult to manage, as fate or an act of aggression against the family, or as a challenge or an overwhelming load. These differences in perception also influence whether family members regard themselves as helpless victims or active agents.

With respect to the familial experience of serious mental illness, Terkelsen (1987) cited the following five variables that influence the process of appraisal: (a) the extent of the family members' involvement in the daily life of the client; (b) the models of causation, symptoms, and outcomes that are assumed by family members; (c) the phenomenology and natural history of the illness; (d) such individual factors as personality and life history, life cycle issues, generic responses to hardship, and prior experience with mental illness; and (e) the social network, which is often disrupted by the presence of mental illness in the family. He noted that the appraisal process is complex and dynamic and that the meaning of mental illness for family members is likely to change during the course of a lifetime. All these considerations are likely to apply to the process of family appraisal in the case of serious emotional disturbance.

The Family Paradigm. Reiss and Klein (1987) have explored the role of the family paradigm in mediating the response to stressful events. The family paradigm consists of the underlying assumptions about reality that are shared by all family members and that guide their construction of reality. For example, families may differ in their sense of mastery, in their commitment to family solidarity, and in their openness to current experience and new coping responses. In the face of severe stress, families may need to reformulate their family paradigm. Families who lack the flexibility to modify their paradigm may be unable to respond effectively to altered circumstances, with the risk of family disintegration.

Meaning and Coherence. Another important component of appraisal is the family's ability to restore a sense of meaning and coherence to their lives. Taylor (1983) has argued that successful adaptation to threatening events often involves a search for meaning in the experience and an effort to regain mastery and to restore self-esteem. Similarly, Thompson and Janigian (1988) maintained that adaptation to a negative event may require changing one's life scheme to restore a sense of order and purpose in life. There is some empirical support for the role of meaning and coherence in adaptation to stressful events. For example, Antonovsky and Sourani (1988) found that family sense of coherence (the extent to which the world is seen as comprehensible, manageable, and meaningful) was associated with successful adaptation to family stressors.

Model of Serious Emotional Disturbance. The family's model of serious emotional disturbance also influences family appraisal, as Terkelsen (1987) discussed regarding the familial appraisal of serious mental illness. He observed that an interpersonal theory of etiology, such as one that assumes family pathogenesis, may significantly increase the familial burden of guilt, whereas a biological model may result in feelings of helplessness and despair in the face of an unalterable illness. Interpersonal and biological models are likely to have a similar impact on families who are dealing with serious emotional disturbance. In contrast to these narrower models, a diathesis-stress model assumes the presence of a predisposing factor, such as biological vulnerability, that interacts with life events that may precipitate, ameliorate, or exacerbate the illness (e.g., Engel, 1980). In the case of serious emotional disturbance, a diathesis-stress model may reduce the subjective burden of families (because a biological predisposition is assumed) and may motivate them to cope effectively with the disturbance (because environmental circumstances may affect its manifestation and course).

X: Family Adaptation

Three general criteria of family adaptation are (a) the effectiveness of family members in coping with the serious emotional disturbance and with other adaptive demands, (b) their sense of well-being and satisfaction, and (c) the level of family distress. Although the ABCX model has not been applied to families who have children and adolescents with serious emotional disturbance, it has been used effectively to examine family adaptation under other circumstances (e.g., Lavee, McCubbin, & Patterson, 1985). In light of the changes that are likely to characterize family adaptation through time (see Zipple & Spaniol, 1987), it is important to conduct longitudinal research that incorporates measures of adaptation. In fact, an expanded double ABCX model has been formulated to reflect changes in all of the relevant variables through time (e.g., Figley, 1989).

Practice: Effective Intervention Strategies

To address the needs of families who have children and adolescents with serious emotional disturbance, it is necessary to develop an array of services that can be matched to their specific needs, desires, and resources. A full continuum of family-oriented services consists of nonclinical services, designed primarily to provide education and support to families, and clinical services, designed to offer treatment (see also Hunter & Friesen, Chapter 2 in this volume).

Nonclinical Intervention

Educational programs and support groups are two effective nonclinical intervention strategies. Educational programs can meet many family needs. For example, such programs can impart information about serious emotional disturbance and its treatment, can assist families in making an accurate appraisal of the disturbance and its consequences for the family, and can teach a range of skills and coping strategies needed by families (see Hatfield, 1990). A 10-week educational program provides a general structure that can be modified to meet needs in specific settings. Weekly topics include the nature and purpose of the program; serious emotional disturbance; services, agencies, and resources; the family experience; developmental perspectives; parent-child relationships; stress, coping, and adaptation; enhancing personal and family effectiveness (2 weeks); and family-professional relations.

Given the many needs of children and adolescents with serious emotional disturbance, it is important to address all service systems that may be required. For example, many children and adolescents receive special education services. Relevant topics for their families include identification, evaluation, the individualized education program (IEP), related services, procedural safeguards, least restrictive environment, confidentiality, parental rights, and legal aspects (e.g., the Education of All Handicapped Children Act of 1975 and the Individuals With Disabilities Education Act of 1990 [IDEA]). If an educational program is offered in a mental health setting, a school psychologist might be invited to discuss the educational system with parents. The general program can be altered to meet the needs of specific populations, such as children and adolescents who are involved with the child welfare or criminal justice system, those who have specific diagnoses, those who also have substance abuse problems, and those who are receiving medication.

Families who are coping with serious emotional disturbance often feel stigmatized by the larger society and alienated from the usual channels of social support. Support groups offer one means of providing social support. Such groups include local affiliates of the National Alliance for the Mentally Ill Children and Adolescents Network (NAMI-CAN) and the Federation of Families, as well as support groups within treatment settings. Strong evidence shows the value of support groups for families under these circumstances (e.g., Hatfield, 1987).

Support groups appear to meet three essential family needs: support, education, and empowerment. The groups support families in mobilizing resources and mastering emotional burdens in a protected and nurturing environment. They provide education about serious emotional disturbance, practical problem solving, and coping strategies. The groups further empower families, acting as a vehicle for consumer advocates to improve the mental health system. Professionals can serve with family members as facilitators or cofacilitators of support groups as well as consultants to existing groups. A number of resources are available for professionals who wish to develop a support group for families (e.g., Donner & Fine, 1987).

In addition to educational programs and support groups, many other nonclinical services may benefit families, including educational seminars focusing on specific topics, skills-oriented workshops, crisis groups, drop-in centers, advocacy groups, written materials, newsletters, multifamily groups, and forums that use professional and community resources. It is important to solicit the input of family members early on, as such programs are developed. In addition, many programs can benefit from the use of professional-family member teams.

A comprehensive program of nonclinical services should include the following components: (a) a didactic component that provides information about serious emotional disturbance and the mental health system; (b) a skills component that offers training in communication, conflict resolution, problem solving, assertiveness, behavioral management, and stress management; (c) an emotional component that provides opportunities for grieving, for sharing, and for mobilizing resources; (d) a family process component that focuses on coping with mental illness and its sequelae for the family; and (e) a social component that increases use of informal and formal support networks.

Clinical Intervention

Clinical intervention also offers a valuable resource for some family members, who can benefit from psychotherapy designed to assist them in resolving problems that are reactive to the serious emotional disturbance of their young family member or in addressing other mental health problems that may have been precipitated or exacerbated by current stress. Initially, professionals can assist families in exploring the nature and purpose of specific nonclinical and clinical services, the potential benefits and risks of these services, the risks of forgoing the services, and the available alternatives. Once families have decided to undertake a course of psychotherapy, a process of differential therapeutics can ensure the best match between professional services and the needs, desires, and resources of specific families (see Frances, Clarkin, & Perry, 1984).

A range of therapeutic variables should be considered, including format (individual therapy, marital therapy, family therapy, and group therapy); orientation (e.g., psychodynamic, cognitive-behavioral, and existential-humanistic); and duration and frequency. Given the diversity among families, each of the clinical formats and orientations is likely to be appropriate under some circumstances. Similarly, a flexible approach to duration and frequency is likely to be most useful to families, who may benefit from professional assistance on an as-needed basis, particularly during crises or periods of inpatient treatment.

There are some general guidelines for clinical practice with families. First, a number of treatment goals are appropriate for families under these circumstances. These include the provision of support, the strengthening of competencies that are relevant to coping with serious emotional disturbance and its sequelae for the family, the enhancement of coping strategies, the reframing of personal and familial experience, and the expression and working through of painful emotions. Bernheim's (1982) supportive family counseling is consonant with these goals and is designed to provide information, to offer emotional support, to acknowledge the needs of family members, and to assist families in coping effectively.

Second, there is the risk of negative treatment effects with this population (see Marsh, 1992a). For example, there are risks associated with family therapy that is based on assumptions of family pathogenesis or dysfunction (Appleton, 1974; Drake & Sederer, 1986; Terkelsen, 1983). There are also risks when family therapy is mandated by agencies as a condition for treating a child or adolescent. Families who are seeking assistance for their relative may not see themselves as needing or wanting treatment (Grunebaum & Friedman, 1988) and may object to being treated as the "unidentified patient" (Bernheim, 1989, p. 562). Such mandatory family therapy also is in conflict with the ethical principle of informed consent.

The third guideline, consistent with the general psychotherapy literature, is the overarching importance of the quality of the therapeutic alliance that is formed with families. Effective professional practice is likely to be fostered by a respectful and empathic attitude toward families, an understanding of their phenomenological reality, an effort to meet their expressed needs, and a goal of family empowerment.

Conclusion

A competence paradigm as portrayed in Table 5.1 can guide theory, research, and practice in mental health services for children and adolescents and their families. It is likely to foster the development of alliances between families and professionals; to facilitate the identification, assessment, and enhancement of the competencies that are relevant to coping with serious emotional disturbance; to offer the potential for more precise theory and research concerned with families; to provide a blueprint for designing, implementing, and evaluating professional services; to improve the service system for children and adolescents; and to promote the empowerment of families.

References

Antonovsky, A., & Sourani, T. (1988). Family sense of coherence and family adaptation. *Journal of Marriage and the Family, 50*, 79-92.

Appleton, W. S. (1974). Mistreatment of patients' families by psychiatrists. *American Journal of Psychiatry, 131*, 655-665.

Backer, T. E., & Richardson, D. (1989). Building bridges: Psychologists and families of the mentally ill. *American Psychologist, 44*, 546-550.

Bandura, A. (1990). Conclusion: Reflections on nonability determinants of competence. In R. J. Stemberg & J. Kolligian (Eds.), *Competence considered* (pp. 315-362). New Haven, CT: Yale University Press.

Beavers, W. R., & Hampson, R. B. (1990). *Successful families: Assessment and intervention.* New York: Norton.

Bernheim, K. F. (1982). Supportive family counseling. *Schizophrenia Bulletin, 8*, 634-641.

Bernheim, K. F. (1989). Psychologists and families of the severely mentally ill: The role of family consultation. *American Psychologist, 44*, 561-564.

Bristol, M. M. (1987). Mothers of children with autism or communication disorders: Successful adaptation and the double ABCX model. *Journal of Autism and Developmental Disorders, 17*, 469-486.

Collins, B., & Collins, T. (1990). Parent-professional relationships in the treatment of seriously emotionally disturbed children and adolescents. *Social Work, 35*, 522-527.

Damrosch, S. P., Lenz, E. R., & Perry, L. A. (1985). Use of parental advisors in the development of a Parental Coping Scale. *Maternal-Child Nursing Journal, 14*, 103-109.

Donner, R., & Fine, G. Z. (1987). *A guide for developing self-help groups for parents of children with serious emotional problems.* Washington, DC: Georgetown University Child Development Center.

Dougherty, D. (1988). Children's mental health problems and services: Current federal efforts and policy implications. *American Psychologist, 43*, 808-812.

Drake, R. E., & Sederer, L. I. (1986). The adverse effects of intensive treatment of chronic schizophrenia. *Comprehensive Psychiatry, 27*, 313-326.

Dunst, C. J., Trivette, C. M., & Deal, A. G. (1988). *Enabling and empowering families: Principles and guidelines for practice.* Cambridge, MA: Brookline.

Education of All Handicapped Children Act of 1975, Pub. L. No. 94-142, 20 U.S.C. § 1401-1461, 34 C.F.R. § 300, Subpt. A.

Engel, G. L. (1980). The clinical application of the biopsychosocial model. *American Journal of Psychiatry, 137*, 535-544.

Figley, C. R. (1989). *Helping traumatized families.* San Francisco: Jossey-Bass.

Frances, A., Clarkin, J., & Perry, S. (1984). *Differential therapeutics in psychiatry: The art and science of treatment selection.* New York: Brunner/Mazel.

Frey, K. S., Greenberg, M. T., & Fewell, R. R. (1989). Stress and coping among parents of handicapped children: A multidimensional approach. *American Journal on Mental Retardation, 94,* 240-249.

Friedrich, W. N., Wiltumer, L. T., & Cohen, D. S. (1985). Coping resources and parenting mentally retarded children. *American Journal of Mental Deficiency, 90,* 130-139.

Friesen, B. J., & Koroloff, N. M. (1990). Family-centered services: Implications for mental health administration and research. *Journal of Mental Health Administration, 17*(1), 13-25.

Grunebaum, H., & Friedman, H. (1988). Building collaborative relationships with families of the mentally ill. *Hospital and Community Psychiatry, 39,* 1183-1187.

Hatfield, A. B. (1987). Social support and family coping. In A. B. Hatfield & H. P. Lefley (Eds.), *Families of the mentally ill: Coping and adaptation* (pp. 191-207). New York: Guilford.

Hatfield, A. B. (1990). *Family education in mental illness.* New York: Guilford.

Hatfield, A. B., & Lefley, H. P. (Eds.). (1987). *Families of the mentally ill: Coping and adaptation.* New York: Guilford.

Hill, R. (1949). *Families under stress.* New York: Harper & Row.

Horowitz, F. D., & O'Brien, M. (1989). In the interest of the nation: A reflective essay on the state of our knowledge and the challenges before us. *American Psychologist, 44,* 441-445.

Individuals With Disabilities Education Act of 1990 (IDEA), 20 U.S.C. § 1400 et seq.

Inouye, D. K. (1988). Children's mental health issues. *American Psychologist, 43,* 813-816.

Institute of Medicine. (1989). *Research on children and adolescents with mental, behavioral, and developmental disorders: Mobilizing a national initiative.* Washington, DC: National Academy Press.

Kessler, R. C., Price, R. J., & Wortman, C. B. (1985). Social factors in psychopathology: Stress, social support, and coping processes. *Annual Review of Psychology, 36,* 531-572.

Knitzer, J. (1988). Policy perspectives on the problem. In J. G. Looney (Ed.), *Chronic mental illness in children and adolescents* (pp. 53-72). Washington, DC: American Psychiatric Press.

Lavee, Y., McCubbin, H. I., & Patterson, J. M. (1985). The Double ABCX Model of family stress and adaptation: An empirical test by analysis of structural equations with latent variables. *Journal of Marriage and the Family, 47,* 811-825.

Lazarus, R. S., & Folkman, S. (1984). *Stress, appraisal, and coping.* New York: Springer.

Lefley, H. P. (1989). Family burden and family stigma in major mental illness. *American Psychologist, 44,* 556-560.

Lourie, I. S., & Katz-Leavy, J. (1991). New directions in mental health services for families and children. *Families in Society: The Journal of Contemporary Human Services, 72,* 277-285.

Maluccio, A. N. (Ed.). (1981). *Promoting competence in clients: A new/old approach to social work practice.* New York: Free Press.

Marsh, D. T. (1992a). *Families and mental illness: New directions in professional practice.* New York: Praeger.

Marsh, D. T. (1992b). *Families and mental retardation: New directions in professional practice.* New York: Praeger.

Marsh, D. T. (1992c). Working with families of people with serious mental illness. In L. VandeCreek & S. Knapp (Eds.), *Innovations in clinical practice: A source book* (Vol. 11, pp. 389-402). Sarasota, FL: Professional Resource Press.

Masterpasqua, F. (1989). A competence paradigm for psychological practice. *American Psychologist, 44,* 1366-1371.

Matheny, K. B., Aycock, D. W., Pugh, J. L., Curlette, W. L., & Cannella, K. A. (1986). Stress coping: A qualitative and quantitative synthesis with implications for treatment. *Counseling Psychologist, 14,* 499-549.

McElroy, E. (Ed.). (1987). *Children and adolescents with mental illness: A parents' guide.* Kensington, MD: Woodbine House.

Minnes, P. M. (1988). Family resources and stress associated with having a mentally retarded child. *American Journal on Mental Retardation, 93,* 184-192.

Modrcin, M. J., & Robison, J. (1991). Parents of children with emotional disorders: Issues for consideration and practice. *Community Mental Health Journal, 27,* 281-292.

Orr, R. R., Cameron, S. J., & Day, D. M. (1991). Coping with stress in families with children who have mental retardation: An evaluation of the Double ABCX model. *American Journal on Mental Retardation, 95,* 444-450.

Ponzetti, J. J., & Long, E. (1989). Healthy family functioning: A review and critique. *Family Therapy, 16,* 43-50.

Reiss, D., & Klein, D. (1987). Paradigm and pathogenesis: A family-centered approach to problems of etiology and treatment of psychiatric disorders. In T. Jacobs (Ed.), *Family interaction and psychopathology* (pp. 203-255). New York: Plenum.

Roberts, R. N., & Magrab, P. R. (1991). Psychologists' role in a family-centered approach to practice, training, and research with young children. *American Psychologist, 46,* 144-148.

Singer, J. E., & Davidson, L. M. (1991). Specificity and stress research. In A. Monat & R. S. Lazarus (Eds.), *Stress and coping: An anthology* (3rd ed., pp. 36-47). New York: Columbia University Press.

Steinglass, P. (1987). A systems view of family interaction and psychopathology. In T. Jacobs (Ed.), *Family interaction and psychopathology* (pp. 25-65). New York: Plenum.

Stroul, B. A., & Friedman, R. M. (1986). *A system of care for severely emotionally disturbed children and youth.* Washington, DC: Georgetown University Child Development Center.

Tarico, V. S., Low, B. P., Trupin, E., & Forsyth-Stephens, A. (1989). Children's mental health services: A parent perspective. *Community Mental Health Journal, 25,* 313-326.

Taylor, S. E. (1983). Adjustment to threatening events: A theory of cognitive adaptation. *American Psychologist, 38,* 1161-1173.

Terkelsen, K. G. (1983). Schizophrenia and the family: II. Adverse effects of family therapy. *Family Process, 22,* 191-200.

Terkelsen, K. G. (1987). The meaning of mental illness to the family. In A. B. Hatfield & H. P. Lefley (Eds.), *Families of the mentally ill: Coping and adaptation* (pp. 128-150). New York: Guilford.

Thompson, S. C., & Janigian, A. S. (1988). Life schemes: A framework for understanding the search for meaning. *Journal of Social and Clinical Psychology, 7,* 260-280.

Tuma, J. M. (1989). Mental health services for children: The state of the art. *American Psychologist, 44,* 188-199.

Walker, A. J. (1985). Reconceptualizing family stress. *Journal of Marriage and the Family, 47*, 827-837.

Wikler, L. M. (1986). Family stress theory and research on families of children with mental retardation. In J. J. Gallagher & P. M. Vietze (Eds.), *Families of handicapped persons: Research, programs, and policy issues* (pp. 167-195). Baltimore: Paul H. Brookes.

Zipple, A. M., & Spaniol, L. (1987). *Families that include a person with a mental illness: What they need and how to provide it: Trainer manual.* Boston: Boston University Center for Psychiatric Rehabilitation.

Family Empowerment

A Conceptual Model for Promoting Parent-Professional Partnership

CRAIG ANNE HEFLINGER
LEONARD BICKMAN

Changes in treatment philosophy during the past two decades that favor community care over institutionalization have resulted in many more children with serious emotional disorders living with or near their families. Researchers, parent advocates, and policy analysts agree that it is important to involve parents and other family members in the process of meeting the mental health needs of children and adolescents. Some propose that parental involvement should be encouraged because of its end product—improved outcomes for children and families (Burns & Friedman, 1989). Others (Dunst, Trivette, & Deal, 1988; Friesen, 1989; Hobbs et al., 1984) support the process itself, arguing that involving parents has intrinsic value and that it satisfies an ethical obligation to parents and families, prior to any consideration of outcome.

AUTHORS' NOTE: Preparation of this manuscript was supported by a grant (R01MH-46136-01) from the National Institute of Mental Health (Principal Investigator: Leonard Bickman).

Regardless of the process versus outcomes orientation, the function of the family system (Bronfenbrenner, 1979; Stucky & Newbrough, 1983) is to facilitate the interaction between the child and the service system. In other words, the relationship between parents and professionals is a central dimension of children's mental health services—a dimension that should be examined and strengthened. This chapter reviews the supports for and barriers inhibiting parent-professional partnership and proposes a conceptual model for promoting and evaluating family empowerment.

Policy and Parental Mandates

The Child and Adolescent Service System Program (CASSP), currently housed in the Center for Mental Health Services within the Substance Abuse and Mental Health Services Administration of the Public Health Service, U.S. Department of Health and Human Services, has promoted the view of families as full participants in all aspects of the planning and delivery of services to children with serious emotional disorders. Furthermore, the CASSP principles stress that the needs of families must be addressed in addition to the needs of the child client (Stroul & Friedman, 1986; Vosler-Hunter, 1989).

In addition to policy directives such as CASSP, family members have begun to express more vocally their needs and desires for involvement in mental health service delivery. Parents have requested a combination of information, education, and support from mental health professionals (Bernheim, 1989; Hatfield, 1983; Holden & Lewine, 1982) and others who work with their children. Furthermore, some parents have reported that they want the opportunity to assume an active role in making decisions about their children's treatment. Parents "want in the game" (Heflinger, 1989, p. 62)—information, resources, and participation. This need is a recurrent theme in parent accounts, whether the focus is on families of children and adolescents with serious emotional disturbance (Collins & Collins, 1990; Sokoly, 1993); of young children with developmental disabilities and other handicapping conditions (Able, 1986; Heflinger, 1989; Sokoly, 1991); or of adults with chronic mental illness (Hatfield & Lefley, 1987; Marsh, 1992).

These policy and parental mandates point toward a partnership model of parent-professional interaction, in which both parties join to determine and meet information and treatment needs (Cunningham & Davis, 1985b). The term *partnership* implies collaboration and sharing to reach some common goal; it suggests "a relationship . . . involving close cooperation and joint rights and responsibilities" (*Webster's*, 1988, p. 859). The acknowledgment of both (a) joining for a common purpose and (b) complementarity of differences between parents and professionals is crucial to attain partnership (Cunningham & Davis, 1985a, 1985b).

Conceptual Strands Supporting Parent-Professional Partnership

The partnership model of parent-professional interaction grows out of and is supported by many converging conceptual strands. Hobbs and colleagues (1984; Moroney & Dokecki, 1984) proposed a needs-based framework for services and policies that has been applied to a broad spectrum of human services. They proposed that services to individual family members should not only promote the development and competence of that individual but also encourage that individual's family and community to become more caring and competent. To accomplish this goal of strengthening families, shared responsibility between parents and professionals and other service providers is encouraged.

This needs-based framework is associated with developmental and social-ecological approaches (Bronfenbrenner, 1976; McConachie, 1986; Munger, 1991) in which the focus moves away from the individual child experiencing problems to the context of his or her family. Families are viewed as moving through developmental stages, each of which requires specific family tasks to be mastered (Carter & McGoldrick, 1988). Supporting families in their abilities to master these tasks is one goal of such a social-ecological approach. Families are also viewed as small systems, transacting with other systems in the community. Providing support as families negotiate the network of social systems is a second goal. A third goal is relieving family stress and helping families develop constructive ways to manage tension and overload. The fourth goal of this approach is recognizing the primacy of social supports to families in the community. "The challenge, then, is to identify ways in which . . . parents are enabled to maintain and enhance their capabilities for making intelligent choices and managing resources in the interests of their children" (Moroney & Dokecki, 1984, p. 231).

A philosophical strand that also supports this model of parent-professional interaction is that of transactionalism. Transactionalism was developed as an epistemological and methodological position by Dewey and Bentley (1949/1973), and "posits the simultaneous and inseparable operation of the person-environment system" (Dokecki, 1978, p. 19). The relationship between the individual and the environment, including that between child and family or between child-in-family and service system, is seen as dynamic, constantly changing, and impossible to separate into distinct entities. A transactional approach to mental health service delivery implies (a) that any definition of a child's problem must include recognition of the context within which the child operates and include the frames of reference of the child and other family members and (b) that any treatment plan must recognize the dynamic and changing interrelationships between the child, the family, the mental health professional, and the broader social system within which they operate (Heflinger & Dokecki, 1989). This formulation, therefore, requires active participation by all family members in treatment planning and decision making.

Yet another converging strand that emphasizes the importance of developing parent-professional partnerships is that of client and family rights. The mid-1960s ushered in an era focused on the autonomy of the individual that questioned government and professionals as benevolent caretakers (Rothman, 1978). This movement promoted the view that clients and family members act as citizens, rather than as "children, to be helped, told what to do, and kept off the streets" (Rappaport, 1981, p. 11). It further assumed a conflict of interest in the power-dependence roles of expert-client. Democratic participation in all aspects of community life, an implicit assumption of American society, also supports the exercise of client and family rights (Zimmerman & Rappaport, 1988). Parental advocacy on behalf of their children and themselves, first in the field of developmental disabilities and more recently in mental health, has grown out of this strand. Perhaps the most widely applied practice of parental rights in treatment planning has been in the area of special education: In 1975, the Education of All Handicapped Children Act (P.L. 94-142) and its subsequent reauthorization included parent participation as a due process provision of a "free and appropriate public education" (Sec. 602) for children with special needs.

Models of Parent-Professional Partnership

With the growing consensus promoting parent-professional partnership, new roles for professionals and models of intervention are being prescribed. Schön (1983) has provided a conceptual model that articulates the desired interaction. Called a *reflection in action* model, it requires both participants (professionals and parents, or clients in a therapeutic relationship, as was the focus of his book) to assume active roles in defining, exploring, and solving the problems that bring them together. Professionals and parents both contribute knowledge in determining what is "in the best interest" of the child and family. Professionals bring expertise in child development and the service system, for instance, yet realize that knowledge is incomplete without the perspective of the parents, especially in formulating goals and making decisions. Parents have the expertise regarding their child and family on the basis of living experiences (Featherstone, 1981). Knowledge from both sources is necessary for informed decision making (Sokoly, 1991). What Schön called reflection in action provides a strong contrast to *technical rationality,* promoted in more traditional practice models whereby professional expertise takes precedence over, and may even disregard, parental knowledge and experience (see Table 6.1). Schön's conceptual framework is particularly helpful in exploring partnership because he describes both professional and parental attitudes and beliefs that underlie these two opposing models.

The ideas captured in the reflection in action model shown in Table 6.1 have been advanced in discussions of new practice models. Bernheim (1989) described *family consultation* as a role for mental health professionals in which consumer satisfaction is a crucial outcome variable. A consultation model implies partnership and full competence, participation, and choice of actions of the consultee, in

Table 6.1 Attitudes and Beliefs of Parents and Professionals in Two Models of Parent-Professional Interaction

	Interaction Model	
	Technical Rationality	*Reflection in Action*
Parent	I put myself into the professional's hands and, in doing this, I gain a sense of security based on faith.	I join with the professional in making sense of my case and, in doing this, I gain a sense of increased involvement and action.
	I have the comfort of being in good hands. I need only comply with the professional's advice and all will be well.	I can exercise some control over the situation. I am not wholly dependent on the professional; he or she is also dependent on me for information and action that only I can undertake.
	I am pleased to be served by the best person available.	I am pleased to be able to test my judgments about my situation. I enjoy the excitement of discovery about the professional's knowledge, about the phenomena of services, and about myself.
Professional	I am presumed to know and must claim to do so, regardless of my uncertainty.	I am presumed to know, but I am not the only one in the situation to have relevant and important knowledge. My uncertainties may be a source of learning for me and for them.
	Keep my distance from the parent and hold on to the expert role. Give the parent a sense of my expertise but convey a feeling of warmth and sympathy as a "sweetener."	Seek out connections to the parent's thoughts and feelings. Allow his or her respect for my knowledge to emerge from discovery of it in situation.
	Look for deference and status in the parent's response to my professional persona.	Look for the sense of freedom and of real connection to the parent as a consequence of no longer needing to maintain a professional facade.

SOURCE: Adapted from Schön (1983) and Sokoly (1993).

this case, the parent. Lefley (1989) has portrayed this type of intervention as forming *alliances* between families and professionals. This also has been called a *consumer* (Cunningham & Davis, 1985b) or *partnership* (Mittler & McConachie, 1983) model of parent-professional relationships in which both parents and professionals acknowledge the need for and seek to establish a collaborative relationship, sharing expertise to achieve some common purpose—to benefit the child, in this instance. Such a model differs from the traditional models of expert and transplant. In the expert model, the professional remains dominant in decision making and service delivery. In the transplant model, the professional expertise is shared with parents in a one-way interaction, not taking parental perceptions or needs into account, as depicted by Schön's (1983) technical rationality model described above.

Additional models include an *enablement model of helping* (Dunst & Paget, 1991; Dunst et al., 1988; Dunst, Trivette, Starnes, Hamby, & Gordon, 1993). This model is based on a philosophy of collaboration and mutuality—in other words, a philosophy grounded in parent-professional partnership. Another example of a parent-professional partnership model, specifically focused on parents of children with emotional and behavioral problems and the professionals who work with them, is the Families as Allies Project promoted by the Research and Training Center on Family Support and Children's Mental Health in Portland, Oregon. In this project, parents and professionals jointly participate in group training and communication sessions aimed at exploring facets of effective collaboration and the barriers to parent-professional partnership (Vosler-Hunter, 1989; see also Hunter & Friesen, Chapter 2 in this volume).

Recognition of parents as experts on their child makes them invaluable members of the treatment team. Not only do parents provide essential experiential information regarding the child's history and behavior, but simultaneously they are the most omnipresent treatment "provider" in their 24-hour-per-day care responsibilities. The inclusion of parents as active participants on the treatment team can benefit the family system by reinforcing the executive function of parents as well as diminishing the traditional role of parents as "patients" or "clients" in favor of a partnership or collaborative role (Friesen & Koroloff, 1990). The Families as Allies model has been implemented nationally through CASSP support and has provided a wealth of materials and information for promoting parent-professional partnership (e.g., Kelker, 1987a, 1987b; Schweitzer & Hankins, 1990).

Some family support programs (Weiss & Greene, 1992) have also focused on parental strengths and creation of partnerships with parents to convey information and support competence and growth.

Barriers to Parent-Professional Partnership

Although active parental participation has been endorsed by many individuals and supported by converging conceptual strands, a great gap continues to exist between the intent to involve family members and the actual experiences of parents and professionals in mental health service delivery. Families of individuals with serious emotional disorders have typically been excluded from meaningful participation or cast as part of the problem (Lefley, 1989; Moroney, 1986). Furthermore, a discrepancy between parent and professional viewpoints often can hamper communication and active participation. McElroy (1987) suggested that families with an emotionally disturbed member "march to the beat of a different drummer" (p. 225) from that of many of the professionals who treat them (Spaniol, Zipple, & Fitzgerald, 1984).

The effect of this discrepancy, and of practice models that continue to be embedded in what Schön (1983) called technical rationality, has been increased stress on parents (Lefley, 1989) and widespread dissatisfaction with mental health services (Holden & Lewine, 1982). Parents are offended by professional stigmatization of the family and strenuously object to being either ignored or treated as an unidentified patient (Bernheim, 1989). These discrepant viewpoints, and the ensuing avoidance of parent-professional partnership, are reinforced in professionals by (a) ignorance of the professionals as to the perceptions and needs of family members, (b) theories that ascribe a causative role in mental illness to parents, and (c) general lack of communication and involvement between professionals and family members (Backer & Richardson, 1989). In addition, the mental health service system, as part of the overall health care system, continues to discourage active parent or patient participation in treatment planning through a myriad of policies and practices. These include a diagnostic process that is based on professional judgment and terminology, a payment or reimbursement system that increasingly applies external review that does not include input from parents or patients, and a referral system based on professional networks and reimbursement-driven decision making.

Two extreme positions taken by parents also have acted as barriers against parent-professional partnership. The first is a marked lack of interest in being involved in treatment planning and decision making. Some parents have learned through past interactions with the service system to maintain a passive role in relationships with professionals and to comply with professionally controlled decision making (Darling, 1988). In contrast, other parents have chosen to become vocal advocates challenging the professional establishment in reaction to their prior treatment (Friesen, 1989). Again, this advocacy seems to be based on a parent-controlled model, not partnership. These two differing parental strategies may be understood through an ecological and developmental context, in which a myriad of competing family stresses, concerns, and needs are constantly in conflict for immediate parental attention. Both also can be characterized as negative reactions to service encounters following the technical rationality model, whereby parents have continued to encounter a lack of collaboration.

Moving Toward Partnership: Family Empowerment

The new practice models that promote parent-professional partnership, as described above, are being implemented in professional training programs and policy and are slowly beginning to make an impact at the "street level" (Lipsky, 1980), where parents and professionals come together in face-to-face interaction (or transaction). More emphasis is needed, however, on the parent side of the interaction. Parents play an equally important role in maintaining the type of parent-professional interaction, whether it be a passive role in technical rationality or an active role in reflection in action, as discussed in Schön's (1983) models above. In addition to professional training programs, programs focused on parents also are needed to promote partnership roles.

Family empowerment is a specific goal toward which parent-focused programs should aspire. The term *family empowerment* has proliferated in the mental health and social services literature during the past decade. Although no single definition has emerged or been widely operationalized (Swift & Levin, 1987), family empowerment descriptions share many elements across authors (e.g., Cochran, 1987; Dunst & Paget, 1991; Dunst et al., 1988; Rappaport, 1981, 1987; Rappaport, Swift, & Hess, 1984) that focus on promoting access to resources, competence, and self-efficacy (Sokoly, 1993). Vanderslice (1984) summarized empowerment as "a process through which people become more able to influence those people and organizations that affect their lives and the lives of those they care about" (p. 2).

Parent-focused empowerment literature thus far has typically focused on two of these three elements, resources and competence. The most widespread parent training efforts have been in the area of advocacy, encompassing (a) knowledge about services, rights, and entitlements and (b) skills for communication, negotiation, and problem solving. The advocacy movement has served children and their families in both the mental health and developmental disabilities fields by fostering policy adoption, advances in practice, and increased funding. At the systems level, and in ensuring the continuation of the progress made so far, it continues to have an important function in the mental health field.

The advocacy movement and many resulting training materials, however, are based on a legalistic, rights-based paradigm that assumes an adversarial relationship between parents and providers. As mentioned above, partnership is not necessarily the goal of the programs and, in response to a professionally controlled service system, an antiprofessional bias often is espoused. Professionals have complained that advocates seemed inclined to view all providers as less than conscientious or as consistently attempting to withhold information, services, or both from children and their families. Such attitudes and actions appear to set up a tension that prohibits the development of partnership.

Needed, especially at the individual client and family level, is a broader conceptualization of empowerment that moves beyond advocacy and aspires toward more cooperative and collaborative parent-professional interaction. Advocacy should be just one of a range of activities for successfully interacting with the mental health service system, rather than the only mode. Family empowerment, therefore, may be operationalized as enabling parents to become collaborators in their children's mental health treatment. Parents could benefit from programs that teach skills to promote access to needed information and resources. Furthermore, a third facet, self-efficacy, should be a direct focus in efforts to promote family empowerment. Self-efficacy in this context is the parents' belief that their involvement in their children's mental health treatment will make a difference. Self-efficacy has been demonstrated to be one of the most influential aspects that determines performance, even independent of underlying skills (Locke, Frederick, Lee, & Bobko, 1984; Schuck, 1984). Competent functioning, or in this case, parental functioning as a partner in interaction with their children's mental health professionals, requires all three facets: skills, resources, and self-beliefs of efficacy (Bandura, 1982). Programs are needed that address all facets.

Parental involvement should not, however, be measured as a unidimensional construct with more parent involvement (e.g., more time involved in treatment planning meetings) as the single focus of family empowerment programs. A relative paucity of time spent by parents directly in treatment planning meetings or other treatment-oriented activities may be interpreted in many ways. Some professionals have attributed apparent noninvolvement to parental neglect or lack of interest in the child. Alternative interpretations are available, however. These parents may have experienced lack of opportunity due to system or professional barriers, or parental beliefs that they should not be involved may have been reinforced by past experience. Competing family needs may also take precedence.

It is tempting to promote high levels of parent participation as the goal of family empowerment. One of the critical elements of family empowerment, however, is that of choice: It is up to each family member to interpret the family context, needs, and resources available and to choose the best course of action for that particular family member in that particular family at that particular time (MacMillan & Turnbull, 1983; Nash, Rounds, & Bowen, 1992). In that regard, an empowered parent may choose *not* to participate at any point in a treatment planning meeting on the basis of the total needs of the parent and family. They may choose, at times, to be more involved with their children and less involved in the treatment process (Winton & Turnbull, 1981). Kaplan (1991) cautioned that health care providers tend to view outcomes narrowly and focus on the symptoms at hand, yet patients take a broader view that encompasses more of their total quality of life. Thus, parents may be empowered by having the knowledge, resources, and opportunities needed and may decide that the professionals are best suited to address formal mental health treatment while the other family members attend to other family needs. In addition, some parents feel relief at professional involvement when a problem has been long-standing and see treatment as an opportunity for respite—for the professional caregivers to take the primary treatment role as the parents attend to their own needs (Turnbull & Turnbull, 1985). The primary issue in each of these scenarios is choice: The empowered parent has the ability actively to choose his or her level of participation. This choice is dictated ideally by parent and family needs rather than by mental health service system limitations in resources or opportunities for involvement. A parent-professional partnership model of interaction should recognize and address this issue of choice of level of parental involvement as one to be discussed openly and nonjudgmentally.

A Model of Family Empowerment

Despite much discussion of the family empowerment concerns, little attention has been focused on demonstrating either (a) how to enhance family empowerment or (b) that increasing family empowerment will lead to greater parental involvement or more positive outcomes for the child. Although parental involvement can certainly be valued without requiring positive child outcomes, it is important to examine the conditions under which parents can add to the child's well-being when dealing with a service system.

A logic model (Bickman, 1987) that visually presents program characteristics and goals can be helpful in ensuring that a program aspiring to enhance family empowerment actually addresses the salient points of the underlying theory and, at the same time, plans for measuring both intermediate and final outcomes of the program. Figure 6.1 portrays a model for implementing a program that corresponds to the elements of family empowerment as described. This model focuses on the personal level of empowerment (Gutierrez & Ortega, 1991) at which a change in behavior is expected to be

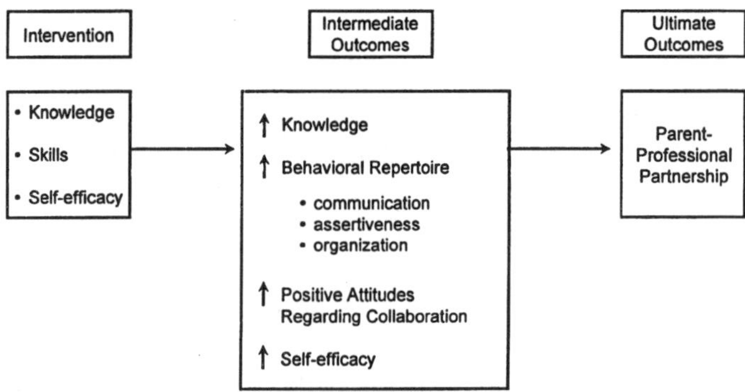

Figure 6.1. Family Empowerment: A Conceptual Model for Promoting Parent-Professional Partnership

demonstrated at the individual case level (Friesen, 1989) as the individual interacts with the service system (Koren, DeChillo, & Friesen, 1992).

As illustrated in Figure 6.1, an intervention program aimed at promoting family empowerment must seek to enhance (a) knowledge, (b) skills, and (c) self-efficacy. The left-most box describing the intervention, a parent-focused training program, includes all three aspects of empowerment. Such a program was designed and implemented as part of a National Institute of Mental Health (NIMH)-funded study of the effects of a group-level intervention on parent participation in their children's mental health services. A training program (Heflinger, Anderson, Digby, Grubb, & Williams, 1994) was developed for parents that focused on the following:

- *Knowledge:* providing information about the nature of the mental health system and other available community resources, understanding and participating in the diagnostic process, assessing the child's and family's needs, and reviewing the rights parents have in dealing with the system
- *Skills:* training in specific areas of assertiveness, communication, and goal setting; assessing the relationship between parents and professionals; problem solving; finding community resources; and building personal information files
- *Self-efficacy* regarding their children's mental health services: reinforcing the motivation for changing parents' behavior and relationships to the service provider, encouraging active participation in decision

making, promoting collaborative relationships between parents and professionals, and modeling participation in a support group

The inclusion of knowledge and skills components is similar to other parent interventions. The focus on self-efficacy, although mentioned in the empowerment literature, is a novel addition and focus of this training program. Bandura's (1977, 1986) theory of self-efficacy has been a focus of a number of studies designed to change behavior. Bandura defined perceived self-efficacy as the judgments of one's capabilities to organize and execute courses of action required to attain designated types of performances. Individuals can believe that a particular course of action will produce certain outcomes but will not act on that belief if they question whether they can actually execute the necessary activities. Thus, to be high in self-efficacy, persons not only must believe that certain actions will lead to specified outcomes but also must believe that they are capable of those actions. Bandura (1986) concluded that those who judge themselves to be highly efficacious will expect favorable outcomes, that self-doubters will expect mediocre performances of themselves and thus negative outcomes, and that these beliefs will function as determinants of behavior. Furthermore, judgments of self-efficacy determine how much effort people will expend and how long they will persist in the face of obstacles or aversive experiences (Bandura & Cervone, 1983). Thus, parents may need to change or modify their self-perceptions to participate more effectively as partners with professionals in the children's treatment planning. These modified self-perceptions may include (a) I can be an important and valued member of my child's mental health treatment team, (b) I have much to contribute to treatment planning and decision making for my child, (c) I can influence professionals and the treatment for my child, (d) I accept responsibility for solving problems and making decisions on behalf of my child, (e) I can take an active and assertive role in planning and implementing the treatment plan for my child, and (f) I believe I am an equal partner with professionals who are treating my child.

These self-perceptions reflect an empowerment stance by promoting parental involvement in seeking appropriate solutions for the problems that brought them and their children into mental health treatment. This stance moves beyond blame for the current situation toward resolution in an environmental context in which problems and barriers to meeting needs are overcome. By doing so, this approach reduces the probability of increasing guilt or diminishing self-esteem and, consequently, emphasizes acquisition of self-supportive behavior and a sense of self-efficacy and competence (Brickman et al., 1982; Dunst & Trivette, 1987).

Supporting the use of self-efficacy theory in changing health behaviors, the authors of a comprehensive review (Strecher, DeVillis, Becker, & Rosenstock, 1986) concluded that "for all health-related areas studied in this review, self-efficacy appears to be a consistent predictor of short- and long-term success. In experimental studies, manipulations of self-efficacy have proven consistently powerful in initiating and maintaining [behavior] change" (p. 87). It should be noted that all of the studies reviewed involved only students and that none dealt with mental health services. This focus on self-efficacy, however, appears to hold promising implications for enhancing parents' involvement in their children's mental health treatment.

One of the characteristics of the self-efficacy theory is its specificity. The theory applies to specific behaviors and expectations versus a general personality trait. Persons are more or less self-efficacious in specific areas. Thus, an intervention to promote family empowerment would aim at affecting not general self-efficacy but instead parental self-efficacy related to their children's mental health services. This specific parental mental health services self-efficacy includes the beliefs that they could engage in the activities that were necessary to affect how their children were treated and that if they did these activities, their children's treatment would improve.

In addition to outlining the focus of the intervention, Figure 6.1 illustrates the expected outcomes. By providing information, skills, and a self-efficacious approach, this parent-focused program was designed to affect (a) parents' knowledge of the mental health system; (b) their repertoire of behavior for interacting with professionals, including communication skills and assertiveness; (c) their attitudes toward professionals and collaborative endeavors; and (d) their mental health services self-efficacy. Each of these outcomes is viewed as a critical and necessary element in parent participation in a collaborative model of parent-professional interaction. Thus, the goal of family empowerment as discussed above, enabling parents to become partners in their children's mental health treatment, would be met through attainment of these outcomes.

Measurement Issues. The logic model as specified in Figure 6.1 also provides a basis for examining the impact of the planned intervention. To test the model, each of the boxes that represents an important construct requires a method for measuring that construct. We implemented a program evaluation of this family empowerment model in Fayetteville, North Carolina. This chapter offers an overview of the conceptual framework underlying the intervention and evaluation. Other manuscripts (Heflinger, Bickman, Northrup, & Sonnichsen, in press; Northrup, Bickman, & Heflinger, 1995) offer more detailed discussions of the intervention and evaluation issues. Research in this area is complicated by a lack of suitable standardized instruments to measure the constructs related to family empowerment, and instrument development had to be undertaken to examine this phenomenon.

Limitations of a Parent-Focused Intervention

Two limitations of this chapter's approach to family empowerment, however, need explication. First, intervention at the personal level is a necessary but insufficient step in empowering families of children with serious emotional problems (Heflinger & Dokecki, 1989; Koren, DeChillo, & Friesen, 1992). This model focuses on the parent side of the parent-professional interaction as one of the critically needed components in improving services to children with emotional and behavioral disorders and their families. This model complements other approaches that have focused on professional training.

Second, Riger (1993) warned that empowerment implies actual personal control and that mere enhancement of the sense of personal control (without actual control) does a disservice to the individual and, in fact, serves to support the status quo. Furthermore, she raised concern that empowerment models typically focus on individualistic approaches that promote conflict rather than cooperation. This criticism corresponds to the limitations of advocacy programs discussed above. The model posed in this chapter offers an approach to family empowerment that focuses on parent-professional partnership, an approach in the tradition of enhancing community (Hobbs, et al., 1984; Moroney & Dokecki, 1984; Sarason, 1984).

Both of these limitations highlight the need to view parent-professional partnership as a complex and multidimensional concept that includes, at a minimum, parent dimensions, professional dimensions, parent-professional interactional dimensions, and societal-policy dimensions (see Sokoly, 1993). The intervention program promoting family empowerment included in this chapter, although focusing on parent dimensions at the personal level, contributes a conceptual model that could be extended and applied to all of these dimensions.

Conclusion

Family-focused intervention and research is becoming more prominent in the field of child and adolescent mental health services. The family empowerment program described above and depicted in Figure 6.1 is but one of a growing number of studies beginning to investigate the mechanisms of parent involvement in their children's mental health services (see also Koren, DeChillo, & Friesen, 1992; Sonnichsen, 1994; Sonnichsen & Heflinger, 1993). This attention is much needed to better understand the mechanisms for enabling parents to collaborate with professionals on behalf of their children. Using logic models to explicate the underlying theory ensures attention to the most salient conceptual issues for program planning and evaluation. Family empowerment in this model includes three critical elements—knowledge, skills, and self-efficacy—all of which must be addressed to promote a partnership model of parent-professional interaction.

References

Able, H. (1986). *Parent-professional communication relative to medical care decision making for seriously ill newborns.* Unpublished doctoral dissertation, Vanderbilt University, Nashville, TN.

Backer, T. E., & Richardson, D. (1989). Building bridges: Psychologists and families of the mentally ill. *American Psychologist, 44,* 546-550.

Bandura, A. (1977). Self-efficacy: Toward a unifying theory of behavioral change. *Psychological Review, 84,* 191-215.

Bandura, A. (1982). Self-efficacy mechanism in human agency. *American Psychologist, 37,* 122-147.

Bandura, A. (1986). *Self-efficacy: Social foundations of thought and action: A social cognitive theory.* Englewood Cliffs, NJ: Prentice Hall.

Bandura, A., & Cervone, D. (1983). Self-evaluative and self-efficacy mechanisms governing the motivational effects of goal systems. *Journal of Personality and Social Psychology, 45*(5), 1017-1028.

Bernheim, K. F. (1989). Psychologists and families of the severely mentally ill: The role of family consultation. *American Psychologist, 44,* 561-564.

Bickman, L. (Ed.). (1987). *Using program theory in evaluation.* San Francisco: Jossey-Bass.

Brickman, P., Rabinowitz, V. C., Karuza, J., Coates, D., Cohn, E., & Kidder, L. (1982). Models of helping and coping. *American Psychologist, 37,* 368-384.

Bronfenbrenner, U. (1976). The experimental ecology of education. *Educational Researcher, 5,* 5-15.

Bronfenbrenner, U. (1979). *The ecology of human development: Experiments by nature and human design.* Cambridge, MA: Harvard University Press.

Burns, B. J., & Friedman, R. M. (1989). The research base for child mental health services and policy: How solid is the foundation? In P. Greenbaum, R. Friedman, A. Duchnowski, K. Kutash, & S. Silver (Eds.), *Conference proceedings: Children's mental health services and policy: Building a research base* (pp. 7-13). Tampa, FL: Research and Training Center for Children's Mental Health.

Carter, B., & McGoldrick, M. (1988). Overview: The changing family life cycle: A framework for family therapy. In B. Carter & M. McGoldrick (Eds.), *The changing family life cycle* (2nd ed., pp. 3-38). New York: Gardner.

Cochran, M. (1987). Empowering families: An alternative to the deficit model. In K. Hurrlemann, F. X. Kaufmann, & F. Losel (Eds.), *Social intervention: Potential and constraint* (pp. 105-120). New York: Walter de Gruyter.

Collins, B., & Collins, T. (1990). Parent-professional relationships in the treatment of severely emotionally disturbed children and adolescents. *Social Work, 35,* 522-527.

Cunningham, C., & Davis, H. (1985a). Early parent counseling. In M. Craft, J. Bicknell, & S. Hollins (Eds.), *Mental handicap: A multidisciplinary approach* (pp. 162-176). London: Bailliere Tindall.

Cunningham, C., & Davis, H. (1985b). *Working with parents: Frameworks for collaboration.* Philadelphia: Open University Press.

Darling, R. B. (1988). Parental entrepreneurship: A consumerist response to professional dominance. *Journal of Social Issues, 44,* 141-158.

Dewey, J., & Bentley, A. (1973). Knowing and the known. In R. Handy & E. C. Harwood (Eds.), *Useful procedures of inquiry* (pp. 89-192). Great Barrington, MA: Behavior Research Council. (Original work published 1949)

Dokecki, P. R. (1978). A transactional perspective on the interrelationship of the societal power structure, the mental health establishment, the individual, and the community. *Journal of Community Psychology, 6,* 19-21.

Dunst, C. J., & Paget, K. D. (1993). Parent-professional partnerships and family empowerment. In M. J. Fine (Ed.), *Collaboration with parents of exceptional children* (pp. 25-44). Brandon, VT: Clinical Psychology Publishing.

Dunst, C. J., & Trivette, C. M. (1987). Enabling and empowering families: Conceptual and intervention issues. *School Psychology Review, 16,* 443-456.

Dunst, C. J., Trivette, C. M., & Deal, A. G. (1988). *Enabling and empowering families: Principles and guidelines for practice.* Cambridge, MA: Brookline.

Dunst, C. J., Trivette, C. M., Starnes, A. L., Hamby, D. W., & Gordon, N. J. (1993). Family support programs for persons with developmental disabilities: Key elements, differential characteristics, and program outcomes. *Family System Intervention Monograph, 3* (No. 1). Morgantown, NC: Center for Family Studies, Western Carolina Center.

Education of All Handicapped Children Act of 1975, Pub. L. No. 94-142, 20 U.S.C. § 1401.

Featherstone, H. (1981). *A difference in the family.* New York: Penguin.

Friesen, B. J. (1989). Parents as advocates for children and adolescents with serious emotional handicaps: Issues and directions. In R. M. Friedman, A. J. Duchnowski, & E. L. Henderson (Eds.), *Advocacy on behalf of children with serious emotional problems* (pp. 68-78). Springfield, IL: Charles C Thomas.

Friesen, B. J., & Koroloff, N. K. (1990). Family-centered services: Implications for mental health administration and research. *Journal of Mental Health Administration, 17,* 13-25.

Gutierrez, L., & Ortega, R. (1991). Developing methods to empower Latinos: The importance of groups. *Social Work With Groups, 14*(2), 23-43.

Hatfield, A. B. (1983). What families want of family therapists. In W. R. McFarland (Ed.), *Family therapy in schizophrenia* (pp. 41-65). New York: Guilford.

Hatfield, A. B., & Lefley, H. P. (Eds.). (1987). *Families of the mentally ill: Coping and adaptation.* New York: Guilford.

Heflinger, C. A. (1989). *Bridging the gap between policy enactment and street level implementation of P.L. 99-457 and related early intervention programs for young children with handicapping conditions and their families.* Unpublished doctoral dissertation, Vanderbilt University, Nashville, TN.

Heflinger, C. A., Anderson, J., Digby, J., Grubb, C., & Williams, C. (1994). *Vanderbilt family empowerment project: Family group curriculum manual* (Rev. ed.). Nashville, TN: Vanderbilt Center for Mental Health Policy.

Heflinger, C. A., Bickman, L. B., Northrup, D. A., & Sonnichsen, S. E. (in press). A theory-driven intervention and evaluation to explore family empowerment. *Journal of Emotional and Behavioral Disorders.*

Heflinger, C. A., & Dokecki, P. R. (1989). A community psychology framework for participating in mental health policy making. *Journal of Community Psychology, 17,* 141-154.

Hobbs, N., Dokecki, P. R., Hoover-Dempsey, K. V., Moroney, R. M., Shayne, M. W., & Weeks, K. H. (1984). *Strengthening families.* San Francisco: Jossey-Bass.

Holden, D. F., & Lewine, R. J. R. (1982). How families evaluate mental health professionals, resources, and effects of illness. *Schizophrenia Bulletin, 8,* 626-633.

Kaplan, R. M. (1991). Health-related quality of life in patient decision making. *Journal of Social Issues, 47,* 69-90.

Kelker, K. A. (1987a). *Making the system work: An advocacy workshop for parents.* Portland, OR: Families as Allies Project.

Kelker, K. A. (1987b). *Working together: The parent/professional partnership.* Portland, OR: Families as Allies Project.

Koren, P. E., DeChillo, N., & Friesen, B. J. (1992). Measuring empowerment in families whose children have emotional disabilities: A brief questionnaire. *Rehabilitation Psychology, 37*(4), 305-321.

Lefley, H. P. (1989). Family burden and family stigma in major mental illness. *American Psychologist, 44,* 556-560.

Lipsky, M. (1980). *Street-level bureaucracy.* New York: Russell Sage.

Locke, E. A., Frederick, E., Lee, C., & Bobko, P. (1984). Effect on self-efficacy, goals, and task strategies on task performance. *Journal of Applied Psychology, 69*(2), 241-251.

MacMillan, D. L., & Turnbull, A. P. (1983). Parent involvement with special education: Respecting individual differences. *Education and Training of the Mentally Retarded, 18,* 4-9.

Marsh, D. T. (1992). *Families and mental illness: New directions in professional practice.* New York: Praeger.

McConachie, H. (1986). *Parents and young mentally handicapped children: A review of research issues.* Cambridge, MA: Brookline.

McElroy, E. M. (1987). The beat of a different drummer. In A. B. Hatfield & J. P. Lefley (Eds.), *Families of the mentally ill: Coping and adaptation* (pp. 225-243). New York: Guilford.

Mittler, P., & McConachie, H. (Eds.). (1983). *Parents, professionals and mentally handicapped people: Approaches to partnership.* Cambridge, MA: Brookline.

Moroney, R. M. (1986). *Shared responsibility: Families and social policy.* New York: Aldine.

Moroney, R. M., & Dokecki, P. R. (1984). The family and the professions: Implications for public policy. *Journal of Family Issues, 5,* 224-238.

Munger, R. L. (1991). *Child mental health practice from the ecological perspective.* Lanham, MD: University Press of America.

Nash, J., Rounds, K., & Bowen, G. (1992). Level of parental involvement on early childhood intervention teams. *Families in Society, 73*(2), 93-99.

Northrup, D. A., Bickman, L., & Heflinger, C. A. (1995). *The mental health services efficacy questionnaire: Psychometric properties.* Nashville, TN: Vanderbilt Center for Mental Health Policy.

Rappaport, J. (1981). In praise of paradox: A social policy of empowerment over prevention. *American Journal of Community Psychology, 9,* 1-25.

Rappaport, J. (1987). Terms of empowerment/exemplars for prevention: Toward a theory for community psychology. *American Journal of Community Psychology, 15,* 121-148.

Rappaport, J., Swift, C., & Hess, R. (1984). *Studies in empowerment: Steps toward understanding and action.* New York: Haworth.

Riger, S. (1993). What's wrong with empowerment. *American Journal of Community Psychology, 21*(3), 279-292.

Rothman, D. J. (1978). The state as parent: Social policy in the progressive era. In W. Gaylin, I. Glasser, S. Marcus, & D. J. Rothman (Eds.), *Doing good: The limits of benevolence* (pp. 67-96). New York: Pantheon.

Sarason, S. B. (1984). Community psychology and public policy: Missed opportunity. *American Journal of Community Psychology, 12,* 199-207.

Schön, D. A. (1983). *The reflective practitioner: How professionals think in action.* New York: Basic Books.

Schuck, D. H. (1984). Enhancing self-efficacy and achievement through rewards and goals: Motivational and informational effects. *Journal of Educational Research, 78*(1), 29-34.

Schweitzer, T. B., & Hankins, B. J. (1990). *Developing Families as Allies: Participant manual.* Jackson: State of Mississippi Department of Mental Health.

Sokoly, M. (1991). *Developing an empowerment approach to family strengths and needs assessment: Rethinking parent-professional relationships.* Unpublished master's thesis, Vanderbilt University, Nashville, TN.

Sokoly, M. (1993). *Parent-professional relationships and family empowerment: Developing a framework for understanding.* Unpublished doctoral dissertation, Vanderbilt University, Nashville, TN.

Sonnichsen, S. E. (1994). *Factors related to parental participation in children's mental health services: Exploratory analysis of the status of parents and families.* Unpublished master's thesis, Vanderbilt University, Nashville, TN.

Sonnichsen, S. E., & Heflinger, C. A. (1993). *Preliminary assessment of parental involvement: Appendix G to the final report of the implementation study of the Fort Bragg Evaluation Project.* Unpublished manuscript, Vanderbilt University Center for Mental Health Policy, Nashville, TN.

Spaniol, L., Zipple, A., & Fitzgerald, S. (1984). How professionals can share power with families: Practical approaches to working with families of the mentally ill. *Psychosocial Rehabilitation Journal, 8*(2), 77-84.

Strecher, V. J., DeVillis, B. M., Becker, M. H., & Rosenstock, I. M. (1986). The role of self-efficacy in achieving health behavior change. *Health Education Quarterly, 13,* 73-91.

Stroul, B. A., & Friedman, R. (1986). *A system of care for children and youth with severe emotional disturbances* (Rev. ed.). Washington, DC: Georgetown University Child Development Center, CASSP Technical Assistance Center.

Stucky, P. E., & Newbrough, J. R. (1983). Mentally retarded persons in the community. In K. T. Kernan, M. Begab, & R. Edgerson (Eds.), *Social influences on the behavior of retarded persons* (pp. 21-38). Baltimore: University Park Press.

Swift, C., & Levin, G. (1987). Empowerment: An emerging mental health technology. *Journal of Primary Prevention, 8,* 71-94.

Turnbull, H. R., & Turnbull, A. P. (1985). *Parents speak out: Then and now.* Columbus, OH: Merrill.

Vanderslice, V. (1984). Empowerment: A definition in progress. *Human Ecology Forum, 14*(1), 2-3.

Vosler-Hunter, R. W. (1989). *Changing roles, changing relationships: Parent-professional collaboration on behalf of children with emotional disabilities.* Portland, OR: Portland State University, Research and Training Center on Family Support and Children's Mental Health.

Webster's ninth new collegiate dictionary. (1988). Springfield, MA: Merriam-Webster.

Weiss, H. B., & Greene, J. C. (1992). An empowerment partnership for family support and education program and evaluation. *Family Science Review, 5,* 131-148.

Winton, P. J., & Turnbull, A. P. (1981). Parent involvement as viewed by parents of preschool handicapped children. *Topics in Early Childhood Special Education, 1*(3), 11-19.

Zimmerman, M. A., & Rappaport, J. (1988). Citizen participation, perceived control, and psychological empowerment. *American Journal of Community Psychology, 16,* 725-750.

Family Research Methods

Issues and Strategies

JOAN M. PATTERSON

Family and health research has expanded dramatically in the last decade (Patterson, 1990). The methodologies for doing family research surrounding health issues have become increasingly more sophisticated as the numbers of studies have grown. These methodologies draw extensively from the field of family science, in which there has been growth in the conceptualization and measurement of family variables (Boss, Doherty, LaRossa, Schumm, & Steinmetz, 1993). In this chapter, the trends in family and health research are reviewed. Issues to be considered by investigators who are studying mental health problems of children in relationship to their families are addressed. Finally, implications and recommendations for future research are considered.

Who and What Are Being Studied?

First, there is a need to address two questions: Who is being studied, and what is being studied? The biopsychosocial paradigm

AUTHOR'S NOTE: Preparation of this chapter was supported by the National Institute on Disability and Rehabilitation Research Grant #H133890012 and by Maternal and Child Health Bureau Grant # MCJ000111.

(Engel, 1977) is the foundation for conceptualizing most family and health research undertaken today. The interactions between biological variables (such as organic impairment in the neurological system), psychological variables (such as temperament), and social variables (such as social support) are examined. Family variables are included as social variables. Most often, the focus or the outcome of interest is the health of an individual, and the biological and social contexts are considered as factors influencing that outcome. From a systemic perspective, however, focusing on one system, the individual, is an arbitrary, linear punctuation in what is really understood to be a circular pattern of effects.

The second question, what is being studied, is focused, in the most generic sense, on health. When conducting family and health research, generally, the concern is about the health of individuals and the health of family systems. Both of these constructs, family and health, encompass multiple dimensions, have subjective and objective elements, and have been discussed and written about extensively by scholars from many disciplines. When undertaking any research study, it is critical to carefully define all the constructs or variables being investigated, beginning with a conceptual definition of each variable, which subsequently influences the operational definition or measure chosen. The following definitions of family and health are intended to provide a conceptual basis for the discussion of research issues that follows.

What Is Family?

A family system is a group of individuals and the pattern of relationships between them. Contained within this definition are two critical aspects of family: family structure and family functioning. *Family structure* is defined as who is in the system. An invisible boundary marks who is in (and who is out) and sets the family apart from its social context. Family structure allows for the family within to create its own identity and sense of itself so that it can function effectively as a unit. One of the important tasks of a family is to define and maintain this boundary—to be clear about who is part of its family unit. There is wide cultural and ethnic variability in what constitutes "family." The U.S. Census Bureau definition that a family is "two or more persons living together who are related by blood, marriage, or adoption" is seldom acceptable for clinical or empirical work. For example, among African Americans, fictive kin—friends and neighbors who function as family members in providing support but who do not live in the household—are often considered family (Fine, 1993). Among most family scholars, *family* is now defined more broadly with a definition such as "the nexus of people, living together or in close contact, who take care of one another and provide guidance for dependent members of the group" (Wood, in press). Furthermore, the definition used by most family clinicians and scientists is that the family itself defines who is and who is not part of the family. (See also Pinderhughes, Chapter 10 in this volume.)

Family functioning refers to the patterns of relationship connecting members of a family system (Bateson, 1972). There are patterns for showing affection, for solving problems, for accomplishing daily tasks, for celebrating holidays and birthdays, and so forth. Family functioning is a property not of an individual but of the whole family unit. It is what is really meant by saying that a family is more than the sum of its parts. Family functioning is a multidimensional construct because many different aspects of family functioning can be considered, such as cohesion, flexibility, communication, and behavioral control. Different theories of family functioning (e.g., systems theory, development theory, communications theory, role theory, and stress theory, and so on) emphasize different dimensions of family functioning. Examples of some of these theories and variables are provided below. (See also Bloom, Chapter 8 in this volume, for more on the measurement of family functioning.)

What Is Health?

As with the concept of family, volumes have been written to define and describe *health.* Individual health has been viewed dichotomously (healthy vs. ill), as a continuum (ranging from good to poor), and as a holistic dynamic state, expressed as the process of living (Anderson & Tomlinson, 1992). The World Health Organization (1976) definition emphasizes the multidimensional nature of health: physical, psychological, social, and spiritual well-being. In a major study of family processes and the health of a community sample of parents,

Fisher, Ransom, Terry, Lipkin, and Weiss (1992) assessed 14 dimensions of adult health, such as general well-being, depression, smoking, and preventive behaviors. Most researchers who have studied chronic illness prefer a definition that recognizes the multidimensional nature of health and portrays each dimension as a continuum. The relationships between these dimensions raises interesting empirical questions. Is change in one dimension (e.g., psychological health) associated with change in other dimensions? Do they improve or decline together? Or if one dimension declines (e.g., physical health due to organ dysfunction), does a person get stronger in another domain (e.g., spiritual health) as a form of compensation? At the family level, there are at least two different ways to conceptualize family health: (a) as the sum of the individual health statuses of all family members or (b) as the health of the unit as a whole, that is, the health of the family's functioning patterns. In the first instance, one could use a definition and measure of individual health and then sum the individual health status measures across all family members. I prefer to call this summary measure "familial health" to distinguish it from a health measure focused on the family unit's functioning patterns. This strategy was used in a study reporting the impact on familial health of caring for a medically fragile child at home (Patterson, Leonard, & Titus, 1992). The second way of conceptualizing family health, as family functioning patterns, is the focus of most of the family assessment measures to be discussed in this chapter.

Family health, like individual health, has been viewed from differing perspectives (Walsh, 1993). For example, a dysfunctional label often is inferred when one or more family members are symptomatic. This dichotomous approach is too simplistic and, furthermore, subject to considerable error because there is not a one-to-one relationship between individual health and family health. Alternatively, average functioning, or the statistical mean for given interactional patterns, is another way of considering normal or healthy functioning. Assessment instruments with statistical norms are based on this perspective. Scoring at the high positive end of a normal distribution, however, is not usually considered unhealthy although, technically, such a score is out of the average range.

Another perspective for conceptualizing family health is as optimal functioning (competence), that is, high ability to accomplish family tasks and promote the development and well-being of individual members. Yet another perspective for considering the health of families is as transactional family processes, which evolve through time in response to varying developmental and social circumstances. There is no absolute standard or best set of processes characteristic of healthy families. These processes are expected to vary depending on a variety of factors, including stage of the family's life cycle, family structural type, race, culture and ethnicity, historical time, sexual orientation, situational stressors (e.g., chronic illness), social class, and economic factors, among others. These latter two perspectives for considering family health, optimal family functioning and transactional family processes, are recommended in conceptualizing family health or functioning for empirical studies related to children's mental health. Both perspectives are able to take into account the various sources of variability listed above when considering family functioning.

A Systems Perspective Linking Individual Health and Family Health

A child's physical or mental illness affects not only the child but the whole family as well. When a child is diagnosed with a chronic condition, the impact on the family leads to changes in its functioning patterns. This new style of functioning, in turn, affects the perception and care of the child, the course of the child's development, and sometimes the course of the condition itself (Patterson, 1991). For example, it has been observed that mothers sometimes become overly protective and too close to their child with a chronic illness—perhaps to ensure that medical needs are met, to show that she still loves the child despite the condition, or to try to compensate for the pain, suffering, and loss associated with the condition. This may be related to a father's pulling away from the mother and/or the child because of high emotional demands. Perhaps the father copes by working harder or pursuing hobbies; further, he may resent the mother's closeness to the child or feel that the mother does not want him around.

The important point is that a chronic condition has an impact on the family and changes its functioning patterns in some way. The reciprocal impacts between the individual and the family are circular and continuous through time, as depicted in Figure 7.1. It is an

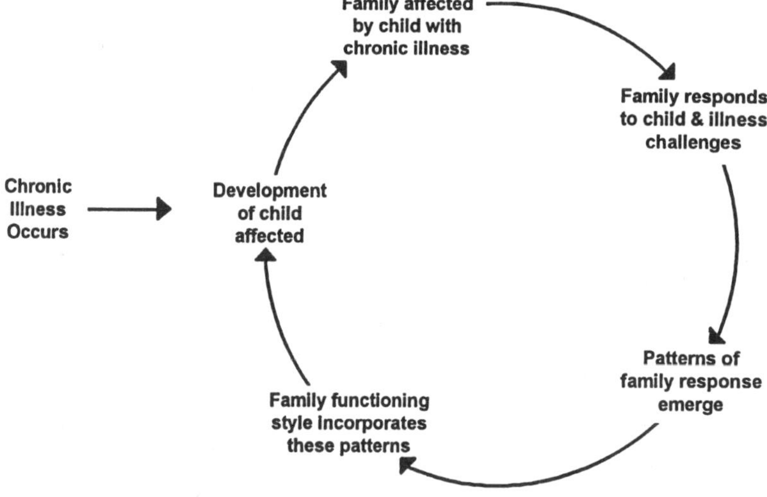

Figure 7.1. Circular Effects Linking Individual Development and Family Functioning When a Child Is Diagnosed With Chronic Illness

arbitrary perspective to focus linearly on only two points in this circular pattern and suggest that the child's problem has an impact on the family, or, as is more often the case, to focus on the family as the starting point and say that it causes the child's problems. It is important to think systemically when studying children and their families. One of the assumptions of systems theory is that a change in one part (e.g., a person) leads to changes in other parts of the system (e.g., family as a whole).

The nature of this relationship is, of course, the essence of research studies focused on family systems and children's mental health. In the past, researchers have been too quick to blame families for children's problems or to blame children for their families' difficulties. Operating from a systems perspective eliminates blame and is more respectful of children and families participating in research. To genuinely understand the nature and direction of reciprocal effects, longitudinal studies are necessary. With repeated measures of the health and functioning of individual family members (child, parents, siblings) through time and repeated measures of family system functioning through time, researchers would be in a better position to explain the magnitude and direction of change. Results of such studies would, of course, offer greater insight about intervention—both when to intervene and with whom.

Research Design Issues

Approaches to Family Research

Knowledge of children's chronic health conditions and their impact on families has developed from several approaches. One approach is the personal descriptive accounts written by parents or children living with chronic conditions, such as Deford's (1983) description of the effect of his daughter's cystic fibrosis on their family, Featherstone's (1980) account of family life with her child with disabilities, Dorris's (1989) account of his son's and family's struggles with fetal alcohol syndrome, and Massie's (1985) reflections on living with hemophilia. In addition, subjective, qualitative reports from clinicians who work with chronically ill children and their families compose the largest body of literature in this area. Sometimes these reports are based on a single case, but more often they represent the distillation of experience from working with many children. These qualitative approaches are particularly rich in identifying critical variables that need to be studied systematically in empirical designs and for generating hypotheses about the relationship between variables.

Within the empirical literature, the primary study design has been cross-sectional, whereby relationships between individual, family, and sometimes biological variables are examined from data collected at one time. A major limitation of such studies is that change through time is not assessed, and the direction of effects between variables cannot be understood (e.g., did family functioning lead to child outcomes, or did child functioning lead to family outcomes?). Unfortunately, investigators with cross-sectional data often imply causal relationships. One improvement in these cross-sectional study designs is the increasing use of comparison groups—comparing different diagnostic conditions or comparing children with chronic conditions to those who have no chronic condition. For example, Hauser et al. (1993) compared adolescent and family functioning among youth with diabetes and youth experiencing acute illness episodes.

Few longitudinal studies examine the dynamic relationships between chronic conditions in childhood and family functioning through time. Those that have been published have used primarily two or three data collection points during a relatively short period, such as 2 to 3 years. For example, the effect of caring for a child who is medically fragile on parental distress was examined during a 2-year period, attempting to explain variability in parent psychological health with child, family, and service delivery system variables (Patterson & Leonard, 1994). Clearly needed are studies that systematically follow children and families during an extended period, using measures that capture change in biopsychosocial variables. This would contribute to the understanding of the dynamic and reciprocal relationships between individual and family functioning and of the processes of adapting to changing social and developmental contexts.

A critically important study design that is only beginning to emerge in families and health research is the experimental study. In this design, an effort is made to manipulate a set of variables, such as family functioning, to effect change in another set of variables, such as child health status. The early work of Minuchin et al. (1975) involved family therapy interventions to improve the health of children with chronic illnesses such as diabetes and asthma. Clinical trials with random assignment to family therapy interventions have been reported recently for children with asthma (Gustafsson, Kjellman, & Cederblad, 1986) and diabetes (Satin, LaGreca, Zigo, & Skyler, 1989).

Finally, more studies of families and health that use qualitative methods are being published, particularly by nurse researchers. For example, investigators are using grounded theory to develop new theoretical models of adaptation (Knafl & Deatrick, 1990). Qualitative methods are particularly valuable in exploring subjective variables, such as the perceived meaning of illness and its relationship to child and family functioning. In addition, there is growing recognition of the need for more studies of ethnically diverse families, particularly using qualitative methods, given the poor (or unknown) reliability and validity of many standardized measures among minority populations (Patterson & Blum, 1993). In 1986, Campbell published a comprehensive review of family and health research studies in which he emphasized study design and methodology. This review is an excellent resource for investigators looking for additional grounding in family research methods.

Measurement of Family-Level Constructs

When the family system is the unit of analysis, measurement issues are more complex. Variables that are characteristics or traits of individuals cannot necessarily be construed as properties of a social system such as the family. It is not uncommon, however, for investigators to ask respondents to consider the family as the referent when completing questionnaires that originally were designed to assess characteristics of individuals. For example, locus of control is an individual construct that is frequently included in health research. Can locus of control be a property of a family system? Possibly, but if applied to the family level, the conceptual definition needs to be clear and differentiated from individual locus of control. Investigators studying family systems need to pay careful attention to the unit of analysis and level of measurement (see also Bloom, Chapter 8 in this volume). Ransom (1986) presented a typology for classifying family data that has considerable heuristic value for investigators designing family and health research studies. He differentiated the three levels of family data discussed below.

Level I data are based on some characteristic possessed by the family unit or one of its members. These measures are often derived from some demographic characteristic and are usually categorical variables. For example, single-parent, two-parent, and stepparent are three different ways of classifying family structure that combine parenting and marital status.

Level II data are derived from an individual family member about the family unit, another family member, or even oneself. The data may be obtained in a variety of ways, usually by self-report questionnaire or interview. Two types of Level II data are IIa, information obtained from only one family member; and IIb, the same information obtained from two or more family members and then combined to create a relational score (e.g., a couple discrepancy score). Level II data are the most common type in family and health studies. There is a long history of using mothers as the primary informants about family life, especially when studying children, probably because mothers have been more available and willing to participate in research studies. In the last decade, however, increasing numbers of studies are including fathers as informants about the family as well, and investigators have found that fathers often report differently about family life. There was a time when discrepancies between mothers' and fathers' reports about their family were viewed as an indication that something was wrong with the family. Fortunately, this pejorative view of families is no longer the case. Most family scientists acknowledge that it is to be expected that individual members of the family will have differing views, given their different roles within the family and their own unique history and experiences that interact with family experiences.

One strategy for using multiple members' reports about the family is to use each member's report separately and to try to determine which one is most predictive of the outcome of interest (Level IIa). Another strategy is to combine individual self-reports in meaningful ways to create a true family-level construct (Level IIb). For example, discrepancy scores can be computed from any pair of individuals' scores. A typology of families that is based on the amount of discrepancy or congruence between family members could be examined. Walters, Pittman, and Norrell (1984) have offered a methodology for combining all the scores of different family members by determining the amount of shared variance (vs. unique variance) in their responses. Other multivariate techniques for creating relational family scores include regression analysis and cluster analysis, for example. Many of these methods, however, are theoretical and do not generalize beyond the research sample used and thus have limited value in the overall advancement of the science of families and health (Fisher, Kokes, Ransom, Phillips, & Rudd, 1985).

Some self-report measures about the family can be converted readily to a family-level score. For example, the Family Inventory of Life Events and Changes (McCubbin & Patterson, 1983) is a measure of the pileup of life events and strains (often called a stress measure).

Respondents check "yes" or "no" to indicate whether each of 71 items occurred in their family during the last year. A family score can be created by combining the responses of all family members and summing all the items that *any* member indicated happened last year. An item is counted only once regardless of whether one or more members endorse it. This method is consistent with the theory underlying the instrument that if an event is experienced by any member, the stress level of the family as a unit is increased.

Another application of the Level IIb family measures is from a recent study of families who have a child with cystic fibrosis (Patterson, Budd, Goetz, & Warwick, 1992). Each parent in the study completed the Coping Health Inventory for Parents (CHIP; McCubbin et al., 1983), which assesses each parent's coping strategies. A family level score (parental dyad score) was created by using each parent's minimum score on each of the three coping patterns assessed by the CHIP. The theoretical rationale for this operationalization is based in family stress theory that argues that families do better if they have a broader repertoire of coping behaviors from which to draw (rather than only one or two ways to cope). The CHIP has three coping subscales focused on the individual, the family unit, and the medical condition. Thus, two-parent families have six scores to combine. The higher the minimum score across all the subscales, the better or more balanced is family coping.

Level III data are derived from family interaction in naturalistic settings (such as eating a meal in their home) or from family interaction during research-specified tasks carried out in their home or in a laboratory. Two levels of quantifiable scores are derived from such family interaction: IIIa, an outside observer rates or counts aspects of family process; and IIIb, a behavioral product score is derived directly from the interaction itself. There are now several different rating systems for outside observers to code family process (see Grotevant & Carlson, 1989; Touliatos, Perlmutter, & Strauss, 1990, for reviews of these coding systems and other family measures). Micro coding systems code moment-by-moment interaction. Macro coding systems assign global ratings to family process after a segment of interaction is observed. Sometimes coding is done in vivo as it happens. In other instances (and more commonly), the interaction is videotaped and coded later. Level IIIb data and scores are produced directly from tasks the family engages in rather than relying on an outside observer rating the family. The best known (although not as yet widely used) method is the Card Sort Procedure (Reiss, 1981), whereby family members simultaneously sort patterned cards while they talk to each other without visual contact (they are in private, adjacent booths). This procedure yields scores that operationalize the family paradigm dimensions of configuration, coordination, and closure, which are part of a theoretical framework for understanding family problem-solving behavior (discussed below). (See also Bloom's discussion, Chapter 8 in this volume, of the Colorado Family Assessment, which combines many of the levels of measurement discussed here.)

The sources of the data are quite different for each of the levels of measurement just described. Included are both an insider's perspective (a family member's report about the family) and an outsider's perspective. Some scientists argue that family process can be measured only from the outsider's perspective (Level III) because one cannot be part of the system being assessed (Ransom, 1986). Wamboldt and Wolin (1988) make a distinction between family *reality* (with a small *r*) and family *Reality* (capital *R*). Family reality is what an individual perceives about different aspects of his or her family. In contrast, family Reality is uninfluenced by the subjectivity of a person who is part of the system and thus can be assessed only by someone outside the system. The choice of levels of family measurement depends on the research question and other pragmatic considerations such as cost. Ideally, more studies should include multiple levels of measurement that would allow investigators to understand the relationships between these different levels. In the section below, specific family constructs based on different theoretical frameworks are discussed. In the examples of family and health studies cited to illustrate these constructs, an effort is made to draw attention to the level of family measurement used. The reader also should note that there are several good reference books describing family measurement methods. Grotevant and Carlson (1989), Touliatos et al. (1990), and Jacob and Tennenbaum (1988) review many instruments for measuring family functioning constructs that produce data at Levels II and III.

Theoretical Frameworks for Family and Health Research

Formulating Research Questions

Any research design should be driven by a clear specification of the research question(s). For those studying family and health issues, clinical observation and experience, complemented by a careful review of the literature, are often the starting place. Increasingly, funding agencies have mandated to ask more "relevant" research questions so that the knowledge generated will have applicability to real-life needs and problems. For example, family members living with chronic illness or disability more often are asked to provide consultation with researchers in the formulation of research questions. In addition, practitioners who provide direct services to families and children are another important source of research questions.

Studies of families and health have varied widely in the degree to which theoretical frameworks have guided the specification of research questions, hypotheses, or empirical models. In an earlier review (Patterson, 1990), less than half of the studies specified a theoretical orientation. Family systems theory often is implied in many of these studies, however. The scientific knowledge base focused on families and health would be strengthened and enhanced if investigators carefully specified a theoretical framework in formulating their research questions and hypotheses. Theoretical frameworks provide conceptual definitions for constructs and variables that inform the operational definition chosen. Empirical results derived from such measures in turn contribute to theory-building efforts, strengthening the knowledge about families and health. To illustrate the ways in which family theory has guided empirical studies of families and health, the conceptual definitions of some of the major constructs from family systems theory, family communication theory, and family stress theory are discussed below. Specific research studies related to families and health are reviewed to illustrate how constructs were operationalized. Family systems theory is a broad, global theory for studying families. The other two are examples of midrange theories that are more focused on a specific aspect of family functioning.

Family Systems Theory

Two important family systems concepts that have been studied by many investigators interested in families and health are cohesion and flexibility. *Cohesion* refers to the emotional bonds of unity and commitment linking family members to each other. It varies on a continuum from low to high. Some theorists (e.g., Moos & Moos, 1983) view the relationship between cohesion and health as linear, with high levels associated with better family health and, hence, individual health. The Family Environment Scale (FES; Moos & Moos, 1981) includes cohesion as 1 of 10 subscales assessing the social climate of families. The FES produces Level II family data. Several investigators, using the FES to measure family cohesion, have reported that high cohesion is associated with better health outcomes in children with chronic illnesses and in their parents (Daniels, Moos, Billings, & Miller, 1987; Thompson, Gustafson, Hamlett, & Spock, 1992; Timko, Stovel, & Moos, 1992).

Other theorists (Beavers, 1993; Olson, 1993) conceptualize cohesion as curvilinear, with either extreme of too much cohesion or too little cohesion associated with less optimal family functioning. These extremes, in turn, are hypothesized to be associated with individual symptoms. In their view, families are faced with finding a balance between the togetherness of being part of a family unit and separateness when autonomy of the individual is emphasized. Methods for assessing these extremes of cohesion include (a) Family Adaptability and Cohesion Evaluation Scales (FACES; Olson, 1993); (b) Clinical Rating Scale (Olson, 1993); (c) Self-Report Family Inventory (Beavers, 1993); and (d) Beavers Interactional Style Scale (Beavers, 1993). FACES and the Self-Report Family Inventory produce Level II data, and the Clinical Rating Scale and Beavers Interactional Style Scale are macro coding systems producing Level III data.

Too much family cohesion has been associated with poorer outcomes for children with chronic diseases: (a) higher hemoglobin A1C in children with diabetes (Gustafsson, Cederblad, Ludvigsson, & Lundin, 1987) and (b) poor peak expiratory flow rate in children with asthma (Gustafsson, Kjellman, Ludvigsson, & Cederblad, 1987).

Flexibility is defined as the ability of the family to change its functioning patterns in response to normative and nonnormative experiences. It too varies on a continuum, with some theorists viewing flexibility as linearly related to family functioning, with high flexibility considered as family competence (Beavers, 1993). Watson, Henggeler, and Whelan (1990) found that family flexibility was associated with better adaptation in families with a child who was hearing impaired. Flexibility, however, like cohesion, is viewed by some theorists as curvilinearly related to family functioning, with the extremes associated with poorer family functioning. Gustafsson and his colleagues reported that extreme family flexibility scores were associated with poorer metabolic control in children with diabetes (Gustafsson, Cederblad et al., 1987) and with greater steroid dependency in children with asthma (Gustafsson, Kjellman et al., 1987).

Some of the earliest family systems theorists to identify the relationship between extreme family cohesion and extreme family flexibility and disease processes were Minuchin et al. (1975). They reported that the family patterns of enmeshment, rigidity, overprotectiveness, inability to resolve conflicts, and triangulation of the chronically ill child in marital conflict were associated with recurrent ketoacidosis in children with diabetes and increased asthmatic episodes in children with asthma. They were able to reduce these symptoms with family therapy interventions. Their results have been challenged, however, for blaming families for illness problems and for inadequate empirical methods (Coyne & Anderson, 1988).

Wood et al. (1989), using more rigorous empirical methods to measure family functioning, found different associations between family functioning and child health. Using observer ratings of family interaction (Level IIIa data), they found that disease activity in children with abdominal illnesses was significantly associated with triangulation and marital dysfunction but not with enmeshment, overprotection, rigidity, or conflict avoidance. They argued that marital dysfunction and triangulation may be a cluster of family functioning patterns that has a maladaptive effect on disease activity and that enmeshment/overprotection may be a separate cluster that has an adaptive or neutral effect on disease activity. In the earlier Minuchin model, it was implied that all of these patterns were maladaptive. Notably, the observed family patterns had stronger associations with medication use than with laboratory measures of disease. Families reported that their children's behavior changed when on corticosteroids (more irritable and emotionally labile), leading the family to respond as though "walking on eggshells." This important research illustrates the reciprocal relationships between disease activity, treatment, individual functioning, and family system response.

Overinvolvement, triangulation, and marital dysfunction are closely related to the family systems concept of boundaries. A *boundary* is that psychological line that sets a system apart from its context. Families have both internal boundaries differentiating the various subsystems within the family, such as the parental dyad or the sibling subsystem, as well as external boundaries that define who is in the family and that set the family apart from the larger community context. It is not uncommon in families in which a child has a chronic condition for one parent to become overly involved with the sick child, while the other parent is excluded or pulls away. This can lead to a parent-child coalition in which generational boundaries (mother-father dyad) are violated, and the executive functioning of the parental-marital dyad needed for optimal family functioning is disrupted. Conversely, Beavers, Hampson, Hulgus, and Beavers (1986) reported that clear generational boundaries in which parents of children with mental retardation worked together to make decisions and in which the marital relationship was nurtured by mutual respect were associated with better health outcomes. Their measures included a global rating score for these family patterns on the basis of macro coding of videotaped family interaction (Level IIIa data).

An external family boundary that is semipermeable is generally viewed as most adaptive. It often becomes too permeable, however, when a child has a chronic condition, and health, education, and social service providers become overly directive with the family about how to manage the child. The family's needs, beliefs, values, culture, and lifestyle, which contribute to family identity and integrity, are often ignored. This has been observed among medically fragile children who receive daily home care from nurses and home health aides (Patterson, Jernell, Leonard, & Titus, 1994). Families reported that their family privacy was invaded and that they felt judged and less in control of managing family life. This was a major source of strain and tension for families that negatively affected the parents' health. These results suggest the need for studying family impact from a systems perspective. In this case, the helping system (home care providers) was a major source of strain for the family. It calls attention to the need to support families in maintaining their external boundaries to retain their viability as a well-functioning system.

Family Communication Theory

A midrange family theory that has been employed extensively in the study of family process and mental health/illness outcomes is communication theory. In particular, investigators have focused on communication difficulties and affective expression within the family to understand and explain health outcomes. *Communication deviance* refers to the lack of commitment to ideas or precepts, unclear or idiosyncratic communication of themes or ideas, language anomalies, and disruptive speech (Campbell, 1986). The results of several studies suggest that communication deviance is present in families before the onset of psychiatric symptoms and that it is relatively specific to the onset of schizophrenia as opposed to other psychiatric conditions (Campbell, 1986). *Expressed emotion* involves intense emotional overinvolvement of a family member with the target person, coupled with frequent critical comments (Cole, Kane, Zastowny, Grolnick, & Lehman, 1993). Vaughn (1989) reviewed a large number of studies examining the relationship between expressed emotion and health outcomes. Collectively, these studies provide strong support for the linkage of expressed emotion to mental and physical illness. Remaining unclear from these studies, however, is the direction of effect. Is the expressed emotion a response of the family to the patient's illness, or is the expressed emotion a more stable, generalized attitude of the family that contributes to the patient's problems (e.g., relapse in schizophrenia)? Most of these studies rely on Level IIIa data derived from macro coding of videotaped family interaction, which often involves a task associated with family conflict (Cole et al., 1993).

The quality of family communication has been studied as a major factor influencing health outcomes in children with chronic physical illness. For example, Hermanns, Florin, Dietrich, Rieger, and Hahlweg (1989) reported that high maternal expressed emotion was associated with more frequent asthma attacks in their children. Blechman and Delamater (1993) have advanced a family communication model to explain variability in metabolic control of children with diabetes. In their model, effective family communication is linked to positive mood states, which in turn are associated with a willingness to learn and perform new tasks such as complying with treatment regimens. Or to state it another way, good moods lead to individual competence, better management of the diabetes, and hence, better health outcomes. The researchers used direct observation of family interaction to code effective family communication (Level IIIa data), which they defined as the ability to send a message, influence behavior, and solve a problem.

The Blechman and Delamater (1993) research focuses on the instrumental aspects of communication, that is, communication contributes to being able to get something done or to solve problems. This aspect is in contrast to affective communication, which is how emotions and feelings are expressed in the family. Both aspects of communication are important family process variables related to health outcomes of family members; they appear to be even more important when a family is challenged by a chronic condition. Usually, there are more decisions to be made and problems to be solved when chronic illness is present, and illness needs may conflict with other family needs, thus requiring greater ability to resolve conflicts. For many families, the communication of affect is more difficult. Steinglass and his colleagues (Reiss, Steinglass, & Howe, 1993; Steinglass & Horan, 1987) have observed that many families repress negative affect associated with grief and anger about the chronic condition because they feel unjustified in their grief response and feelings of anger. Open expressiveness of feelings in families, however, has been associated with better health outcomes in children with cancer (Spinetta, Murphy, Vik, Day, & Mott, 1988); diabetes (Borrow, AvRuskin, & Siller, 1985; Marteau, Bloch, & Baum, 1987); and leukemia (Kupst & Schulman, 1988).

Family Stress Theory

Another theoretical framework that has been used frequently in conceptualizing family and health studies is family stress theory. Given the increasing evidence for the relationship between stress and illness at the individual level, it is not surprising that family scientists have looked to family stress models as the basis for conceptualizing their research. For illustrative purposes, the major constructs from the Family Adjustment and Adaptation Response (FAAR) Model (Patterson, 1988, 1989) are discussed here. The constructs are similar to those concepts advanced by Boss (1988) in her Contextual Model of Family Stress and by McCubbin and McCubbin (1993) in their Resiliency Model of Family Stress. In the FAAR Model, five major constructs are emphasized: pileup of demands, resources, coping behaviors, family meanings, and family adaptation. Families attempt to maintain balanced functioning by using their resources and coping behaviors to meet the stressors and strains they face. The meaning that family members ascribe to the demands they face, as well as their resources, is a critical factor in achieving balanced functioning. The outcome of family efforts to achieve balanced functioning is conceptualized as family adaptation, which ranges on a continuum from good to poor. Good outcomes are reflected in (a) positive physical and mental health of individual members, (b) optimal role functioning of individual members (such as in work, school, parenting, etc.), and (c) maintenance of a family unit that can accomplish its life cycle tasks.

In attempting to understand the impact of chronic health problems on families as well as the family's ability to manage the health condition, it is important to recognize that families are never dealing with a single event. Rather, there are multiple sources of demands that change through time. Illness events cause added hardships. For example, Stein and Reissman (1980) have developed a measure, the Impact on Family Scales, that systematically assesses personal, family/social, and financial hardships associated with caring for a child with a chronic condition. Combining mothers' and fathers' reports from the Impact on Family Scales (Level IIb data), Patterson, Leonard et al. (1992) found that more hardships were associated with adverse health outcomes in family members.

Normative developmental tasks are also part of the pileup of demands and often are more difficult when a chronic condition is present. For example, youth with diabetes have been found to experience delayed ego development compared with youth without chronic illness (Hauser, Jacobson, Noam, & Powers, 1983). Furthermore, the family's response to the diabetes, as reflected by family members' interaction patterns, appears to mediate the relationship between chronic illness and ego development (Hauser et al., 1993). Several investigators have systematically assessed the pileup of demands in families by using self-report life events scales (Level IIa data) and found that higher stress was associated with poorer outcomes. For example, higher family stress was associated with poorer adherence to treatment regimens for cystic fibrosis (Patterson, 1985) and poorer physiological health outcomes for children with diabetes (Hamlett, Pellegrini, & Katz, 1992).

Resources are those traits or characteristics of the family unit, of individual members, or of the community that can be used by families to manage their pileup of demands. In the FAAR Model, family functioning characteristics such as cohesion, flexibility, communication skills, and clear organization of roles and rules are included as part of family resources. Many family and health studies focus on identifying the presence or absence of these resources relative to health outcomes of interest. Investigators are interested in knowing what "protects" a child and family from adverse outcomes when a known risk factor is present, such as disability in a child. As already mentioned, several self-report instruments produce Level II data for assessing some of these resources present in families, such as FACES and FES (see Grotevant & Carlson, 1989, for descriptions of others).

Social support is one of the most important resources that buffer high levels of stress in families. When chronic conditions are present, supportive relationships outside of the family have been shown to be associated with better family and child outcomes (Jessop, Riessman, & Stein, 1988; Varni, Wilcox, & Hanson, 1988; Wallender & Varni, 1989). Unfortunately, the risk of losing sources of support often is associated with chronic conditions because of stigma, fear, or less time in the family for social relationships. Usually, social support is assessed through interviews or self-report instruments (Level II data).

Do resources have a direct or indirect effect on outcomes of interest under conditions of chronic stress? Does the absence of family resources matter more for children with chronic illness than for children without chronic illness? Breslau (1993) compared psychiatric sequelae in children with brain dysfunction with children with no chronic condition and with children with chronic illnesses with no brain dysfunction. Her focus was on the resource of family cohesion (Level IIa data) as a potential buffer between stress associated with chronic illness and child outcomes. Family cohesion was protective against psychiatric sequelae across all groups. In addition, there were no interaction effects between family cohesion and group, suggesting a direct main effect of resources on outcomes (vs. a buffering or moderating effect). Although children with chronic illnesses showed higher levels of depression, this did not appear to be related directly to family functioning but rather to the stress of living with a chronic illness.

Another important variable in stress theory is coping. In the FAAR Model, coping is defined as the specific effort of an individual or family to maintain or restore balance between demands and resources. Hauser et al. (1993) used audiotaped family interviews to code family coping with diabetes (Level III data). Their emphasis was on family coping rather than individual coping. Hence, the referent for the use of any strategy had to be the family as a group versus an individual family member (e.g., "we did it" vs. "I did it"). In families with a member with diabetes (compared with a member with an acute illness), there were more frequent problem-focused coping efforts, greater coping efforts directed at expressing feelings to others, and more effort in being self-reliant.

In a study of parental coping when a child had cystic fibrosis, Patterson, Budd et al. (1992) found that parents who used a *balanced* coping strategy that included the behaviors of taking care of the family, taking caring of themselves personally, and actively seeking information and managing the child's medical condition had children with better pulmonary function trends during a 10-year period. The coping score was an example of Level IIb data because the independent scores of a mother-father dyad were combined to create a balanced coping score, which was the minimum score of either parent on the six coping subscales. This measure was based on family stress theory, in which a broad repertoire of coping behaviors is viewed as most adaptive.

This issue of balancing multiple family needs is a central concept in understanding family adaptation to stress. Reiss et al. (1993) emphasized the importance of balancing illness needs with other family needs to minimize the distortion of normal family regulatory processes and distortion of the family's developmental course. In the study of mortality in patients with end-stage renal disease, the family's sense of mastery, coordination, and closure were assessed using a family interaction task that directly scores these dimensions (Level IIIb data). Surprisingly, families high on coordination (a positive aspect of family functioning) had patients who died earlier. Paradoxically, strict patient adherence with renal dialysis treatment also predicted early death. In interpreting these findings, Reiss et al. proposed that integrated cohesive families become vulnerable as the intense medical needs of the patient threaten the family's ability to meet other needs and stay strong. To protect the family unit as a whole from disintegration, the patient with terminal illness voluntarily withdraws from the family, which the family allows. As the patient withdraws, he or she becomes more integrated into the dialysis unit and adheres to its rules as a way to join this social community. This important study illustrates the complexity of the interactions between patients, family structure and functioning, and relationships with the health service system. Furthermore, it illustrates the level of complexity and sophistication that can be brought to bear in studying family process in relationship to health. More studies of this level of conceptual and empirical rigor and richness are needed.

Future Directions

Given the mounting evidence for the relationship between individual health and family health, there clearly is a need for more research to advance the understanding of these relationships. Good empirical studies provide the basis for primary prevention efforts, public policy related to health, and the provision of health and related services to children and families. Research recommendations to enhance the knowledge base about children's mental health and families are detailed below.

1. More epidemiologic studies to determine the incidence and prevalence of children's mental health problems should be undertaken. How are children's mental health problems distributed in the population—which groups are more vulnerable, at what ages, living in what types of families, living in what geographic areas, and so forth?

2. Research should be theoretically based. Conceptualization and assessment of family functioning need to grounded in a theoretical orientation. Greater sophistication in conceptualizing complex family processes will lead to greater clarity in the specification of variables and the relationships between variables, as well as to improved operational measures for assessing these variables. As Fisher et al. (1992) have pointed out, early family and health studies have been too restricted and simplistic in assessing the dimensions of family functioning. More studies that include multiple, independent dimensions of family functioning are needed.

3. Whenever possible, family assessment should involve multiple methods and multiple informants to obtain the richest picture of family process. Most early studies relied principally on mothers as informants of family process. Not only are the perspectives of other family members needed, but efforts to combine two or more family members' self-reports should be included (Level IIb data). In addition, more data about the family from an outsider's perspective (Level III data) need to be obtained to complement the insider view obtained from family self-report instruments.

4. Better research designs are needed to answer the research questions posed. Needed also are better sampling techniques to improve the generalizability of findings as well as larger samples to ensure adequate power for finding significant effects when they exist (avoid Type-II error). Meaningful comparison and/or control groups should be incorporated in research designs.

5. Longitudinal studies are needed to improve the understanding of family process, of change through time, and of the direction of effects between child, family, and community variables.

6. Intervention studies in which the family system is the unit of intervention should be undertaken. It is important to keep the unit of analysis conceptually clear so that an individual property is not construed as a family characteristic. More randomized controlled trials are needed to evaluate the real impact of the intervention more clearly. Long-term as well as short-term outcomes should be assessed. These intervention studies are critical to good theory building, which contributes to the advancement of science.

7. Biopsychosocial studies that combine the methodologies of several disciplines to measure biologic, psychologic, and family

system variables are needed. These studies will require greater collaboration across disciplines.

8. Studies that involve diverse and understudied children and families should be greatly expanded. This diversity may include race, ethnicity, culture, religious beliefs, and socioeconomic status. Every aspect of the research process, its underlying assumptions and methods, needs to be scrutinized in regard to issues of diversity. For example,

Are persons from diverse backgrounds on the research team?

Are the research questions or hypotheses biased or driven by values or beliefs that are too narrow or culturally specific?

Do the sampling procedures encourage and allow for diversity?

Are the assessment methods reliable and valid for diverse groups?

Do the dissemination methods include ways of reaching underserved populations?

9. Qualitative studies of family process are needed to complement the knowledge generated from quantitative studies. Many aspects of family process involve not only individual family member subjectivity but also shared family constructions of meaning. Assessment of these subjective constructs often requires qualitative methods that allow for the participant's reality to be brought forth.

10. Needed are studies that focus on health and resiliency rather than on illness and pathology. This will involve studies designed to identify those protective factors that contribute to good outcomes in children and families. One should not assume that the absence of illness or pathology necessarily means health. Although health and illness may be the end points along the same continuum, the range of pathology and the range of competence are distinct, each with its own normal distribution. Perhaps it is only one standard deviation on the low end of competence that overlaps with one standard deviation on the high end of pathology.

Conclusion

Families are complex social units. Good family research methods will contribute to the understanding of the variability in adaptive capacities of families. Research should be both theoretically grounded and driven by rigorous and clear specifications of the important questions. In addition to building theory, such findings will contribute to improved services for children and families who face and must learn to live with a wide variety of stressful circumstances.

References

Anderson, K., & Tomlinson, P. (1992). The family health system as an emerging paradigmatic view for nursing. *Image: Journal of Nursing Scholarship, 14*(1), 57-63.

Bateson, G. (1972). *Steps to an ecology of mind.* New York: Ballantine.

Beavers, J., Hampson, R. B., Hulgus, Y. F., & Beavers, W. R. (1986). Coping in families with a retarded child. *Family Process, 25,* 365-378.

Beavers, R. (1993). Measuring family competence: The Beavers systems model. In F. Walsh (Ed.), *Normal family processes* (2nd ed., pp. 73-103). New York: Guilford.

Blechman, E. A., & Delamater, A. M. (1993). Family communication and Type 1 diabetes: A window on the social environment of chronically ill children. In R. Cole & D. Reiss (Eds.), *How do families cope with chronic illness?* (pp. 1-24). Hillsdale, NJ: Lawrence Erlbaum.

Borrow, E., AvRuskin, T., & Siller, J. (1985). Mother-daughter interaction and adherence to diabetes regimens. *Diabetes Care, 8,* 146-151.

Boss, P. (1988). *Family stress management.* Newbury Park, CA: Sage.

Boss, P., Doherty, W., LaRossa, R., Schumm, W., & Steinmetz, S. (Eds.). (1993). *Sourcebook of family theories and methods: A contextual approach.* New York: Plenum.

Breslau, N. (1993). Psychiatric sequelae of brain dysfunction in children: The role of family environment. In R. Cole & D. Reiss (Eds.), *How do families cope with chronic illness?* (pp. 57-70). Hillsdale, NJ: Lawrence Erlbaum.

Campbell, T. L. (1986). Family's impact on health: A critical review. *Family Systems Medicine, 4,* 135-328.

Cole, R. E., Kane, C., Zastowny, T., Grolnick, W., & Lehman, A. (1993). Expressed emotion, communication, and problem solving in the families of chronic schizophrenic young adults. In R. Cole & D. Reiss (Eds.), *How do families cope with chronic illness?* (pp. 141-172). Hillsdale, NJ: Lawrence Erlbaum.

Coyne, J., & Anderson, B. (1988). The "psychosomatic family" reconsidered: Diabetes in context. *Journal of Marital and Family Therapy, 14,* 113-123.

Daniels, D., Moos, R., Billings, A., & Miller, J. (1987). Psychosocial risk and resistance factors among children with chronic illness, healthy siblings, and healthy controls. *Journal of Abnormal Child Psychology, 15,* 295-308.

Deford, F. (1983). *Alex: The life of a child.* New York: Viking.

Dorris, M. (1989). *The broken cord.* New York: HarperPerennial.

Engel, G. (1977). The need for a new medical model: A challenge for biomedicine. *Science, 196,* 129-136.

Featherstone, H. (1980). *A difference in the family.* New York: Basic Books.

Fine, M. (1993). Current approaches to understanding family diversity: An overview of the special issue. *Family Relations, 42*(3), 235-237.

Fisher, L., Kokes, R., Ransom, D., Phillips, S., & Rudd, P. (1985). Alternative strategies for creating "relational" family data. *Family Process, 24,* 213-224.

Fisher, L., Ransom, D., Terry, H., Lipkin, M., & Weiss, R. (1992). The California family health project: I. Introduction and a description of adult health. *Family Process, 31,* 231-250.

Grotevant, H., & Carlson, C. (1989). *Family assessment: A guide to methods and measures.* New York: Guilford.

Gustafsson, P., Cederblad, M., Ludvigsson, J., & Lundin, B. (1987). Family interaction and metabolic balance in juvenile diabetes mellitus: A prospective study. *Diabetes Research and Clinical Practice, 4,* 7-14.

Gustafsson, P., Kjellman, N., & Cederblad, M. (1986). Family therapy in the treatment of severe childhood asthma. *Journal of Psychosomatic Research, 30*(3), 369-374.

Gustafsson, P., Kjellman, N., Ludvigsson, J., & Cederblad, M. (1987). Asthma and family interaction. *Archives of Disease in Childhood, 62,* 258-263.

Hamlett, K., Pellegrini, D., & Katz, K. (1992). Childhood chronic illness as a family stressor. *Journal of Pediatric Psychology, 17*(1), 33-47.

Hauser, S., Jacobson, A., Bliss, R., Vieyra, M., Willett, J., Cole, C., DiPlacido, J., Paul, E., Lavori, P., Wolfsdorf, J., Herskowitz, R., & Wertlieb, D. (1993). The family and the onset of its youngster's insulin-dependent diabetes: Ways of coping. In R. Cole & D. Reiss (Eds.), *How do families cope with chronic illness?* (pp. 25-55). Hillsdale, NJ: Lawrence Erlbaum.

Hauser, S., Jacobson, A., Noam, G., & Powers, S. (1983). Ego development and self-image complexity in early adolescence: Psychiatric and diabetic patients. *Archives of General Psychiatry, 40,* 325-332.

Hermanns, J., Florin, I., Dietrich, M., Rieger, C., & Hahlweg, K. (1989). Maternal criticism, mother-child interaction, and bronchial asthma. *Journal of Psychosomatic Research, 33,* 469-476.

Jacob, T., & Tennenbaum, D. (1988). *Family assessment: Rationale, methods, and future directions.* New York: Plenum.

Jessop, D., Riessman, C., & Stein, R. (1988). Chronic childhood illness and maternal mental health. *Journal of Developmental and Behavioral Pediatrics, 9,* 147-156.

Knafl, K. A., & Deatrick, J. A. (1990). Family management style: Concept analysis and development. *Journal of Pediatric Nursing, 5*(1), 4-14.

Kupst, J., & Schulman J. (1988). Long-term coping with pediatric leukemia: A six-year follow-up study. *Journal of Pediatric Psychology, 13,* 7-22.

Marteau, T., Bloch, S., & Baum, J. (1987). Family life and diabetic control. *Journal of Child Psychology and Psychiatry, 28,* 823-833.

Massie, R. (1985). The constant shadow: Reflections on the life of a chronically ill child. In N. Hobbs & J. Perrin (Eds.), *Issues in the care of children with chronic illness* (pp. 13-23). San Francisco: Jossey-Bass.

McCubbin, H., McCubbin, M., Patterson, J., Cauble, A., Wilson, L., & Warwick, W. (1983). CHIP: Coping health inventory for parents: An assessment of parental coping patterns in the care of the chronically ill child. *Journal of Marriage and the Family, 45,* 359-370.

McCubbin, H., & Patterson, J. (1983). Stress: The family inventory of life events and changes. In E. Filsinger (Ed.), *Marriage and family assessment* (pp. 275-297). Beverly Hills, CA: Sage.

McCubbin, M., & McCubbin, H. (1993). Family coping with health crises: The resiliency model of family stress, adjustment, and adaptation. In C. Danielson, B. Hamel-

Bissell, & P. Winstead-Fry (Eds.), *Families, health and illness* (pp. 21-63). New York: C. V. Mosby.

Minuchin, S., Baker, L., Rosman, B., Liebman, R., Milman, L., & Todd, T. (1975). A conceptual model of psychosomatic illness in children. *Archives of General Psychiatry, 32,* 1031-1038.

Moos, R., & Moos, B. (1981). *Family environment scale manual.* Palo Alto, CA: Consulting Psychologists Press.

Moos, R., & Moos, B. (1983). Clinical applications of the family environment scale. In E. Filsinger (Ed.), *Marriage and family assessment* (pp. 253-273). Beverly Hills, CA: Sage.

Olson, D. (1993). The circumplex model of marriage and family function. In F. Walsh (Ed.), *Normal family processes* (2nd ed., pp. 104-137). New York: Guilford.

Patterson, J. (1985). Critical factors affecting family compliance with cystic fibrosis. *Family Relations, 34,* 173-213.

Patterson, J. (1988). Families experiencing stress: The family adjustment and adaptation response model. *Family Systems Medicine, 5*(2), 202-237.

Patterson, J. (1989). A family stress model: The family adjustment and adaptation response. In C. Ramsey (Ed.), *The science of family medicine* (pp. 95-118). New York: Guilford.

Patterson, J. (1990). Family and health research in the 1980s: A family scientist's perspective. *Family Systems Medicine, 8*(4), 421-434.

Patterson, J. (1991). A family system's perspective for working with youth with disability. *Pediatrician, 18,* 129-141.

Patterson, J., & Blum, R. (1993). A conference on culture and chronic illness in childhood: Conference summary. *Pediatrics, 91*(5), 1025-1030.

Patterson, J., Budd, J., Goetz, D., & Warwick, W. (1992). Family correlates of a ten-year trend in pulmonary health trend in cystic fibrosis. *Pediatrics, 91*(2), 383-389.

Patterson, J., Jernell, J., Leonard, B., & Titus, J. (1994). Caring for medically fragile children at home: The parent-professional relationship. *Journal of Pediatric Nursing, 9*(2), 98-106.

Patterson, J., & Leonard, B. (1994). Caregiving and children. In E. Kahana, D. E. Biegel, & M. Wykle (Eds.), *Family caregiving across the lifespan.* Thousand Oaks, CA: Sage.

Patterson, J., Leonard, B., & Titus, J. (1992). Home care for medically fragile children: Impact on family health and well-being. *Journal of Developmental and Behavioral Pediatrics, 13*(4), 248-255.

Ransom, D. (1986). Research on the family in health, illness and care: State of the art. *Family Systems Medicine, 4,* 329-336.

Reiss, D. (1981). *The family's construction of reality.* Cambridge, MA: Harvard University Press.

Reiss, D., Steinglass, P., & Howe, G. (1993). The family's organization around the illness. In R. Cole & D. Reiss (Eds.), *How do families cope with chronic illness?* (pp. 173-213). Hillsdale, NJ: Lawrence Erlbaum.

Satin, W., LaGreca, A., Zigo, M., & Skyler, J. (1989). Diabetes in adolescence: Effects of multifamily group intervention and parent simulation of diabetes. *Journal of Pediatric Psychology, 14*(2), 259-275.

Spinetta, J., Murphy, J., Vik, P., Day, J., & Mott, M. (1988). Long-term adjustment of children with cancer. *Journal of Psychosocial Oncology, 6,* 179-191.

Stein, R. K., & Reissman, C. K. (1980). The development of an impact-on-family scale: Preliminary findings. *Medical Care, 18,* 465-472.

Steinglass, P., & Horan, M. (1987). Families and chronic medical illness. *Journal of Psychotherapy and the Family, 3,* 127-142.

Thompson, R., Gustafson, K., Hamlett, K., & Spock, A. (1992). Stress, coping, and family functioning in the psychological adjustment of mothers of children and adolescents with cystic fibrosis. *Journal of Pediatric Psychology, 17*(5), 573-585.

Timko, C., Stovel, K., & Moos, R. (1992). Functioning among mothers and fathers of children with juvenile rheumatic disease: A longitudinal study. *Journal of Pediatric Psychology, 17*(6), 705-724.

Touliatos, J., Perlmutter, B., & Strauss, M. (1990). *Handbook of family measurement techniques.* Newbury Park, CA: Sage.

Varni, J., Wilcox, K., & Hanson, V. (1988). Mediating effects of family social support on child psychological adjustment in juvenile rheumatoid arthritis. *Health Psychology, 7,* 421-431.

Vaughn, C. E. (1989). Annotation: Expressed emotion in family relationships. *Journal of Child Psychology and Psychiatry, 30,* 13-22.

Wallender, J., & Varni, J. (1989). Social support and adjustment in chronically ill and handicapped children. *American Journal of Community Psychology, 17,* 185-201.

Walsh, F. (1993). Conceptualization of normal family processes. In F. Walsh (Ed.), *Normal family processes* (pp. 3-69). New York: Guilford.

Walters, L., Pittman, J., & Norrell, J. (1984). Development of a quantitative measure of a family from self-reports of family members. *Journal of Family Issues, 5,* 497-514.

Wamboldt, F., & Wolin, S. (1988). Reality and myth in family life: Changes across generations. *Journal of Psychotherapy and the Family, 4,* 141-165.

Watson, S. M., Henggeler, S. W., & Whelan, J. P. (1990). Family functioning and the social adaptation of hearing impaired youths. *Journal of Abnormal Child Psychology, 18,* 143-163.

Wood, B., Watkins, J., Boyle, J., Nogueria, J., Zimand, E., & Carroll, L. (1989). The "psychosomatic family" model: An empirical and theoretical analysis. *Family Process, 28,* 399-417.

Wood, B. L. (in press). A developmental biobehavioral systems approach to the treatment of chronic illness in children. In R. Mikesel, D. Lusterman, & S. McDaniel (Eds.), *Family psychology and systems therapy: A handbook.* Washington, DC: American Psychological Association.

World Health Organization. (1976). *Statistical indices of family health* (Rep. No. 589). Geneva, Switzerland: World Health Organization.

The Colorado Family Assessment

A Computer-Based Procedure for Multilevel Family Evaluation

BERNARD L. BLOOM

In 1965, Handel introduced his review of the psychological study of whole families by calling attention to Burgess's (1926) felicitous phrase, "the family as a unity of interacting personalities." Handel described the fundamental question in the study of families as "how do the several personalities in a family cohere in an ongoing structure that is both sustained and altered through interaction?" (p. 21). In recent years, there has been a growing realization that any comprehensive family assessment must take this interactional conception of family functioning into account. For example, Pearlin and Turner (1987) have written,

---

AUTHOR'S NOTE: I thank Mark Roland, Senior Systems Analyst for the Computer Laboratory for Instruction in Psychological Research, Department of Psychology at the University of Colorado, for his extraordinary skill and unfailing good humor in writing the program code that made possible the implementation of the Colorado Family Assessment.

> The family . . . is a very complex and differentiated institution and its very complexity invites a variety of conceptual orientations and research questions. . . . To assess such elements, it is necessary to observe the functioning of the family unit, not its separate members. This is a difficult task at best and is usually done under laboratory conditions. Strictly speaking, most studies that purport to be family studies are not. Instead, they are studies of the individual-in-family. (p. 144)

Another compelling evaluation of the complexity of family assessment can be found in the work of Ransom, Fisher, Phillips, Kokes, and Weiss (1990), who wrote,

> The variety of meanings of the term "family," the multidimensional and multileveled nature of those meanings, and the extraordinary range of assessment and measurement techniques available to tap them all combine to create a condition of complexity that easily leads to confused and confounded investigating and reporting. With the increased popularity of family systems theory and the attending pressure to report results in terms that reflect the "whole" family, the confusion and confounding of family concepts and measures and the discussion of family research results have grown worse. (p. 48)

The assessment of families as differentiated from the assessment of family members is especially important because measures of individual personality or cognitive functioning seem to account for a relatively small proportion of variance in individual behavior. Because the family may represent the single most important environmental setting within which most individuals function, assessing the family, over and above the individuals who compose it, has the potential for making a significant additive contribution to the understanding of individual behavior (Brown & Kidwell, 1982; Christensen & Arrington, 1987; Gottman, 1982).

Family assessment procedures can be divided into two separate domains as a function of whether data are provided by "outsiders" or "insiders" (Olson, 1977, 1985). Outsider assessments provide a view of the family as interpreted by observers and are based on clinical interview procedures, observation of families in naturalistic settings, or observation of unrestricted behavior in laboratory settings (e.g., Drechsler & Shapiro, 1961; Fleck, 1980; Grotevant & Carlson, 1987; Quinton, Rutter, & Rowlands, 1976; Riskin & Faunce, 1970; Steinglass,

1980; Straus & Tallman, 1971). Insider assessments, of which the Colorado Family Assessment (CFA) is an example, require little indirect interpretation and come from family member self-reports; from laboratory studies in which family members work together to complete a specified task, produce a product, or resolve a disagreement; and, more recently, from the analysis of physiological data (e.g., Filsinger, 1983; Humphrey & Benjamin, 1986; Levenson & Gottman, 1985; Miller, Epstein, Bishop, & Keitner, 1985).

Regarding insider views of the family, Fisher (1982) and his colleagues (Fisher, Kokes, Ransom, Phillips, & Rudd, 1985) have proposed distinguishing between (a) the individual level of assessment, in which "data from a single family member are utilized with no reference to the views, perceptions, or actions of other family members" (1985, p. 214); (b) the relational level of assessment, in which "individual-level data collected from two or more family members are 'related' to each other in some way" (p. 214); and (c) the transactional level of assessment that reflects "some product of the system or behavioral interchange among system members . . . [resulting in] a whole that is significantly different from the sum of its parts" (p. 215; see also Ransom et al., 1990).

Fisher et al. (1985) have concluded that individual-level data, made up of statements by an individual family member about the family, are not family data as such, although they may provide useful information. Relational-level data, on the other hand, can yield meaningful descriptions of a family, as can transactional-level data, obtained directly from the analysis of actual contingent behavior of the family members.

Problems inherent in family assessment based on data obtained from a single family member are particularly important when research interests focus on the mental health of children or adolescents. Most family data based on the observations of a single family member are collected from mothers—a state of affairs that led Safilios-Rothschild (1969) to coin the phrase "wives' family sociology" in characterizing these research studies (see also Larsen & Olson, 1990). To the extent that interventions are designed to affect children's mental health through some form of family intervention, assessment of that mental health must take into account that children are embedded in families. Under these circumstances, assessment of family functioning needs to include the evaluation of how children interact with their parents and siblings.

Two implications seem clear from these and other related methodological and conceptual analyses of the recent family assessment literature (e.g., Forman & Hagan, 1984; Hannum & Mayer, 1984; Miller, Rollins, & Thomas, 1982; Olson, 1985; Sigafoos & Reiss, 1985; Sigafoos, Reiss, Rich, & Douglas, 1985; Sprey, 1988; Szinovacz, 1983; Thompson & Walker, 1982; Thomson & Williams, 1982): (a) Family assessment requires data from more than one family member, and (b) a comprehensive family assessment requires obtaining data at both relational and transactional levels.

Characteristics of Healthy Family Functioning

Although most family researchers are interested in some specific aspect of family functioning, several have attempted to formulate a set of overall general principles regarding what is often referred to as healthy or normal family functioning (see Walsh, 1982, for a review of these formulations). Often these formulations constitute the basis for an omnibus inventory of family functioning such as the CFA.

Although different family theorists often emphasize different aspects of healthy family functioning, there is enough similarity in these formulations that Barnhill (1979) identified four basic common themes. The first theme, identity processes, includes individuation, "independence of thought, feeling, and judgment of individual family members" (p. 95), and mutuality, "a sense of emotional closeness, joining, or intimacy which, however, is only possible between individuals with clearly defined identities" (p. 95). The second theme, change, includes flexibility—"the capacity to be adjustable and resilient in response to varied conditions and to the process of change" (p. 95), and stability, "consistency, responsibility, and security in family interactions" (p. 95).

Barnhill's (1979) third theme, information processing, includes clear perception, "undistorted awareness of self and others" (p. 95), and clear communication, "clear and successful exchange of information between family members" (p. 96). The fourth theme, role structuring, includes role reciprocity, "mutually agreed upon behavior patterns or sequences in which an individual complements the role of a role partner" (p. 96), and clear generational boundaries, "certain specific types of role reciprocity among family members . . . between marital, parent-child, and sibling relationships" (p. 96).

These themes can be seen, for example, in the earlier work of Glasser and Glasser (1970), who identified five criteria of what they called "adequate family functioning": (a) internal role consistency among family members, (b) consistency of family roles and norms and actual role performance, (c) compatibility of family roles and norms with community norms, (d) the ability of the family group to meet the psychological needs of family members, and (e) the ability of the family group to respond to change (p. 291). Similarly, these themes are seen in the work of Beavers (1976, 1982), who has urged evaluating families in the adequacy of their functioning in five fundamental dimensions: (a) intrafamilial power structure, (b) family tolerance for individuation and autonomous functioning, (c) capacity for the acceptance of separation and loss, (d) perception of reality, and (e) family affect or feeling tone.

Using an entirely different approach to the identification of healthy family characteristics, Curran (1983) surveyed some 500 family therapists, school counselors and teachers, family physicians, social workers, pastoral counselors, and directors of family agencies and asked them what they felt to be the most important traits of the happy family. Curran found the results to suggest 11 traits with a remarkable degree of similarity to the Barnhill formulation. According to Curran, the happy family (a) communicates and listens, by encouraging the expression of individual feelings and independent thinking, recognizing nonverbal messages, and attempting to resolve disagreements; (b) affirms and supports family members by making sure that the family mood is positive, by helping all family members develop self-esteem, and by expecting that all family members will be supportive of each other; (c) teaches respect for others, by respecting individual differences and decisions within the family, by showing respect to those outside the family, and by respecting the property of others; (d) has a sense of trust in each family member, by giving children the opportunity to earn trust, by encouraging parents as well as children to be trustworthy, and at the same time, by recognizing that broken trust can be mended; (e) spends time together, recognizing when stress is high and when there is a need to have fun together, and by discouraging the formation of divisive coalitions and cliques within the family; (f) exhibits a sense of shared responsibility, by understanding that responsibility means more than doing chores, that responsibility should be geared to the capability of individual family members, and that members of the family need to live with the consequences of irresponsibility; (g) teaches a sense of right and wrong, by making sure that parents share major important values, provide guidelines about right and wrong behavior, and teach children to live morally and to be responsible for their own moral behavior; (h) has a strong sense of family, seeing itself as a link between the past and the future, honoring its elders and welcoming its babies, and cherishing its religious and secular traditions and rituals; (i) respects each family member's privacy, not only regarding space but also regarding friends, confidences, and the wish to be alone; (j) values service to others, by being basically empathic, altruistic, and hospitable, and by serving others in need; and (k) admits to and seeks help with problems, considering problems a normal part of family life and working toward developing problem-solving skills.

These four perspectives on healthy family functioning, although far from identical, have enough similarities to identify their parallels. Table 8.1 illustrates this comparison.

Although it seems unlikely that any omnibus family assessment procedure can assess every aspect of healthy family functioning that has received the attention of family researchers, the CFA has been designed to assess an array of important aspects of family functioning consistent with the dimensions just identified, attending particularly to family characteristics that have to be examined at different levels of empirical and theoretical abstraction. The CFA is a new instrument, however, and its validity needs to be established through research.

The Colorado Family Assessment

Insider views of the family are obtained with the CFA at three increasingly complex levels that differ not only in the nature of the data but also in the evaluated family attributes. In keeping with the

Table 8.1 Comparative Approaches to the Conceptualization of Healthy Family Functioning

Barnhill (1979)	*Curran (1983)*	*Glasser and Glasser (1970)*	*Beavers (1976)*
Identity processes: individuation with mutuality	Affirms and supports each other; teaches respect for others; shared responsibility; trust in each other; service to others	Ability to meet psychological needs of family members	Tolerance for individuation and for autonomous functioning
Change: flexibility with the capacity for stability	Admits to and seeks help with problems	Ability of the family group to respond to change	Capacity to accept separation and loss
Information processing: clear perception and clear communication	Communicates and listens; teaches sense of right and wrong	Role performance matches family norms	Accurate perception of reality; appropriate affect and tone
Role structuring: role reciprocity and clear generational boundaries	Spends time with family; sense of family; sense of privacy	Role consistency; compatibility of family norms with community norms	Appropriate intrafamilial power structure

terminology employed in the methodological approaches to family assessment that have been briefly reviewed, the CFA includes both relational and transactional data. Data are provided by two, three, or four family members regarding individual family members as well as the family as a whole. (For more on levels of analysis in family measurement, see Patterson, Chapter 7 in this volume.)

The procedure requires about 1 hour for three-person families and 90 minutes for four-person families and takes place in a setting in which up to four family members, seated in front of computer terminals, carry out a series of fully automated assessment procedures. The software program is written in FORTRAN and operates on Digital Equipment Corporation equipment using the VMS operating system, a system unusually well suited to this particular application. At the conclusion of the CFA, a report can be generated that provides information regarding the purposes of each of the assessment procedures, as well as specific scores obtained by the family throughout the procedure (see Burke & Normand, 1987; Mathisen, 1987). A sample of the CFA report is available from me.

Levels of Analysis

First-Person Self-Report Measures. First-person self-report measures ("What do I think about my family?") constitute the backbone of the family assessment literature (e.g., Bloom, 1985; Forman & Hagan, 1984; McCubbin & Thompson, 1987; van der Veen, 1965). There are two groups of self-report measures: (a) single-dimension scales that assess a concept of interest to a particular research group, such as intimacy (Schaefer & Olson, 1981), cohesion (Bilbro & Dreyer, 1981), conflict tactics (Straus, 1979), marital satisfaction (Wampler & Powell, 1982), or dyadic trust (Larzelere & Huston, 1980), and (b) multidimensional measures that assess a variety of aspects of family functioning within a single test instrument, such as the Family Environment Scale (Moos & Moos, 1976), the Family Evaluation Scales (Green, Kolevzon, & Vosler, 1985), the Family Assessment Device (Miller et al., 1985), the Family Adaptability and Cohesion Evaluation Scales (Olson, Sprenkle, & Russell, 1979), and the Family Assessment Measure (Skinner, Steinhauer, & Santa-Barbara, 1983).

Self-report measures combine ease of data collection with simplicity of data analysis. Two difficulties with these measures are increasingly recognized, however. First, there is clearly a ceiling on the proportion of variance of family behavior that can be accounted for by these measures, largely because there seem to be a limited number of uncorrelated self-reported domains of family functioning. Second, certain aspects of family functioning, such as family interaction, cannot be adequately assessed without examining actual family behavior.

In the self-report component of the CFA, family members respond in a four-choice format (very true, fairly true, fairly untrue, or very untrue for my family) to a 60-item measure. Twelve different aspects of family functioning are assessed: (a) cohesion (how much family members are concerned about and committed to the family, spend time together, and are helpful and supportive of each other); (b) expressiveness (how much family members are allowed and encouraged to express their opinions and their feelings to each other); (c) conflict (how often family members get angry, criticize, and fight with each other); (d) organization (how important it is to the family to be well organized, prompt, and neat); (e) sociability (how much family members seek and get pleasure from social interactions with others); (f) external locus of control (how much family members believe that things that happen to them are largely a matter of good or bad luck and, therefore, beyond their control); (g) family idealization (how much the family is prized and valued by its members); (h) disengagement (how often family members are too independent of each other and fail to communicate with each other); (i) democratic family style (how often family decisions are made with the full participation of all family members); (j) permissive family style (how much the family functions without the existence and enforcement of rules, allowing family members to go their own ways); (k) authoritarian family style (how often parents make the rules regarding family behavior, order others around, and punish children for breaking rules); and (l) enmeshment (how much family members insist on always being together, without allowing time for individual family members to lead their own lives). These scales were developed in a series of studies (Bloom, 1985) that sought to identify the essential nonduplicated components of four commonly used self-report measures of family functioning and seem to encompass the most important dimensions of these scales.

In examining these aspects of family functioning in the context of characteristics of healthy family functioning previously discussed (see Table 8.1), it can be seen that Barnhill's (1979) concept of identity processes is indexed by high scores on democratic family style, permissive family style, family sociability, and family idealization and low scores on enmeshment, disengagement, and authoritarian family style. Barnhill's concept of flexibility with capacity for change is indexed by high scores on organization. Barnhill's concept of information processing is indexed by high scores on expressiveness and low scores on conflict, external locus of control, and disengagement. Finally, Barnhill's concept of role structuring is indexed by high scores on cohesion.

These 12 aspects of family functioning constitute dimensions that should distinguish well-functioning from poorly functioning families. In keeping with general formulations of healthy family functioning, I have hypothesized that in contrast to members of poorly functioning families, well-functioning family members should describe their families as more cohesive and expressive, less conflicted, better organized, more sociable, with a lower sense of external locus of control, with a greater sense of family idealization, more engaged with each other, more democratic, and less permissive and authoritarian in their general ways of interacting with each other, and less enmeshed.

The CFA report provides scores on each of the 12 scales for each individual family member. In addition, average scores across all family members are provided, as well as differences in scale scores between all family dyads. In addition to the absolute score differences between well-functioning and poorly functioning family members on the 12 self-report measures, I hypothesize that differences in scores among dyads of well-functioning families should be significantly smaller than among dyads of poorly functioning families.

Third-Person Self-Report Measures. The second component of the CFA assesses predictability and predictive accuracy of family members ("What do I think other family members think about my family?") in the context of a measure of family child-rearing behavior. This instrument consists of 15 items derived from a factor analysis of two major child-rearing scales (Bloom & Lipetz, 1987; Schaefer, 1965; Siegelman, 1965; also see Cross, 1969; Schludermann & Schludermann, 1970; Schwarz, Barton-Henry, & Pruzinsky, 1985). Three aspects of child rearing are assessed using the same four-choice format described for the self-report measure: (a) affection or acceptance (how often parents express affection and acceptance of their children and enjoy, help, support, and praise them); (b) punitiveness (how often parents punish their children by such methods as scolding, spanking, or making them do extra work); and (c) psychological control (how much parents take an active role in monitoring the behavior of their children and setting specific limits on their activities away from home). In addition to providing an opportunity for family members to describe their own impressions of parental child-rearing styles, the procedure also asks family members to predict how they think other members of their family will describe parental child-rearing behavior on the same 15 items.

As in the case of the first-person self-report measures, results are calculated on each of the three child-rearing scales for individual family members along with averages of all family members and differences in scale scores between all family dyads. In addition, measures are obtained of the predictability of family members (differences between each family member's actual scale scores and aggregated predictions of that family member by other family members).

The third-person self-report measure is clearly related to Barnhill's (1979) concept of information processing (see Table 8.1). One expects that clear perception and clear communication could be indexed by scores on the third-person self-report measure that reflect a high level of predictability of other family members' behaviors.

Although the principal purpose of the third-person self-report is to assess family member predictability and accuracy in the prediction of other family members' child-rearing attitudes, the nature of the child-rearing attitudes can be examined directly. I hypothesize that members of well-functioning families, when contrasted with members of poorly functioning families, will describe parental child-rearing behavior as more affectionate, less punitive, and more moderate in their control, and that dyadic differences in reports of parental child-rearing behavior among family members will be smaller. In addition, I hypothesize that responses to these child-rearing questions will be more predictable by other family members in well-functioning than in poorly functioning families.

Transactional Family Measures. The third, and most complex, level of family assessment on the CFA is designed to examine interactional aspects of family functioning. A number of objective family interactional assessments have been reported in the literature (e.g., Bauman, Roman, Borello, & Meltzer, 1967; Floyd, O'Farrell, & Goldberg, 1987; Miller et al., 1982; Oliveri & Reiss, 1981; Reiss, 1967; Reiss & Sheriff, 1970; Strodtbeck, 1951; Usandivaras, Grimson, Hammond, Issaharoff, & Romanos, 1967). Such procedures for family assessment provide a task that requires family members to interact in some way and derive measures of family functioning from an analysis of that interaction.

Of all interactional measures of family behavior, perhaps most attention has been directed toward those procedures that examine how families deal with conflict or disagreement. The CFA includes a computerized version of the revealed differences experiment (RDE), first described by Strodtbeck (1951) and later employed in a number of different research settings (Caputo, 1963; Cheek, 1964; Farina, 1960; Jacob, 1975, 1987; Mishler & Waxler, 1968; Stabenau, Tupin, Werner, & Pollin, 1965).

The RDE asks family members to make individual judgments regarding some issue, and then members attempt to reconcile differences in their judgments through face-to-face interaction. Strodtbeck believed that the RDE provided a unique view of conflict resolution and permitted the identification of balance of power and modes of influence among members of a group.

To create the automated version of the RDE for the CFA, 26 of the 38 items (all of the items that were directly related to family issues) used by Mishler and Waxler (1968) were first administered to a group of 300 undergraduate students at the University of Colorado. Students were asked to choose one of two alternatives for each question and then to describe in a sentence or two why they chose that alternative. From the analysis of the results, a unique set of five reasons for each alternative was developed that could be chosen for each of the 26 questions.

In the CFA, each family member is given the opportunity to choose a preferred alternative for each question. If the members of the family agree with each other, they are informed of that agreement and then go on to the next question. If the members of the family do not agree with each other, one of the two lists of reasons is displayed for each family member, depending on which alternative was chosen, and the family members are asked to identify which reason was most salient to them as the basis for their choice. After each family member has examined the list of alternatives and has chosen the most pertinent one, each is then provided with a display of all family members' choices and reasons. Finally, after family members have learned about each other's choices and reasons, the original problem is presented again for their consideration, and family members are encouraged to change their minds if they wish to do so.

Analysis of the RDE provides information regarding the level of disagreement in the family and about the coalitions among family members when disagreements occur. In addition, an analysis is made of patterns of influence among family members, that is, the extent to which family members influence and are influenced by each other when disagreements do occur.

In examining the RDE in the context of Barnhill's (1979) concepts of healthy family functioning (see Table 8.1), the concept of flexibility with the capacity for stability should be indexed by a high level of willingness of family members to be influenced by each other. Barnhill's concept of role structuring should be indexed by a relatively low level of disagreement among family members and by the presence of appropriate coalitions among family members in the event of disagreement.

I hypothesize that in well-functioning families, as contrasted with poorly functioning families, less initial disagreement will occur among family members. When disagreements do occur, parents and children in well-functioning families will disagree with each other less frequently than in the case of poorly functioning families, and family members will influence each other and will be more often influenced by each other in the process of conflict resolution.

In summary, at the level of self-report, I hypothesize that members of well-functioning families will see themselves as relatively unconflicted about their families, happy to be part of their families, and optimistic about their abilities to resolve issues of concern to them. Members of well-functioning families will think of themselves as democratic, rather than authoritarian or permissive, in their approaches to the solutions of family problems. I hypothesize that well-functioning families will be made up of individuals who enjoy being with each other without feeling they cannot get away from each other and, at the same time, will enjoy being with other people. Members of well-functioning families will be cohesive, will feel free to express themselves to each other, and will be able to carry out the tasks of family functioning in a well-organized manner. Members of well-functioning families will share a general orientation to child rearing that is characterized by relatively high levels of parental affection and acceptance, low levels of parental punitiveness, and age-appropriate levels of parental behavior control of children.

At the level of interpersonal appraisal, members of well-functioning families should see each other realistically in that they can predict each other's attitudes and behavior relatively accurately. Finally, at the level of family interaction, specifically when dealing with disagreements, situations requiring resolution should come up relatively infrequently in well-functioning families. When disagreements arise, they should not be the result of consistent and predictable differences of opinion between parents and children. I hypothesize that while working toward the resolution of disagreements, members of well-functioning families will listen to and be influenced by each other, and listen to and be moved by each other, without inappropriate regard to status or role within the family.

Potential Uses of the Colorado Family Assessment

The CFA was designed to have three specific areas of application: (a) as a procedure for the collection of data useful in the evaluation of hypotheses regarding family functioning and its vicissitudes; (b) as a diagnostic instrument used for the identification of specific dysfunctional family characteristics (Hazelrigg, Cooper, & Borduin, 1987); and (c) as the foundation of an educationally oriented family-based preventive intervention program. Its principal advantages as an assessment instrument are its relatively comprehensive multilevel and multidimensional characteristics; its ease, speed, and high reliability of administration and scoring; and its high level of acceptability to families as a technique for family evaluation. Computer-based procedures for assessment are becoming increasingly common and appreciated. Clients of mental health and other human service professionals appear to be quite comfortable and increasingly accustomed to using computer terminals (Bloom, 1992), and the reliability of computer-assisted assessments appears to be indistinguishable from that of more traditionally administered assessment procedures (Blouin, Perez, & Blouin, 1988).

The CFA provides a method for assessing family functioning and, thus, for testing hypotheses in which family functioning serves as either a dependent or independent measure. In the case of family functioning as a dependent measure, for example, the CFA permits the examination of the effects of illness, bereavement, marital difficulties, and external stressful life events on family functioning. In addition, the CFA can be used as an indicator of progress in a family undergoing family therapy or counseling, that is, as an objective measure of improvement. As an independent measure of family functioning, CFA scores can be used, for example, to study how families that differ in the nature of their functioning will differentially cope with adversity.

As a diagnostic instrument, the CFA can be used to alert therapists to issues that need to be considered as families enter a treatment relationship. The CFA can identify families with abnormally high levels of disagreement among the members regarding many aspects of the family. Moreover, it can identify families that are unusually conflict-ridden and can help pinpoint the specific nature of some of those conflicts. The CFA can help identify family members who are isolated by others in the family or who are outliers in their belief systems. In preventive intervention objectives, the CFA shares much in common with MATESIM (Lehtinen & Smith, 1985), an automated marriage assessment that "predicts problem areas in the marriage, areas in which the marriage is especially satisfying, and identifies areas in which the clients can individually direct self-change to improve the overall quality of the relationship" (p. 117; also see Aradi, 1985; Friedman, 1985).

The CFA report describes and defines each of the assessment components and is designed to be a nontechnical document that can, in conjunction with the debriefing session, lead the family members through the quantitative analysis of their scores. Furthermore, the report can be given to the family and can be examined in greater detail by family members in the privacy of their own home.

The analysis of the first-person self-report measure provides an opportunity for family members to find out what they think about their family on a number of important family dimensions and how their evaluations compare with each other. Family members can contrast their assessments of their family with their aspirations for the family and can begin a change process that continues beyond the debriefing session.

Analyses of the first-person measures of child-rearing behavior provide an opportunity to compare notes on family member perceptions of parental child-rearing practices. Measures of predictability identify differences in the degree to which family members can accurately predict each other's responses to the child-rearing questionnaire and the extent to which family members differ in their degree of predictability.

Finally, analysis of the revealed differences experiment describes how family members cope with disagreements and, perhaps, how they cope with conflict more broadly. The report identifies the nature of intrafamilial coalitions when there are disagreements and evaluates the extent to which family members are willing to change their minds when faced with evidence that other family members disagree with them.

Conclusion

The usefulness of the CFA ultimately will be determined by the extent to which it achieves its three objectives in both research and clinical settings. In general, the CFA will need to provide valid information about family functioning that can be used in the development and examination of family theory, clinically useful diagnostic evaluations, and an educational experience that can result in positive changes in family functioning.

References

Aradi, N. S. (1985). The application of computer technology to behavioral marital therapy. *Journal of Psychotherapy and the Family, 1,* 167-177.

Barnhill, L. (1979). Healthy family systems. *Family Coordinator, 28,* 94-100.

Bauman, G., Roman, M., Borello, J., & Meltzer, B. (1967). Interaction testing in the measurement of marital intelligence. *Journal of Abnormal Psychology, 72,* 489-495.

Beavers, W. R. (1976). A theoretical basis for family evaluation. In J. M. Lewis, W. R. Beavers, J. T. Gossett, & V. A. Phillips (Eds.), *No single thread* (pp. 46-82). New York: Brunner/Mazel.

Beavers, W. R. (1982). Healthy, midrange, and severely dysfunctional families. In F. Walsh (Ed.), *Normal family processes* (pp. 45-66). New York: Guilford.

Bilbro, T. L., & Dreyer, A. S. (1981). A methodological study of a measure of family cohesion. *Family Process, 20,* 419-427.

Bloom, B. L. (1985). A factor analysis of self-report measures of family functioning. *Family Process, 24,* 225-239.

Bloom, B. L. (1992). Computer-assisted psychological intervention: A review and commentary. *Clinical Psychology Review, 12,* 169-197.

Bloom, B. L., & Lipetz, M. E. (1987). *Child-rearing scales on the Colorado Family Checkup* (Tech. Rep. No. 1). Unpublished manuscript, University of Colorado, Center for Family Studies, Department of Psychology, Boulder.

Blouin, A. G., Perez, E. L., & Blouin, J. H. (1988). Computerized administration of the diagnostic interview schedule. *Psychiatry Research, 23,* 335-344.

Brown, L. H., & Kidwell, J. S. (1982). Methodology in family studies: The other side of caring. *Journal of Marriage and the Family, 44,* 833-839.

Burgess, E. W. (1926). The family as a unity of interacting personalities. *Family, 7,* 3-9.

Burke, M. J., & Normand, J. (1987). Computerized psychological testing: Overview and critique. *Professional Psychology: Research and Practice, 18,* 42-51.

Caputo, D. V. (1963). The parents of the schizophrenic. *Family Process, 2,* 339-356.

Cheek, F. E. (1964). The "schizophrenogenic mother" in word and deed. *Family Process, 3,* 155-177.

Christensen, A., & Arrington, A. (1987). Research issues and strategies. In T. Jacob (Ed.), *Family interaction and psychopathology: Theories, methods, and findings* (pp. 259-296). New York: Plenum.

Cross, H. J. (1969). College students' memories of their parents: A factor analysis of the CRPBI. *Journal of Consulting and Clinical Psychology, 33,* 275-278.

Curran, D. (1983). *Traits of a healthy family.* Minneapolis, MN: Winston.

Drechsler, R. J., & Shapiro, M. I. (1961). A procedure for direct observation of family interaction in a child guidance clinic. *Psychiatry, 24,* 163-170.

Farina, A. (1960). Patterns of role dominance and conflict in parents of schizophrenic patients. *Journal of Abnormal and Social Psychology, 61,* 31-38.

Filsinger, E. E. (1983). A machine-aided marital observation technique: The dyadic interaction scoring code. *Journal of Marriage and the Family, 45,* 623-632.

Fisher, L. (1982). Transactional theories but individual assessment: A frequent discrepancy in family research. *Family Process, 21,* 313-320.

Fisher, L., Kokes, R. F., Ransom, D. C., Phillips, S. L., & Rudd, P. (1985). Alternative strategies for creating "relational" family data. *Family Process, 24,* 213-224.

Fleck, S. (1980). *Yale guide to family assessment.* New Haven, CT: Yale University School of Medicine, Department of Psychiatry.

Floyd, F. J., O'Farrell, T. J., & Goldberg, M. (1987). Comparison of marital observational measures: The marital interaction coding system and the communication skills test. *Journal of Consulting and Clinical Psychology, 55,* 423-429.

Forman, B. D., & Hagan, B. J. (1984). Measures for evaluating total family functioning. *Family Therapy, 11,* 1-36.

Friedman, P. H. (1985). The use of computers in marital and family therapy. *Journal of Psychotherapy and the Family, 1,* 37-48.

Glasser, P. H., & Glasser, L. N. (1970). Adequate family functioning. In P. H. Glasser & L. N. Glasser (Eds.), *Families in crisis* (pp. 290-301). New York: Harper & Row.

Gottman, J. M. (1982). Temporal form: Toward a new language for describing relationships. *Journal of Marriage and the Family, 44,* 943-962.

Green, R. G., Kolevzon, M. S., & Vosler, N. R. (1985). The Beavers-Timberlawn model of family competence and the circumflex model of family adaptability and cohesion: Separate, but equal? *Family Process, 24,* 385-398.

Grotevant, H. D., & Carlson, C. I. (1987). Family interaction coding systems: A descriptive review. *Family Process, 26,* 49-74.

Handel, G. (1965). Psychological study of whole families. *Psychological Bulletin, 63,* 19-41.

Hannum, J. W., & Mayer, J. M. (1984). Validation of two family assessment approaches. *Journal of Marriage and the Family, 46,* 741-748.

Hazelrigg, M. D., Cooper, H. M., & Borduin, C. M. (1987). Evaluating the effectiveness of family therapies: An integrative review and analysis. *Psychological Bulletin, 101,* 428-442.

Humphrey, L. L., & Benjamin, L. S. (1986). Using structural analysis of social behavior to assess critical but elusive family processes. *American Psychologist, 41,* 979-989.

Jacob, T. (1975). Family interaction in disturbed and normal families: A methodological and substantive review. *Psychological Bulletin, 82,* 33-65.

Jacob, T. (Ed.). (1987). *Family interaction and psychopathology: Theories, methods, and findings.* New York: Plenum.

Larsen, A., & Olson, D. H. (1990). Capturing the complexity of family systems: Integrating family theory, family scores, and family analysis. In T. W. Draper & A. C. Marcos (Eds.), *Family variables: Conceptualization, measurement, and use* (pp. 19-47). Newbury Park, CA: Sage.

Larzelere, R. E., & Huston, T. L. (1980). The dyadic trust scale: Toward understanding interpersonal trust in close relationships. *Journal of Marriage and the Family, 42,* 595-604.

Lehtinen, M. W., & Smith, G. W. (1985). MATESIM: Computer assisted marriage analysis for family therapists. *Journal of Psychotherapy and the Family, 1,* 117-131.

Levenson, R. W., & Gottman, J. M. (1985). Physiological and affective predictors of change in relationship satisfaction. *Journal of Personality and Social Psychology, 49,* 85-94.

Mathisen, K. S. (1987). Issues in research on clinical computer applications for mental health. In J. H. Greist, J. A. Carroll, H. P. Erdman, M. H. Klein, & C. R. Wurster (Eds.), *Research in mental health computer applications: Directions for the future* (DHHS Pub. No. (ADM) 87-1468, pp. 79-88). Washington, DC: Government Printing Office.

McCubbin, H. I., & Thompson, A. I. (Eds.). (1987). *Family assessment inventories for research and practice.* Madison: University of Wisconsin, Family Stress Coping and Health Project.

Miller, B. C., Rollins, B. C., & Thomas, D. L. (1982). On methods of studying marriages and families. *Journal of Marriage and the Family, 44,* 851-872.

Miller, I. W., Epstein, N. B., Bishop, D. W., & Keitner, G. I. (1985). The McMaster family assessment device: Reliability and validity. *Journal of Marital and Family Therapy, 11,* 345-356.

Mishler, E. G., & Waxler, N. E. (1968). *Interaction in families: An experimental study of family processes and schizophrenia.* New York: John Wiley.

Moos, R. H., & Moos, B. S. (1976). A typology of family social environments. *Family Process, 15,* 357-371.

Oliveri, M. E., & Reiss, D. (1981). A theory-based empirical classification of family problem-solving behavior. *Family Process, 20,* 409-418.

Olson, D. H. (1977). Insiders' and outsiders' views of relationships: Research studies. In G. Levinger & H. L. Raush (Eds.), *Close relationships: Perspectives on the meaning of intimacy* (pp. 115-135). Amherst: University of Massachusetts Press.

Olson, D. H. (1985). Commentary: Struggling with congruence across theoretical models and methods. *Family Process, 24,* 203-207.

Olson, D. H., Sprenkle, D. H., & Russell, C. S. (1979). Circumflex model of marital and family systems: I. Cohesion and adaptability dimensions, family types, and clinical applications. *Family Process, 18,* 3-28.

Pearlin, L. I., & Turner, H. A. (1987). The family as a context of the stress process. In S. V. Kasl & C. L. Cooper (Eds.), *Stress and health: Issues in research methodology* (pp. 143-165). New York: John Wiley.

Quinton, D., Rutter, M., & Rowlands, O. (1976). An evaluation of an interview assessment of marriage. *Psychological Medicine, 6,* 577-586.

Ransom, D. C., Fisher, L., Phillips, S., Kokes, R. F., & Weiss, R. (1990). The logic of measurement in family research. In T. W. Draper & A. C. Marcos (Eds.), *Family variables: Conceptualization, measurement, and use* (pp. 48-63). Newbury Park, CA: Sage.

Reiss, D. (1967). Individual thinking and family interaction. *Archives of General Psychiatry, 16,* 80-93.

Reiss, D., & Sheriff, W. H. (1970). A computer-automated procedure for testing some experiences of family membership. *Behavioral Science, 15,* 431-443.

Riskin, J., & Faunce, E. E. (1970). Family interaction scales: I. Theoretical framework and method. *Archives of General Psychiatry, 22,* 504-512.

Safilios-Rothschild, C. (1969). Family sociology or wives' family sociology? A cross-cultural examination of decision-making. *Journal of Marriage and the Family, 31,* 290-301.

Schaefer, E. S. (1965). Children's reports of parental behavior: An inventory. *Child Development, 36,* 413-424.

Schaefer, M. T., & Olson, D. H. (1981). Assessing intimacy: The pair inventory. *Journal of Marital and Family Therapy, 7,* 47-60.

Schludermann, E., & Schludermann, S. (1970). Replicability of factors in children's report of parent behavior (CRPBI). *Journal of Psychology, 76,* 239-249.

Schwarz, J. C., Barton-Henry, M. L., & Pruzinsky, T. (1985). Assessing child-rearing behaviors: A comparison of ratings made by mother, father, child, and sibling on the CRPBI. *Child Development, 56,* 462-479.

Siegelman, M. (1965). Evaluation of Bronfenbrenner's questionnaire for children concerning parental behavior. *Child Development, 36,* 163-174.

Sigafoos, A., & Reiss, D. (1985). Rejoinder: Counterperspectives on family measurement: Clarifying the pragmatic interpretation of research methods. *Family Process, 24,* 207-211.

Sigafoos, A., Reiss, D., Rich, J., & Douglas, E. (1985). Pragmatics in the measurement of family functioning: An interpretive framework for methodology. *Family Process, 24,* 189-203.

Skinner, H. A., Steinhauer, P. D., & Santa-Barbara, J. (1983). The family assessment measure. *Canadian Journal of Community Mental Health, 2,* 91-105.

Sprey, J. (1988). Current theorizing on the family: An appraisal. *Journal of Marriage and the Family, 50,* 875-890.

Stabenau, J. R., Tupin, J., Werner, M., & Pollin, W. (1965). A comparative study of families of schizophrenics, delinquents, and normals. *Psychiatry, 28,* 45-49.

Steinglass, P. (1980). Assessing families in their own homes. *American Journal of Psychiatry, 137,* 1523-1529.

Straus, M. A. (1979). Measuring intrafamily conflict and violence: The conflict tactics (CT) scales. *Journal of Marriage and the Family, 41,* 75-88.

Straus, M. A., & Tallman, I. (1971). SIMFAM: A technique for observational measurement and experimental studies of families. In J. Aldous, T. Condon, R. Hill, M. Straus, & I. Tallman (Eds.), *Family problem solving: A symposium on theoretical, methodological, and substantive concerns* (pp. 381-438). Hinsdale, IL: Dryden.

Strodtbeck, F. L. (1951). Husband-wife interaction over revealed differences. *American Sociological Review, 16,* 468-473.

Szinovacz, M. E. (1983). Using couple data as a methodological tool: The case of marital violence. *Journal of Marriage and the Family, 45,* 633-644.

Thompson, L., & Walker, A. J. (1982). The dyad as the unit of analysis: Conceptual and methodological issues. *Journal of Marriage and the Family, 44,* 889-900.

Thomson, E., & Williams, R. (1982). Beyond wives' family sociology: A method for analyzing couple data. *Journal of Marriage and the Family, 44,* 999-1008.

Usandivaras, R. J., Grimson, W. R., Hammond, H., Issaharoff, E., & Romanos, D. (1967). The marbles test: A test for small groups. *Archives of General Psychiatry, 17,* 111-118.

van der Veen, F. (1965). The parent's concept of the family unit and child adjustment. *Journal of Counseling Psychology, 12,* 196-200.

Walsh, F. (1982). Conceptualizing normal family functioning. In F. Walsh (Ed.), *Normal family processes* (pp. 3-42). New York: Guilford.

Wampler, K. S., & Powell, G. S. (1982). The Barrett-Lennard relationship inventory as a measure of marital satisfaction. *Family Relations, 31,* 139-145.

The Cultural Competence Model

Implications for Child and Family Mental Health Services

JAMES L. MASON
MARVA P. BENJAMIN
SARAH A. LEWIS

Increasingly, the issue of cultural diversity is becoming more widely addressed by health and human service delivery systems and professionals (Jacobs & Bowles, 1988; Lefley & Pedersen, 1986). This newfound focus on cultural diversity is not new, however (Green, 1982; Ponterotto & Casas, 1991; Solomon, 1976). This issue is currently gaining attention because culturally diverse belief systems are becoming better understood (Ho, 1992), the demographic profile of American society is changing (Lum, 1992), patterns of restrictive service alternatives for certain cultural groups have become apparent (Cross, Bazron, Isaacs, & Dennis, 1989), and consideration has been given to historical underuse and premature termination of service issues (Flaskerud, 1986; Ponterotto & Casas, 1991; Sue & Sue, 1990).

In an attempt to shed light on issues of cultural diversity, this chapter provides insight into the Child and Adolescent Service System Program (CASSP; Stroul & Friedman, 1986) cultural competence model. It will cover the rationale for cultural relevance in the delivery of human services to children and youth of color and their families, the major points of the model, theoretical barriers to implementing or using culturally appropriate service delivery models, and implications for human service professionals and service delivery systems in providing child and family services.

Rationale for Culturally Appropriate Service Delivery

Since World War II, there have been numerous attempts to institutionalize human service delivery approaches that are sensitive to cultural differences (Green, 1982; Solomon, 1976). Many approaches have been identified that have little theoretical or research foundation. It has become increasingly apparent that some people of color have values and belief systems that are different from the mainstream population. Furthermore, families and children of color often face greater poverty (Edelman, 1987) and differential treatment (Cross et al., 1989; Knitzer, 1982; Sue & Sue, 1990) or experience linguistic barriers, diagnostic errors, problematic screening instruments, and failure of professionals to distinguish between culturally adaptive and maladaptive behavior (Lefley & Pedersen, 1986).

This most recent concern regarding diversity has yielded cross-cultural training and service delivery models that are much more concerned with worker behavior (Lefley & Pedersen, 1986). One recent iteration is the CASSP cultural competence model, defined as a set of congruent attitudes, practices, policies, and structures that come together in a system, agency, or group of professionals and enable that system, agency, or those professionals to work effectively in cross-cultural situations. This model reflects the new genre of service delivery approaches that makes benign distinctions on the basis of culture and views culture as a factor in service delivery. The CASSP cultural competence model was specifically developed for children, youth, and families of color who come into contact with the mental health system (Cross et al., 1989). Perhaps the real value of the model is the emphasis placed on the behavioral domains of clinical practices, agency administration, organizational governing structures, and physical plant characteristics. The model also focuses on worker attitudes, as do traditional cultural sensitivity or awareness models.

The nuances of the cultural competence model are important because many see it simply as "being nice" to people, not being overtly biased, or treating everyone the same. Professionals and systems need to develop a value base that outlines why becoming culturally competent is an important agenda as the United States enters the 21st century (Woody, 1992). To help develop the rationale, we list below several important concerns including changing demographics, values and belief systems, and general barriers to cultural pluralism.

Changing Demographics

It is important to recognize that American society is rapidly becoming more culturally and racially diverse. By the year 2000, people of color will number about one third of the total U.S. population (Wilson & Gutierrez, 1985). Between 1970 and 1980, the U.S. Census recorded marked increases in the populations of cultural groups of color. African Americans increased by 17%, from 22.6 million to 26.5 million, and Hispanics by 61%, from 9.1 million to 14.6 million; Asian Americans more than doubled their numbers, from 1.5 million to 3.5 million (133% increase); and the number of Native Americans/Alaskan Natives grew from 800,000 to 1.4 million, a 75% increase (Lum, 1992).

In addition to the rapidly increasing birthrates among people of color, significant growth also came from legal immigration, particularly in Mexican, Filipino, and Korean populations. Undoubtedly, this growth does not include undocumented persons entering the country. The shift in demographics has been equaled only by the European influx of the late 19th and early 20th centuries. Hawaii, Alaska, New Mexico, and soon California will have minority populations that will constitute a plurality of the states' total population. The implications of these realities affect the complexion both of consumer populations and of the people who work on their behalf. The demographic picture alone suggests a need to accommodate cultural differences. Recruitment and retention of new workers who are prepared to work cross-culturally are critical as well (Fernandez, 1991; Woody, 1992).

Values and Belief Systems

Another major consideration is the beliefs, norms, and values of people of color (Ho, 1987, 1992; Sue & Sue, 1990). The acknowledgment that Eurocentric values have dominated the sciences and have been propagated as cultural universals (Ehrlich & Feldman, 1977) begins to set in motion the inevitable clash between dominant and nondominant culture behaviors. This distinction often represents a point of friction between systems (and the professionals therein) and consumers.

One example is the different ways in which families have been defined and perceived. Often, people of color are within family systems that include intergenerational, extended, and fictive dimensions that depart from the biological-nuclear configuration that most systems are designed to serve (Cross et al., 1989; Ho, 1987; Sue & Sue, 1990). Stereotypically, with dominant cultural families, biological parents live with their biological children. Conversely, people of color are more likely to be in an extended family configuration, live in close proximity to one another, and generally have familial resources that can go unacknowledged (Ponterotto & Casas, 1991; see also Albee & Canetto, Chapter 3, and Patterson, Chapter 7, in this volume for discussions on family definitions).

Another example is the concept of time, which for many people of color is more past- or present-based as opposed to future-oriented for people of European descent (Sue & Sue, 1990). Given this time orientation, clashes may occur when children and families of color with culturally specific perspectives of time show up late for an appointment or appear casual with respect to formal appointment or check-in times; although the client may see nothing wrong with this behavior, it can be interpreted by service providers as disrespectful. Although no insult is intended, (un)spoken conflicts or attributions can emerge. Ponterotto and Casas (1991) assert that this more casual belief of time conflicts with the Western perspective of time. Although the non-Westerner perceives time as circular—it cannot be wasted (it comes again)—the Westerner sees time as linear—specific moments can be forever lost. One group may view the other as wasteful and disrespectful of (other people's) time, whereas the others may view this obsession with time as too rigid or inflexible, to the point of being offensive. Again, clashes emerge around this little-understood cultural difference that can confuse or even preclude the therapeutic process.

Little known are the culturally distinct perspectives of illness and health. As Sue and Sue (1990) suggest, many Native American, Asian American/Pacific Islander, African American, and Hispanic American individuals and families may have non-mainstream views of illness, etiology, help seeking, help providers, relevant providers, and appropriate treatments. Some people of color in the United States reflect behavior that is fairly consistent with many Third World cultures in that what is sought in service delivery are concrete responses such as advice, an opportunity for confession, consolation, and medication (Sue & Sue, 1990). Growing out of, perhaps, the past- and present-time orientation, something tangible and immediate should happen as a result of treatment. In many cases, long-term goals can be broken into incremental steps with periodic measurable objectives. In many situations, the ability to broker concrete services to children and their families may bestow greater credibility on the professional. For example, quality-of-life enhancements or empowerment services (e.g., socialization and recreational opportunities, skill development classes, cultural enrichment programs, self-advocacy training) can be brokered concomitantly. It is not unusual to see culturally diverse families turn to spiritualists, natural healers, medicine people, herbalists, or clergy at times of physical, emotional, or social turmoil. Working cooperatively with these individuals should be pursued by mental health professionals.

Because of different perspectives of etiology, sharing intimate information during the treatment process can cause anxiety, hardship, or stigma, and, thus, disclosure may work differently with people of color (Lum, 1992; Pinderhughes, 1989). By mainstream standards, the ability to disclose often is seen as an indication of a healthy personality (Sue & Sue, 1990); for children and families of color, however, this inhibition to openly share may have cultural or sociopolitical roots. Cultural roots emerge because social and emotional (even physical) problems are not only attributed to the client but can be extended to family members or even ancestors. Sociopolitical roots become evident when children and families of color may not disclose because the professionals (particularly when mainstream in orientation) may not have experienced bias or racism or may be unable to relate to or even hear such comments.

Moreover, the history of family and child social service systems, law enforcement, education, and others may engender feelings of what Sue and Sue (1990) call a *paranorm.* Derived from the word *paranoid,* it suggests that people of color have been victims of oppression and discrimination and, as a result, have developed cultural antennae that help them survive and adapt. Grier and Cobbs (1968) called it *cultural paranoia,* observing that the absence of this trait may be a better indication of pathology than its presence. In worst-case scenarios, some personal information can come back to haunt clients (e.g., a man living in the home, a welfare recipient "working under the table," and child-rearing practices that conflict with local laws). Self-disclosure can unnecessarily embarrass the family or have real or perceived consequences. Hence, practitioners should be aware of this reluctance to self-disclose and may have to model this behavior for children and their families (Pinderhughes, 1989).

Beliefs of cause and effect constitute another area in which conflict may emerge. The Western perspective of how and why things happen may differ from that of children and families of color. The imposition of Western cause-effect linear models may be in itself a bias so subtle that it is not acknowledged. These rational models, which from a Western standpoint appear so universally salient, consider left-brain functioning; in other words, they are distinctly analytical, rational, and verbal and seek linear cause-effect relationships. In contrast, Ornstein (1972) viewed Native American culture as right-brain functioning. Thus, conflicts between Western and non-Western modes of constructing reality can occur. One overlooked strategy to engage in with clients is asking their perspective of cause and effect around the presenting problem, providing an opportunity to take a cross-cultural journey.

Another cross-cultural issue concerns communication and greeting behavior, for which the styles and patterns can be remarkably dissimilar between Western and non-Western cultures. Sue and Sue (1990) assert that standard English is a low-context language, requiring little in affect, gestures, and tones to be optimally expressive. High-context language uses a variety of gestures, tones, and behaviors to convey meaning. Words or phrases that exist in English may not have counterparts in Spanish or in some of the Asian dialects. The discrepancies between low- and high-context communication styles can be subtle.

Greeting behavior, social etiquette (Green, 1982), kinesics, proxemics, and culturally specific affect (Sue & Sue, 1990) are also important issues to consider. Although the use of different languages has become more widely known, little has been done to standardize the use of interpreters (Randall-David, 1989). Often people who use nonstandard English or English as a second language may see communication problems as a barrier that stymies many therapeutic efforts, leads to conflicts, or drives consumers away.

Barriers to Cultural Pluralism

In addition to differences in norms, values, and beliefs of Western and non-Western-oriented groups, other differences pertain to social learning about cultural and racial diversity. Ehrlich and Feldman (1977) believe that scientific foundations for studying cultural differences are based on racially biased research and theory. These early foundations in science explained the various racial categories in dehumanizing ways (Sillen & Thomas, 1972). Such social phenomena as conquest, colonization of societies of color, enslavement of African peoples (Stampp, 1956), and exploitation of Third World human and natural resources all lead to a variety of conclusions that were painted by the benign, if not noble, behaviors of European peoples. Thus, deficit-oriented perspectives have been initially fueled and subsequently sustained. Intentional or not, this romanticizing of Western expansionism allows one to reframe racial and cultural genocide and subjugation and general denigration of non-Western civilization (Edson, 1989). These barriers are mentioned not to reopen old wounds but to help understand how social learning and formal education, when combined with changing demographics, herald the urgency in understanding the role that culture plays in how social and behavioral problems are defined (Green, 1982; Ho, 1992; Sue & Sue, 1990); how help is sought (Neighbors & Taylor, 1985); how treatment is provided and perceived (Gibbs, Huang, & Associates, 1989; Ho, 1992); how programs are managed and developed (Gallegos,

1982); and, in general, how services to culturally diverse populations are evaluated (Orlandi, 1992).

An additional hindrance to promoting cultured pluralism is the current education and training of professionals. Most graduate education and professional training contains curricula that are bereft of cultural information (Jacobs & Bowles, 1988; Lefley & Pedersen, 1986; Pinderhughes, 1989). The notion that the panacea will come in the form of racially and culturally diverse people in graduate and professional schools who will soon enter the professional field also is overly optimistic. Although this is a nice solution to an entrenched problem, the numbers currently enrolled do not reflect the proportions in the general population (Sanchez, Demmler, & Davis, 1990).

An additional barrier is the tendency to take an aggregate approach in viewing minority populations. This perspective ignores minority between-group differences and lumps all minorities together. This is inappropriate because the respective groups, although having overlapping problems, also have problems that are group-specific. Both between- and within-group perspectives are important to pursue, as well as to attend to general group distinctions within a given cultural rubric, to ensure that the full spectrum of a given group can be adequately served. Perhaps most important, such perspectives serve to preclude the invoking of new stereotypes.

Using the concept of minority is, in itself, problematic to the degree that in describing various racial and cultural groups, within- and between-group differences are blurred. Even the major racial categories can be an issue. The term *African American* may reveal something about the client but can conjure up such a picture that many demographic variables affecting service delivery will go ignored. Such variables can include sex, age, income, education, national origin, religious orientation, marital status, sexual preference, physical ability, and facility with the language. One danger is that the newfound information is used as a protocol for work with an entire group. This is particularly troublesome given that historically, most research on racial and ethnic groups used samples that were largely low-income populations and focused primarily on their problems and not on their cultural strengths (Ponterotto & Casas, 1991).

Thus, when one begins a multicultural initiative, identifying which populations need to be addressed is critical. Yet the term *minority* has been used so often in reference to numeric minorities that it has become confusing. Pinderhughes (1989) notes that the simple lack of numbers is not necessarily what makes a group vulnerable. For example, women are not a numeric minority but receive minority status, and black South Africans are not a minority but are treated as an out-group in their native land.

Cultural competence efforts require a more specific perspective of the target population; minority as a concept is too broad. It also can encompass people of color and non-ethnic cultural groups (e.g., people who are homeless, gays and lesbians, and people with disabilities). Interventions or programs designed for African Americans may lose utility with nonblack immigrant or refugee populations. Transition issues and programs for gay and lesbian adolescents could overlook issues of urban children of color. To work with culturally diverse families, one must determine which group(s) are being targeted. Approaches that target minority populations in general may be obsolete.

The Cultural Competence Model

As a result of the ever increasing trends acknowledging diversity, many cross-cultural models are emerging. The CASSP cultural competence model was developed for the field of children's mental health but appears to have the necessary theoretical foundation to lend itself to various service disciplines involving children, families, communities of color, and, at least theoretically, to non-ethnic cultural groups. Its major emphasis is on behavior inasmuch as it (a) covers attitudes, practices, policies, and structures and (b) has implications for both line staff and administrative personnel. In contrast to earlier models, the principles and elements of the model are more concerned with behavior than awareness and sensitivity (Lefley & Pedersen, 1986). The major values and elements of the model are described below.

The Cultural Competence Values

Valuing Diversity. Cultural diversity should be framed as a strength, not only in clientele but also in line staff, administrative personnel, board membership, and volunteers. An agency can manifest this concern in many ways, such as convening events that celebrate diversity of food, holidays, heroes, music, and clothing. Certainly, members of a given group are able to suggest meaningful ways to recognize a given community. Approaches such as these should not be viewed as the product but as a process that heals and brings communities together.

Conducting Cultural Self-Assessment. This value is concerned with the degree to which an agency or professional is aware of cultural blind spots. For example, as previously stated, most systems work on a linear time orientation, yet if a community or its members view time differently, conflicts may arise. Similarly, systems anticipate that people will disclose freely; many people of color, however, are not likely to share information without a personal relationship (Ho, 1987, 1992; Pinderhughes, 1989; Sue & Sue, 1990). Randall-David (1989) compiled several self-study guides that help professionals identify cross-cultural blind spots. LaFromboise, Coleman, and Alexis (1991); D'Andrea, Daniels, and Heck (1991); and Ho (1992) have each developed measures that can help professionals identify various aspects of their cultural awareness.

Understanding the Dynamics of Difference. This principle suggests that one needs to understand what happens when people of different cultural backgrounds interact. An example is when the professional puts his or her best foot forward and is dubiously received by the child or family. For many, relations between people of the dominant culture and people of color can be strained because of historic or even contemporary mistrust (Grier & Cobbs, 1968; Sue & Sue, 1990). For others, it may be important for the professional to model self-disclosing behavior (Lum, 1992). In addition, body language, gestures, and communication styles need to be understood (Kuramoto, Morales, Munoz, & Murase, 1983; Sue & Sue, 1990). In other instances, clients will test the mettle of majority culture professionals, which may be uncomfortable (Lum, 1992). Some individuals of color may be distrustful of even the most well-intentioned professional.

Incorporating Cultural Knowledge. Agencies and professionals need continuing access to cultural information. Appropriate books, videotapes, and other media may be viable sources of information; it may be necessary, however, to create one's own personal library, in addition to creating one for the agency. Other relatively inexpensive endeavors include investigating federal archives and clearinghouses and county and college libraries as well as linking with institutions of higher education, advocacy groups, minority business and ministerial alliances, and natural helpers as a means of staying current with respect to cultural issues. Perhaps some of the most underused resources are former consumers and personnel from collateral agencies who may have personal and external perspectives, respectively.

Adapting to Diversity. Adapting to diversity entails the actual modifications either to direct service approaches or to agency administration. Questions such as the following can steer providers in the right direction: Does the assessment approach mesh with the client's language and belief system? Does treatment planning incorporate natural helpers and supports? Is staff training provided on a continuing basis? And do workers conduct business in enclaves or neutral settings? These issues must be viewed contextually, for even when the population is the same, certain factors will render an adaption useful or not. For example, an approach may prove viable with Hispanics in Tucson, Arizona, but may lose impact with the nominally same group in Houston, Texas, or Omaha, Nebraska. Perhaps one important aspect of the model is that culturally competent programs must reflect contextual realities of a given catchment area (Isaacs & Benjamin, 1991). Hence, even when the population and service discipline are the same, the program may vary.

The Elements of the Cultural Competence Model

Four key elements underline the CASSP cultural competence model: attitude, practice, policy, and structure. Each is discussed in detail below.

Attitude. This element reflects earlier cross-cultural models in its concern with worker knowledge and beliefs, or the area of cognition (Lefley & Pedersen, 1986). One initial concern involves cultural and color blindness—the concept that practitioners should and can treat everyone the same. Cultural or color blindness suggests that humans do not have biases or predispositions about certain groups or people. Getting in touch with these feelings and biases, however, is important. In particular, antibias training proves important as a precursor to more in-depth training. Other general activities include staff training and development, developing a value base for cultural competence (Cross et al., 1989; Woody, 1992), and creating an environment conducive to diverse staff and consumers.

Practice. The practice element considers such issues as the interview process (Green, 1982); diagnostic and assessment approaches (Ho, 1992; Lum, 1992; Pinderhughes, 1989); treatment planning techniques (Gibbs et al., 1989; Ho, 1992; Lum, 1992); and other practice skills that are culturally appropriate. Practice skills may be adapted to accommodate within- and between-group differences. Fortunately, some current research is sensitive to practice and cultural diversity; moreover, such things as moderator variables and culturally specific scales exist to a greater extent than before. In some regions of the country are culturally specific providers who can serve as resources for training and consultation on cultural issues.

Policy. This element suggests that much professional behavior is tied to agency policy. Policies often are used as a means for routinizing behavior related to numerous aspects of service delivery. In many instances, policies were created prior to the concern for cultural diversity and need to be revisited and perhaps revised (Cross et al., 1989; Woody, 1992). Issues regarding new employees, assessment approaches, available services, facility location, natural networks that are consulted and used, and supports that are provided during treatment can be aspects of policy. Other examples of areas that can be influenced or upheld by policy include mission statements, hiring practices (that go beyond affirmative action guidelines), and board membership. Informal policies can wax or wane given organizational culture or circumstance, and gains made can be lost if not anchored in the formal policies of the agency.

Structure. The concept of structure includes both governing structure and physical structure. The former refers to who governs the agency in leadership roles (e.g., board members, consultants, contractors, and key informants). No longer is it feasible to have token representation or persons who may emanate from a culture but no longer maintain direct ties with the culture. This suggests that members of the community need a bigger investment in agency operations and need to share in the economy of health care. For example, one approach might be to hire a minority firm for bookkeeping, catering or food preparation, child care, transportation, legal services, or realty services.

The second aspect of structure concerns the physical plant itself. The decor, location, name, and even hours of operation are important. For example, the artwork on the wall or reading material in the waiting room can reflect diversity and actually jump-start a positive relationship. Isaacs and Benjamin (1991) note that the names and characteristics of facilities can invite use and boost community and client esteem.

The Cultural Competence Continuum

The cultural competence continuum is an imaginary six-point spectrum that includes, in ascending order, cultural destructiveness, cultural incapacity, cultural blindness, cultural precompetence, cultural competence, and cultural proficiency. The purpose of the continuum is to help one assess cross-cultural movement and growth in striving toward cultural proficiency (Cross et al., 1989). The points on the continuum notwithstanding, the goal is to become more competent with a given group or with multiple groups. In addition, it is quite possible to be more competent with middle-class African Americans but to lose effectiveness with working-class members; similarly, one may be competent with Hispanic Americans but not with Asian Americans/Pacific Islanders. Given the increasing diversity and mobility of society in the United States, ethnic enclaves will not remain static with respect to community demographics, thus requiring that people have at least cursory skills for populations that are seldom encountered or slowly emerging. Cultural competence is not an all-or-nothing state of affairs; it is a developmental process. Moreover, a static perspective of culture or cultural differences should be avoided. It is also a dynamic phenomenon; one never really "arrives" because culture is dynamic and subject to change. One must stay forever vigilant in the pursuit of cross-cultural skills.

Consequently, cultural competence should be viewed as any other academic discipline in that skills need to be aimed through time by proper training and attention to practice and research.

The continuum is useful for self-examination through time, perhaps using single subject designs, pre- and posttest designs, or time series analyses. In either instance, one can identify positive growth as well as areas needing additional growth. By identifying cross-cultural blind spots on a continuing basis, relevant training and education activities can be pursued.

Identifying Barriers to Service Delivery

As a precursor to the development of the CASSP cultural competence model, a conference was held in Atlanta in 1986 during which cultural key informants from the four major groups of color (African Americans, Asian Americans/Pacific Islanders, Hispanic Americans, and Native Americans) were asked to identify factors affecting the mental health of minority youth and their families. This process in and of itself was important. The process enumerated stressors that should be identified as an aspect of culturally competent assessment and treatment planning.

The stressors were delineated into external and internal dimensions and can be viewed as areas of vulnerability affecting the various communities of color. The external factors included (a) the impact of institutional racism (Jones, 1988; Mann, 1993); (b) the impact of the media (Phinney & Rotheram, 1987; Wilson & Guiterrez, 1985); (c) the economy and availability of employment (Thomas, 1990; Tienda, 1990; Tienda & Jensen, 1988; Wilson, 1987); (d) the urban environment (Cross et al., 1989; Edelman, 1987; Mann, 1993; Wilson, 1987); (e) language and communication styles (Green, 1982; Ho, 1987, 1992; Jones, 1988; Lum, 1992; Randall-David, 1989; Sue & Sue, 1990; Van-Si, 1992); (f) geographic isolation/resource-poor environments; (g) middle-class flight (Wilson, 1987); (h) the strain of acculturation (Huang, 1989; Jones, 1988); (i) inter- and intragroup conflicts (Tienda, 1990); and (j) the American sociopolitical environment (Edelman, 1987).

The internal factors are best understood as issues endemic to a given group and, to some degree, within the group's control. These included (a) differential family structure (Gibbs et al., 1989; Ho, 1987, 1992; Pinderhughes, 1989; Sue & Sue, 1990); (b) the conflict of cultures (Jones, 1988); and (c) the abuse of alcohol and drugs (Isaacs, 1986).

Implications for Professionals and Service Delivery Systems

All the stressors listed in the previous section can and do have a serious impact on self-concept and sense of efficacy for people of color (Isaacs, 1986) but should not simply be superimposed on all groups in equal degrees; variance should be anticipated. Professionals and systems can benefit from knowing which factors strain or even preclude the therapeutic or helping process. Therefore, community assessments that are similar to the key informant approach used at the Atlanta conference will be helpful.

Service Provision

In work with children of color and their families, conducting both community and cultural self-assessment is an important issue in providing culturally competent services. Often the barriers affecting service delivery can be ignored when using a culturally blind approach. Jones (1988) comments,

> The cultural blind approach assumes that the problem is somehow biological. It asserts that there are no meaningful biological differences and that race doesn't matter, we are all the same. Although race may not matter, culture does. We are not all the same, as we have evolved from and continue to evolve different cultural legacies. (p. 130)

Treating everyone the same (if it is actually possible) can lead to ignoring the effect that the above factors have on service delivery. For example, if children in a given community are undernourished, there may be consequences in other domains such as educational attainment, emotional or physical development, or even career choices (Edelman, 1987). If institutional bias occurs in the children's mental health system, children of color may end up being served in disproportionate numbers by special education or juvenile justice systems

(Isaacs, 1986; Knitzer, 1982). If the child welfare system has limited culturally diverse foster and adoptive homes, children of color will be overrepresented in more restrictive settings, transracial adoptive or foster placements, and in institutional settings (Cross et al., 1989). The culturally blind approach can also ignore culturally specific coping strategies, community resources, and traditional healing approaches.

Two critical points emerge. First, environmental stressors need to be assessed because when unnoticed, they can jeopardize the quality of life and treatment (Cross et al., 1989; Isaacs, 1986). Second, individualized services must be sensitive to cultural and community contexts (Pinderhughes, 1989). Ho (1992) argued that culturally competent professionals need to focus on six phases in the therapeutic process: precontact, problem identification, problem specification, mutual goal formation, problem solving, and termination. He added that when consumers have limited or bad experiences with a given social service system, negative feelings about professionals can arise. Therefore, the culturally competent professional constantly gathers information about how children, families, and people of color are vulnerable in their respective ecosystems.

Furthermore, Ho (1992) asserted the importance of precontact skills that involve an understanding of the client's individual needs and circumstances. Such awareness includes sensitivity to such issues as the consumer's ethnicity, nationality, gender, religious beliefs, sexual orientation and practices, class affiliation, education, regional characteristics, social history, and cultural identity. Hence, it becomes hard to comprehensively serve a client and provide individualized services if critical aspects of the client's world are ignored.

Lum (1992) added that psychosocial assessment of people of color begins with identifying critical aspects of the client and the client's community. Open discussions concerning racial awareness, family and social history, and personal and cultural beliefs about the presenting problem and its etiology are important. Such discussions can provide an indication of the client's ethnic awareness and esteem (Pinderhughes, 1989), self-concept, and other significant areas (Lum, 1992). Paying attention to dress, holiday celebrations, musical or food interests, and even family networks and authority figures can give key insights into the client's level of acculturation or assimilation. Professionals should keep in mind, however, that relationships are important and may be impeded by asking strangers intrusive or personal questions. Personal questions can be broken up by more mundane questions that afford key insights as to the client's perception of his or her own ethnicity.

Discussions about the family's coping strategies might uncover hidden resources such as natural helpers and healers and even culturally specific therapies or indigenous treatments that may be compatible with that of the formal provider. Natural helpers and leaders (e.g., elders, clergy, and merchants) and support systems (e.g., cultural organizations, religious institutions, and minority community-based organizations) also need to be identified as possible collaborators in treatment planning, service delivery, and evaluation of services. Rappaport (1981) feels that these natural structures allow consumers to affirm their sense of self-determination to experience growth. Further, such structures can actually provide concrete services that complement a formal continuum of care and extend resources beyond those of the provider agency. This evinces the need for professionals to delineate specific client needs that cannot be provided by their agency but might be provided by a natural helping network.

Access to such networks can help culturally competent providers seek creative methods of meeting child and family needs. Culturally competent professionals acknowledge that the consumer, à la Maslow, is a human being with basic needs (as with all humans) but that his or her cultural orientation often influences choices the client makes (Cross et al., 1989). Moreover, movement between emic and etic perspectives is a creative experience for both client and worker (Lum, 1992). As mentioned previously, often communication styles and linguistics, kinesics (e.g., affect and gestures), and proxemics (e.g., personal space and boundaries) are distinct from the mainstream and can easily be misinterpreted. Opportunities for viewing such behaviors occur during treatment (Sue & Sue, 1990). Family members and even children and youth can be guides to understanding behavioral and linguistic nuances (Green, 1982). Lum (1992) warns that smiling, humor, averted gazes, reticence to speak, silent agreement, and other behaviors may be cultural manifestations that can be quickly converted to labels of depression, avoidance, detachment, enmeshment, or inappropriate affect when viewed through a monocultural lens. This is a critical concern and must be acknowledged. Kuramoto et al. (1983) pointed out that people of the majority culture often see cultural differences as indicators of deviance by unwittingly imposing their cultural expectations and penalizing the client when they are not fulfilled.

As mental health professionals consider becoming competent and engaging in a growth process, they should focus on one culture but should consider several cultural communities. A natural beginning is one's own culture orientation or that of the agency with regard to its similarities and distinctions from other cultures. How professionals feel about their own cultural identity is also important to acknowledge. Professionals who do not understand the role culture plays in their own lives will have trouble understanding what it means for consumers. As Pinderhughes (1989) suggested, "Practitioners who value their ethnicity are in a better position to value that of their clients, more ready to help clients learn to value themselves and to use ethnic identity as yet another avenue for building self-esteem" (p. 40). She argued that the color/cultural blind response is often espoused by people who are not in touch with their own cultural identity.

Indeed, there are many approaches for learning about cultural diversity in general and specifically its role in the delivery of human services. Didactic approaches involve workshops, seminars, classes, and lectures. Interactive methods include such techniques as dialogues, town hall meetings, discussion groups, and brown-bag sessions. Experiential techniques involve immersion activities, trips to ethnic enclaves, visiting diverse communities or friends, and various other approaches. Typically safe venues include worship services (e.g., churches, synagogues, temples, mosques, and lodge houses) and cultural ceremonies and rituals (e.g., Cinco de Mayos, Juneteenth celebrations of the date Abraham Lincoln signed the Emancipation Proclamation, Asian New Year festivals, and powwows). Often the goals are not only to enhance understanding as it concerns cognitive awareness (group strengths, social histories, systemic barriers, and general norms and values) but also to improve behavioral skills (e.g., listening and greeting skills, communication skills, and interviewing techniques).

In addition, many aspects of any culture are cloaked. For example, culture in many people's mind is limited to such things as music, food, clothing, art, and other popularly acknowledged manifestations. On the other hand, culture also influences how people construe their relationships with the planet, view aging, define male-female relationships, define illness and health, perceive and use time, and even understand life and death. Awareness here might involve theoretical awareness or knowledge.

Organizational Implications

Key leadership figures in bureaucracies and agencies should acknowledge several important factors. To begin with, a value base must be developed that addresses why systems and individuals need to change (Cross et al., 1989; Fernandez, 1991; Woody, 1992). For example, as discussed previously, some reasons include that the population of communities of color (particularly children of color) is increasing at a much faster rate than that of the dominant culture; that racial, cultural, and linguistic barriers still exist that can perpetuate social problems stemming from historic and institutional oppression that may create more, rather than fewer, social and emotional problems (Ponterotto & Casas, 1991); and that services should be provided in a way that allows the client to experience himself or herself as competent, valuable, and worthwhile, both as an individual and as a member of his or her own cultural group (Pinderhughes, 1989). Ultimately, a value base needs to be developed that considers how services will differ by community and the benefits of a culturally competent workforce (to professionals, consumers, provider agencies, and the community at large).

To serve diverse children and families effectively, it is important to know how the respective groups are negatively affected by specific psychosocial stressors and institutional structures. This information must be updated and disseminated to all agency personnel. Also, the governing structures of systems must be culturally competent for staff attitudes, clinical practices, and agency policies to be in step with the growing culturally diverse society.

With respect to the attitudinal dimension, agencies can (co)sponsor cultural events that celebrate diversity and cultural strengths. Agency staff also can assess their cultural blind spots and participate in antibias training. Information needs to be periodically disseminated that outlines whom the agency serves well and whom it does not serve so well. In addition, data should be circulated that include service outcomes by group, demographic profiles of communities of color (particularly as related to dominant culture profiles), natural helping networks, and potential key informants and cultural consultants.

Often, people who guide organizations lose sight of current and projected demographic trends and the agency implications for meeting the needs of a given consumer group. Such data as infant mortality and life expectancy, income and educational attainment differentials, home ownership rates, dropout and crime rates, and population growth or loss are routine yet important information that can be easily disseminated (Casas, 1984). In many systems, this may mean a revamping of management information systems to capture family- or culturally based information that was previously ignored. Using cultural descriptors such as *white-nonwhite, white-black-other,* and other archaic forms of labeling a multicultural society may do more harm than good in the long run. Simple racial categories that do not include nationality, primary language, family configuration, immigrant or refugee status, and the generation one represents exclude critical components of a consumer's reality.

Pinderhughes (1989) asserted that culture shapes how problems are identified and expressed and how treatment is sought. Sometimes cultural insensitivity is the reason for premature termination of services (Cross et al., 1989; Ho, 1992; Sue & Sue, 1990). In other instances, clients retreat because of the system's focus on deficits and pathology rather than on cultural strengths and assets (e.g., respect for elders, religiosity, harmony with nature or others, extended family support, and community loyalty). Thus, Pinderhughes concluded that clients of color respond to programs emphasizing vital aspects of their culture.

Agencies also must engage in a self-assessment process that helps to determine who resides in their catchment area and whom they serve (noting within- and between-group distinctions); the barriers to service delivery (e.g., transportation and access, hours of operation, language, and history/trust) by group, again noting the above distinctions; line staff and administrator access to cultural key informants including professionals and consumers of color; and the cross-cultural success stories as well as the often overlooked cross-cultural assets of agency personnel (languages spoken, religious affiliations, and experiences in ethnic enclaves).

Concrete suggestions emanating from the 1986 Atlanta conference concerning program development for communities of color included the following: greater awareness of the impact of environmental factors on intrapsychic functioning, the psychic or emotional toll of acculturation on diverse populations, culturally specific definitions of mental health, differential communication styles and languages, culturally specific perspective and practical limitations of confidentiality and anonymity, holistic approaches to service delivery, outreach strategies to involve natural networks of support, accessibility issues and supports, types of services and resources needed to empower consumers of color, community development and empowerment, and leadership development in communities of color (Isaacs, 1986).

One important caveat is that attention to within-group diversity is essential. The above factors will have different degrees of applicability. In some groups, the factors may be absent or only reflective of subgroups. Woody (1992) indicated that providing relevant services requires an examination of unique environmental characteristics of the respective communities of color. Thus, creating a need for consumer involvement in setting goals on the basis of the needs and realities as viewed by the prospective consumers is important. Again, a value base is needed, acknowledging why the agency is making modifications based on values that undergird the efforts. It may prove helpful to answer and develop rationales for the following questions: What is the organization's responsibility in meeting the needs of diverse populations? How can the presence of culturally competent workers help the organization accomplish its goals? How might the provision of culturally competent services differ (between- and within-groups) by cultural group? What is the vision of culturally competent services? How will the organization evaluate services to diverse populations? (Woody, 1992).

In moving toward cultural competence, the organization should solicit input from a variety of individuals and organizations in the diverse communities. Service needs should be defined by group, along with intended outcomes and impact on the lives of the recipient group(s). Certainly, development of such a foundation and its implications will need to be disseminated to all employees. This can serve as rhetoric and rationale for workers who may need to know why changes are being made.

Any efforts to enhance services to culturally diverse populations should consider which elements (attitude, practice, policy, and/or structure) will be affected. In some cases, several elements can be addressed simultaneously; in other situations, only one element is targeted. Attempts to "fix" all elements at once can be overwhelming and can be disheartening when everything does not fall into place; thus, some setting of priorities should prove helpful.

In addition to identifying elements to be affected, it is important to consider whether efforts are short-term, intermediate, or long-range in nature. For example, facility decor may be achievable in the short term by virtue of borrowing prints from libraries, creating culturally diverse collages from old magazines, or even renaming the program or subcomponent therein. Staff development activities may be initiated in the short term but will probably be at least an intermediate effort because of their continuing nature. Creating a culturally competent workforce is likely to be a long-range goal with measurable objectives in short-term, intermediate, and long-term perspectives. While this planning is taking place, likely collaborators to this process should be considered (i.e., key informants, cultural organizations, advocacy organizations, and natural helpers). Moreover, breaking the large goal into achievable subcomponents may help to stave off frustration and generate a sense of accomplishment and credibility on the basis of fulfilling incremental steps.

Formulation of tasks groups should include discussions about group process issues such as problem identification approaches, decision-making strategies, problem-solving techniques, and conflict management concepts to be adopted by the task group. This will be necessary to maintain group cohesiveness and productivity (Zastrow, 1985); it is likely that the more diverse the group, the greater potential for tension and conflict. Managed conflict should be viewed as an asset and not as something to be avoided.

Conclusion

The many benefits of cultural competence become more evident as time passes and diversity increases. There is room for everyone, and there is much work to be done. In addition to the concerns discussed above, too little knowledge has been generated that concerns management information systems and program evaluation (Orlandi, 1992). Epidemiological data are needed regarding incidence and prevalence by group, better ethnic identity formation models, institutional prejudice and racism, models for helping people overcome bias and understanding white racial identity, coping skills and strategies by group (not with impoverished samples only), bicultural identity development, and culturally appropriate assessment and treatment approaches (Ponterotto & Casas, 1991).

Furthermore, cultural competence needs to unfold in a variety of disciplines. Much work has been done in the area of mental health, but additional work is needed that lends itself more easily to fields such as criminal and juvenile justice, maternal and child health, public health, education and higher education, substance abuse services, child and family welfare, teenage pregnancy prevention, and employment training, for example. Cultural competence is a forgiving model that has implications for everyone. As a concept, it is not new (Green, 1982; Ponterotto & Casas, 1991; Solomon, 1976); when not infused into every aspect of service delivery, however, it stands the risk of being minimized, used purely as a marketing tool, or relegated to political correctness. It also is a harbinger of the times that suggests that providers get on the bandwagon or get left behind lamenting "aren't people all the same."

Thus, cultural competence takes culture into account as it relates to creating individualized systems of care (Stroul & Friedman, 1986); planning and delivery of treatment (Cross et al., 1988); recruitment and development of staff (Sanchez et al., 1990; Woody, 1992); graduate and professional training (Jacobs & Bowles, 1988; Lefley & Pedersen, 1986; Parker, 1988); and agency administration (Benjamin, 1993; Woody, 1992). It is both daunting and encouraging that there is more than enough work to go around and that there is a place for everyone who is committed to cultural and racial equity as it relates to the delivery of health and human services.

References

Benjamin, M. P. (1993). *Child and adolescent service system program minority initiative research monograph.* Washington, DC: Georgetown University Child Development Center/CASSP Technical Assistance Center.

Casas, J. M. (1984). Policy, training and research in counseling psychology: The racial/ethnic minority perspective. In S. D. Brown & R. Lent (Eds.), *Handbook of counseling psychology* (pp. 785-831). New York: John Wiley.

Cross, T. L., Bazron, B. J., Isaacs, M. R., & Dennis, K. W. (1989). *Towards a culturally competent system of care: A monograph on effective services for minority children who are severely emotionally disturbed.* Washington, DC: Georgetown University Center for Child Health and Mental Health Policy, CASSP Technical Assistance Center.

D'Andrea, M., Daniels, J., & Heck, R. (1991). Evaluating the impact of multicultural counseling training. *Journal of Counseling & Development, 70,* 143-150.

Edelman, M. W. (1987). *Families in peril: An agenda for social change.* Cambridge, MA: Harvard University Press.

Edson, C. H. (1989). Barriers to multiculturalism: Historical perspectives on culture and character in American society. *Coalition Quarterly, 6*(2-3), 3-9.

Ehrlich, P. R., & Feldman, S. S. (1977). *Race bomb: Skin color, prejudice and intelligence.* New York: Quadrangle/New York Times Books.

Fernandez, J. P. (1991). *Managing a diverse work force: Regaining the competitive edge.* Lexington, MA: Lexington.

Flaskerud, J. H. (1986). Diagnostic and treatment differences among five ethnic groups. *Psychological Reports, 58*(1), 219-235.

Gallegos, J. S. (1982). Planning and administering services for minority groups. In J. J. Austin & W. E. Hershey (Eds.), *Handbook on mental health administration: The middle manager's perspective* (pp. 87-105). San Francisco: Jossey-Bass.

Gibbs, J. T., Huang, L. N., & Associates. (1989). *Children of color: Psychological interventions with minority youth.* San Francisco: Jossey-Bass.

Green, J. W. (1982). *Cultural awareness in the human services.* Englewood Cliffs, NJ: Prentice Hall.

Grier, W., & Cobbs, D. (1968). *Black rage.* New York: Basic Books.

Ho, M. K. (1987). *Family therapy with ethnic minorities.* Newbury Park, CA: Sage.

Ho, M. K. (1992). *Minority children and adolescents in therapy.* Newbury Park, CA: Sage.

Huang, L. N. (1989). Southeast Asian refugee children and adolescents. In J. T. Gibbs, L. N. Huang, & Associates (Eds.), *Children of color: Psychological interventions with minority youth* (pp. 278-321). San Francisco: Jossey-Bass.

Isaacs, M. R. (1986). *Developing mental health programs for minority youth and their families.* Washington, DC: Georgetown University Child Development Center/CASSP Technical Assistance Center.

Isaacs, M. R., & Benjamin, M. P. (1991). *Towards a culturally competent system of care* (Vol. 2). Washington, DC: Georgetown University Child Development Center/CASSP Technical Assistance Center.

Jacobs, C., & Bowles, D. (Eds.). (1988). *Ethnicity and race: Critical concepts in social work.* Silver Spring, MD: National Association of Social Workers.

Jones, J. M. (1988). Racism in black and white: A bicultural model of reaction and evolution. In P. A. Katz & D. A. Taylor (Eds.), *Eliminating racism: Problems in controversy* (pp. 117-134). New York: Plenum.

Knitzer, J. (1982). *Unclaimed children: The failure of public responsibility to children and adolescents in need of mental health services.* Washington, DC: Children's Defense Fund.

Kuramoto, F. H., Morales, R. F., Munoz, F. U., & Murase, K. (1983). Education for social work practice in Asian and Pacific Islander communities. In J. C. Chunn II, P. J. Dunston, & F. Ross-Sheuff (Eds.), *Mental health and people of color: Curriculum development and change* (pp. 127-155). Washington, DC: Howard University Press.

LaFromboise, T. D., Coleman, H., & Alexis, H. (1991). Development and factor structure of the cross-cultural counseling and inventory: Revised. *Professional Psychology: Research and Practice, 22*(5), 380-388.

Lefley, H. P., & Pedersen, P. B. (Eds.). (1986). *Cross-cultural training for mental health professionals.* Springfield, IL: Charles C Thomas.

Lum, D. (1992). *Social work practice and people of color: A process-stage approach* (2nd ed.). Belmont, CA: Brooks/Cole.

Mann, C. R. (1993). *Unequal justice: A question of color.* Indianapolis: Indiana University Press.

Neighbors, H. W., & Taylor, R. (1985). The use of social service agencies by black Americans. *Social Service Review, 59,* 259-268.

Orlandi, M. (Ed.). (1992). *Cultural competence for evaluators: A guide for alcohol and other drug abuse prevention practitioners working with ethnic/racial communities.* Washington, DC: U.S. Department of Health and Human Services.

Ornstein, R. E. (1972). *The psychology of consciousness.* San Francisco: Freeman.

Parker, W. M. (1988). *Consciousness raising: A primer for multicultural counseling.* Springfield, IL: Charles C Thomas.

Phinney, J. S., & Rotheram, M. J. (Eds.). (1987). *Children's ethnic socialization.* Newbury Park, CA: Sage.

Pinderhughes, E. B. (1989). *Understanding race, ethnicity and power: The key to efficacy in clinical practice.* New York: Free Press.

Ponterotto, J. G., & Casas, J. M. (1991). *Handbook of racial/ethnic minority counseling research.* Springfield, IL: Charles C Thomas.

Randall-David, E. (1989). *Strategies for working with culturally diverse communities and clients.* Washington, DC: Association for the Care of Children's Mental Health.

Rappaport, J. (1981). In praise of paradox: A social policy of empowerment over prevention. *American Journal of Community Psychology, 9,* 1-25.

Sanchez, A. M., Demmler, J., & Davis, M. (1990). *Toward pluralism in the mental health disciplines: Status of minority student recruitment and retention in the western states.* Boulder, CO: Western Interstate Commission for Higher Education.

Sillen, S., & Thomas, A. (1972). *Racism and psychiatry.* New York: Brunner/Mazel.

Solomon, B. B. (1976). *Black empowerment: Social work in oppressed communities.* New York: Columbia University Press.

Stampp, R. (1956). *The peculiar institution: Slavery in ante-bellum south.* New York: Knopf.

Stroul, B. A., & Friedman, R. M. (1986). *A system of care for children and youth with severe emotional disturbances.* Washington, DC: Georgetown University Child Development Center, Center for Child Health and Mental Health Policy, CASSP Technical Assistance Center.

Sue, D. W., & Sue, D. (1990). *Counseling the culturally different.* New York: John Wiley.

Thomas, G. E. (1990). Postscript: The road ahead in American race relations: Challenges for the 1990s. In G. E. Thomas (Ed.), *U.S. race relations in the 1980s and 1990s: Challenges and alternatives.* New York: Hemisphere.

Tienda, M. (1990). Race, ethnicity and the portrait of inequality: Approaching the 1990s. In G. E. Thomas (Ed.), *U.S. race relations in the 1980s and 1990s: Challenges and alternatives* (pp. 137-159). New York: Hemisphere.

Tienda, M., & Jensen, L. (1988). Poverty and minorities: A quarter century profile of color and socioeconomic disadvantage. In G. D. Sandefur & M. Tienda (Eds.), *Minority, poverty and social policy* (pp. 23-61). New York: Plenum.

Van-Si, C. (1992). *Understanding Southeast Asian cultures.* Oak Grove, OR: Asian American United Press.

Wilson, C. C., II, & Gutierrez, F. (1985). *Minorities and media: Diversity and the end of mass communication.* Beverly Hills, CA: Sage.

Wilson, W. J. (1987). The black community in the 1980's: Questions of race, class and public policy. In R. Takaki (Ed.), *Different shores: Perspectives on race and ethnicity in America* (pp. 233-240). New York: Oxford University Press.

Woody, D. L. (1992). *Recruitment and retention of minority workers in mental health programs.* Washington, DC: National Institute of Mental Health, Human Resource Development Program.

Zastrow, C. (1985). *Social work with groups.* Chicago: Nelson-Hall.

Alternate Paths to Family Status and Implications for Mental Health Service Delivery and Policy

Adoptive and Foster Families

ELLEN E. PINDERHUGHES

There are several ways to define family patterns (Sussman & Steinmetz, 1987): by structure or constellation (e.g., single-parent, two-parent, or stepparent); by ethnicity (e.g., African American, Mexican American, or Italian American); or by the path taken in becoming a family (e.g., biological, adoptive, or foster). Historically, research on families has focused on two-parent, biologically related families, typically called the nuclear family. Efforts to understand family functioning have used the nuclear family as the standard (e.g., Beavers, 1977; Hill, 1970; Rhodes, 1981). Although such a focus has facilitated the understanding of nuclear family functioning, this emphasis unfortunately has limited the understanding of family functioning among other

AUTHOR'S NOTE: An earlier version of this chapter was presented at the 1993 American Orthopsychiatric Association Annual Meeting, San Francisco, California. I thank Robert Nix for his contributions on open adoptions. I also gratefully acknowledge the comments of Kenneth A. Dodge, Vera A. S. Chatman, Howard M. Sandler, and Craig Anne Heflinger on this chapter.

types of families. An understanding of the unique strengths of and challenges confronting all types of families has been obscured (also see Patterson, Chapter 7 in this volume). As a result, mental health service delivery to families has been based almost exclusively on the characteristics and needs of the nuclear family, with an implicit assumption that this family pattern is the prototypical and desirable family structure. As people recognize increasing diversity within U.S. society, we must also recognize the increasing diversity of family patterns and examine their respective mental health needs. In discussing the needs of diverse families, this chapter will focus on alternate paths to family status.

Numerous paths to becoming a family exist. For some families, the involvement of an external agent such as the court system or a donor parent (surrogate parenting or artificial insemination) is necessary. Among adoptive and foster families, the legal system is required to be involved in the union between parent and child. In addition, for other families, such as families with single parents, stepfamilies, and families with homosexual parents, involvement of the legal system for unifying parent and child may be required. Thus, the traditional path of marriage and procreation within the original marital union is unique in that it typically does not require external involvement. Although the traditional path to family status historically has been the norm in this society, it is the norm no longer. As a result of dramatic changes in demographics and in individual and societal values about the paths to family status, the nuclear family now represents the numerical minority. Thus, it is important to understand family functioning in other family structures, not only for the sake of diversity but also for appropriate and sensitive mental health services delivery to all families. This chapter will review the extant literature on adoptive and foster families, two family types that are legitimated via the legal system, and will explore implications of this literature for mental health services delivery and policy.

Adoptive Families

Among adoptive families, great diversity exists—families who adopt infants, families who adopt children with special needs (i.e., children who are older, members of a sibling group, members of a minority group, and/or children who have an emotional, developmental, or physical disability), and families who adopt transracially or transculturally. Moreover, families differ in their choice of facilitating agent: a public agency, a private agency, or an independent lawyer. Families also vary in the degree of openness characterizing the relationship between adoptive and birth parents. Families adopting children with special needs engage either in an outright adoption process, in which the adopted child enters the home as a new adoptive placement, or in a foster-to-adoption process, in which the adopted child is placed originally as a foster child with the placement and subsequently becomes adopted.

Adopted individuals are estimated to represent 2% to 4% of the population in the United States (Rosenberg, 1993). Between 1987 and 1990, yearly numbers of adoption ranged between 118,000 and 120,000 (Flango, 1990; Flango & Flango, 1993). Estimates of those touched by adoption, that is, members of adoptive nuclear families, as well as members of adoptive-extended and birth-extended families, approach 30% of the U.S. population (Clare, 1991).

As a result of increased scholarly focus on adoption in the last decade (e.g., Barth & Berry, 1988; Berry, 1991a; Brodzinsky, 1987, 1990; Rosenberg, 1993; Rosenthal & Groze, 1992), there are converging perspectives that adoptive status poses unique and often greater challenges for families than exist for nonadoptive families. These challenges generally are considered to exist across the life span, although certain developmental periods are viewed as more vulnerable. Inasmuch as a developmental approach to the discussion of these challenges can be found elsewhere (i.e., Brodzinsky, Schechter, & Henig, 1992; Rosenberg, 1992; Schaffer & Lindstrom, 1989), this section will discuss several generic issues that are relevant across the life span, although the salience of each may vary with development. These issues that directly affect the mental health of family members and must be considered by mental health professionals include openness in the adoption, family appraisal of and communication about adoption, and searching by a member of the triad.

Openness in Adoptions

Openness in adoption refers to the degree of mutually consented contact between birth and adoptive families (Baran & Pannor, 1990).

Although open adoptions are widely believed to be a recent phenomenon, actually they date to the 1800s in the United States and several centuries worldwide. In concert with increasing societal concern about legally protecting children's rights, laws were created to seal adoptive records, eventually prohibiting anyone from accessing the original birth certificate (Baran & Pannor, 1990; Benet, 1976; Cole & Donley, 1990). The mental health community played a critical role in establishing this process, having theorized without sound data how the knowledge of illegitimacy would be damaging to one's self-concept (Cole & Donley, 1990). For a thorough discussion of the history of openness in adoption, see Baran and Pannor (1990) and Cole and Donley (1990).

In recent years, adoption practices have begun to be more flexible in offering birth parents and adoptive parents options about how open adoptive placements could be (Demick & Wapner, 1988). This change was prompted by the dramatic decrease in the availability of healthy infants for adoption since the *Roe v. Wade* (1973) decision that legalized abortion. As a result of the decrease and subsequent lengthy delays in the adoption process, adoptive parents sought alternatives to the traditional agency-facilitated closed adoption. In the process, adoptive parents became more willing to engage in open adoptions. Most critical, however, was the increasing empowerment of birth parents who insisted on greater involvement in the selection process of adoptive parents and in open adoptions (Norris, 1993; Severson, 1993).

Current adoption practices operate within a continuum of openness. At one pole of this continuum is a traditionally closed placement, characterized by limited exchange of nonidentifying information with no actual contact between birth parents and the adoptive family. At the other pole of this continuum is maximal openness, characterized by initial meetings of birth and adoptive parents for exchange of information, followed by contact at a mutually consented rate. Between the two extremes of the continuum lie a myriad of possibilities for exchange of information and contact. For the sake of simplicity, those placements involving any person-to-person contact with the exchange of identifying information between birth and adoptive parents are referred to as open adoptions. Open adoptions are highly controversial with strong arguments leveled by proponents and opponents alike. Benefits and risks to each member of the triad have been delineated (Berry, 1991a, 1991b; Demick & Wapner, 1988; McRoy, Grotevant, & White, 1988). Unfortunately, no sound national statistics exist regarding the frequency of open adoptions in the United States.

Because openness in adoption has been revived only recently, little extant research exists about this phenomenon (Nix, 1993). Several small studies on the adoption of infants have focused on adoptive parents' experiences with and perceptions of openness in adoption (Belbas, 1986; Etter, 1993; Gross, 1993; McRoy et al., 1988; Siegel, 1993), as well as birth parents' experiences and perceptions (Blanton & Deschner, 1990; Fish & Speirs, 1990; Groth, Bonnardel, Davis, Martin, & Vousden, 1987; McRoy et al., 1988; Silber & Dorner, 1990). These studies employed research methods involving one-time interviews with small samples of birth parents or adoptive parents, thereby limiting the understanding of the direct impact of open adoptions on family functioning. Furthermore, an emphasis on the functioning of the family and adopted child has been lacking. Needed are longitudinal studies that target the family as the unit of study (e.g., Berry, 1993).

When the research findings are aggregated, themes emerge about adoptive parents' views of open adoption, its advantages and disadvantages, and the impact of these characteristics on aspects of family functioning. Siegel (1993) found that 81% of her sample of 21 adoptive couples were initially hesitant to engage in an open adoption, expressing concerns about the birth parent reversing her decision, coping with the birth parent's loss, and embarking on an experience without the benefit of others' experiences. Although adoptive parents who have experienced open adoption identify few disadvantages (Belbas, 1986; Berry, 1993; Gross, 1993), those identified include envisioned future difficulties, such as the impact on the adopted child's development, potential problems with the degree of contact with birth parents, or integrating birth parents into the family system (Gross, 1993). Silverstein and Demick (1994) reported that an additional disadvantage for mothers engaging in open adoption is lower self-esteem. Drawing from the self-in-relation perspective, Silverstein and Demick observed that lower esteem actually may reflect increased sensitivity to the birth mother's pain. Mothers who engage in closed adoptions, in contrast, are not faced with the reality of this pain. The concerns and disadvantages expressed by adoptive parents illustrate areas that need focus in mental health service delivery. Most salient among these concerns, however, is that families engaging in open adoptions lack sufficient role models and normative standards.

Adoptive parents who have experienced open adoptions tend to be pleased with their decision (Belbas, 1986; Etter, 1993; Gross, 1993). One advantage that adoptive parents have reported about open adoptions is that as a result of meeting birth parents, they feel more entitled to parent the adopted child (Belbas, 1986; McRoy et al., 1988), a process that clinicians and adoption scholars have noted is critical to successful parenting (e.g., Bourguignon & Watson, 1988; Cohen, Coyne, & Duvall, 1995). Furthermore, Silverstein and Demick (1994) found that parents in open adoptions expressed fewer concerns about their attachment to their adopted infant. In addition, adoptive parents have noted that they have access to more information about the birth parent and not only can share more information with the adopted child when appropriate but also feel more comfortable anticipating this process. Finally, adoptive parents have reported that in the context of open adoption, they feel more in control of the adoption process. Highlighting the significance of control in the process of open adoptions, Etter (1993) reported on the outcome of mediation between adoptive and birth parents in open adoptions. She found that when adoptive and birth parents chose and then formally contracted for the desired amount of contact, both parties not only adhered to the written contract but also expressed high levels of satisfaction with the adoption.

In contrast to the small-scale studies reported above, two studies have employed methodologies that warrant description. In both cases, the studies reported are first waves of longitudinal research.

Grotevant, McRoy, Elde, and Fravel (1994) examined consequences on adoption-related family functioning associated with varying levels of openness. They interviewed a sample of 190 adoptive couples recruited through private adoption agencies in 15 states who were involved in a fully disclosed adoption, a mediated adoption (involving a third party), or a confidential adoption. Critical findings that emerged included (a) high levels of satisfaction among parents regardless of level of openness, (b) a negative relation between fear of birth mother reclaiming the adoptee and level of openness, and (c) a positive relation between level of openness and empathy for adoptee and for birth parent. With more than 70% of parents expressing satisfaction, there were no significant differences in satisfaction with one's control over the birth parent's involvement in the adoption. Two thirds of families in fully disclosed adoptions reported a change from either a confidential or mediated adoption. Apparently, as trust and mutual respect developed, adoptive parents and birth parents both increased their levels of openness. The establishment of trust was an important factor cited by adoptive parents when discussing their lack of fear that the birth mother would reclaim the adoptee. In contrast, parents in confidential adoptions expressed greater fear that the birth mother would reclaim the adoptee. Moreover, these fears were not grounded in the specific adoption experience but rather reflected parents' stereotyped impressions of birth parents. In a related finding, parents in fully disclosed adoptions displayed greater degrees of empathy toward the adoptee and the birth parent than did parents in confidential adoptions. Thus, more positive levels of functioning were associated with fully disclosed adoptions.

Berry (1993) has launched a longitudinal study with a large sample of adoptive families ($N = 1{,}268$) in California. Included in her sample are families who adopted independently as well as families who adopted through public and private agencies. Two critical findings have emerged from the first wave of this longitudinal study. First, experiences and comfort levels with open adoptions have differed as a function of the facilitating source—public agency, private agency, or independent lawyer. Among independent adoptions, the key casework service was facilitating preplacement contact with the birth family, whereas the key casework services for public and private agency adoptions apparently were preparing the adoptee and adoptive family for the placement and the provision of supplemental resources for the adoptive family. Second, adoptive parents who experienced higher levels of contact with birth parents expressed greater levels of comfort. This level of comfort was moderated, however, by the amount of control families have had over the degree of contact, that is, comfort has been highest when preplacement arrangements for contact have been met by both adoptive and birth parents after placement. Thus, Berry (1993) noted that adoptive families are "cautiously comfortable" with their open adoptions (p. 231). A critical factor is having an agreed-on plan for the amount of contact there will be between birth and adoptive families.

Adoptions of older children constitute a unique class of open adoptions. Older children, whose birth parents' parental rights have been terminated, retain memories and knowledge of their families that often affect their functioning in new families. Thus, for some children, contact with birth parents is explicitly prohibited. Despite termination of parental rights, however, adoption workers often encourage that contact be maintained among birth siblings who are placed separately, with prior caretakers, and, where indicated, with certain nonparental members of the birth family. Even less is known about the impact of open adoptions on families adopting older children than about infant adoptions. The limited extant data on adoptions of older children indicate that adoptive parents have mixed attitudes about openness. Partridge, Hornby, and McDonald (1986) found that 14% of adoptive parents in disrupted placements blamed birth parent contact. In her study of families' satisfaction with adoption services, Nelson (1985) noted that 20% of children in the study (N = 257) maintained contact with birth parents. Among this subgroup, 43% of their adoptive parents were ambivalent or regretful about this contact. Barth and Berry (1988) noted an important moderator in adoptive parents' perceptions about openness. Those who felt greater control over contacts with birth parents and other prior caretakers felt the contact was helpful. Adoption workers anecdotally observed that contact between adoptive parents and prior caretakers tended to weaken the adopted child-adoptive parent relationship, although the child's extreme externalizing behaviors were minimized. One consistent theme emerging from the limited research on open adoptions of infants and older children is that the control adoptive parents perceive they have is an important factor related to outcomes. This finding warrants further study.

Adoption-Related Appraisals

However open the adoption is, the appraisals of and family communication about the adoption are critical aspects of family functioning. One appraisal salient for adoptive families is whether a difference exists between adoptive and birth family status. Historically, simultaneous with the resealing of adoptive records, adoption workers moved to close adoptions and encouraged adoptive families to function "as if" they were biological families (Baran & Pannor, 1990; Cole & Donley, 1990). The acknowledgment or rejection of differences between adoptive and biological family life was first observed by Kirk (1964) as a major challenge for the adoptive family. This challenge can be magnified internally by individual family dynamics or externally by societal pressure. Kirk observed that adoptive families who acknowledged differences were likely to create an atmosphere for optimal family and individual functioning. In contrast, families who rejected the possibility that differences existed were likely to establish a context in which open and frank exploration of the family's adoptive status, its attendant issues of loss, and, ultimately, the adopted child's identity, could not occur.

In the three decades since Kirk's (1964) influential work, appraisals about differences and similarities between adoptive family life and biological family life have received little empirical interest. Recent research on families in traditionally closed adoptions (Brodzinsky, 1990; Hoffman-Riem, 1990; Kaye, 1990), however, indicates the significance of appraisals of differences or similarities in adoptive family functioning. In contrast to Kirk's proposal of a positive linear relation between acknowledgment of differences and family functioning, Brodzinsky suggested that the relation is curvilinear with rejection and acknowledgment at the extremes, both associated with poorer family and adopted child outcomes. Furthermore, contrary to Kirk's proposed causal relationship between acknowledgment of differences and subsequent family functioning, in a sample of 40 adoptive families with adolescents, Kaye (1990) found that parents' retrospective reports of behavior problems among adoptees as young children were positively associated with a current level of acknowledgment of differences between adoptive and biological families (perhaps as a post hoc distancing and defensive mechanism).

Drawing from a sociological study of 30 middle-class adoptive parents, Hoffman-Riem (1990) explored how families normalized their nonbiological family status. She noted two patterns: an *as-if normalization,* in which families deny differences in their family status; and an *own-type normalization,* in which families attempt to construct an open awareness of their adoptive status. Those families adopting some time previously tended to engage in an as-if normalization, whereas families adopting more recently tended to practice an own-type normalization.

Thus, there are two apparently contradictory perspectives about appraisals related to differences between adoptive and biological family life. Drawing from his own work as well as that of Kaye (1990), Brodzinsky (1990) noted that a family's coping patterns associated with differences actually may need to be flexible to adapt to the demands of the family's life cycle. For example, Brodzinsky suggested that for families adopting young infants and toddlers, rejection of differences may be important in facilitating the establishment of relationships. This task may compete with those challenges posed by open adoptions for which the presence of birth parents may highlight differences in adoptive family life. Similarly, families who adopt older children with their own history, memories, and expectations of family functioning will need to acknowledge differences from biological family life. In apparent contrast to Brodzinsky, Hoffman-Riem (1990) emphasizes the adaptive value of an own-type normalization that acknowledges differences. She noted that the valence of this pattern differs as a function of the age of the adopted child when placed.

Despite the differences, these writers collectively illustrate the significance of appraisals about adoption and differences that may exist between adoptive and biological families that warrant further research. The relation between these appraisals and child and family functioning also warrants attention from mental health professionals, as does the relation between appraisal of adoption and the current developmental tasks confronting the child and the family.

Adoption Searching

An adoption search involves the process of finding the identity of and perhaps meeting one's birth family. With state laws protecting the identities of adoption triad members, learning the names of birth relatives is an active and sometimes difficult process. For some individuals, learning the identity of family members is sufficient, whereas for others, meeting family members is necessary for the search process to feel complete. Both adoptees and birth parents initiate searches. Adopted women who are married and aged 25 to 34 constitute the modal group of searchers (e.g., Pacheco & Eme, 1993; Sachdev, 1992; Schechter & Bertocci, 1990; Silverman, Campbell, Patti, & Style, 1988). Triseliotis (1984) estimated that 15% of all adoptees search for birth families in their lifetime.

As Schechter and Bertocci (1990) noted, the literature on adoption searches has gradually evolved during the last two decades. Initial writings primarily were journalistic and autobiographical (e.g., Lifton, 1975, 1979). More recently, however, researchers (e.g., Campbell, Silverman, & Patti, 1991; Pacheco & Eme, 1993; Sachdev, 1992; Silverman et al., 1988) have focused on adoption searches and their outcomes. Most of these studies have used sampling and measurement procedures that limit the ability to summarize across different studies as well as to generalize to the adult adoptee population. Nevertheless, themes related to search activity have emerged that warrant attention. These themes include influences on the search and search-related cognitions and reunion themes.

Precipitants. Normative precipitants commonly associated with the adoptee's decision to engage in a search for his or her birth parents include major life cycle transitions such as marriage, pregnancy and birth, and death (Pacheco & Eme, 1993; Silverman et al., 1988). Other precipitants include a hope for a relationship with one's birth family and a wish for greater self-understanding (Silverman et al., 1988). Furthermore, some adoptees wish to assure their birth parents that they are alive and well and were well cared for as children (Sachdev, 1992).

Satisfaction with adoptive family relationships is another factor associated with whether adoptees initiate a search. Findings from early studies implicated dissatisfaction with restricted and limited adoptive family communication about adoption issues as a factor prompting the adoption search (Schechter & Bertocci, 1990). More recent studies, however, suggest that satisfaction, not dissatisfaction, with adoptive family life is critical in who searches (Campbell et al., 1991; Pacheco & Eme, 1993; Sachdev, 1992). Using the most geographically representative sample to date, Campbell et al. studied reunions between adoptees and birth parents. In a sample of 133 adoptees recruited from 18 states who had used different search strategies, the researchers found that adoptive families had been open and responsive in discussing adoption. Thus, it may be that family communication about adoption, moderated by the degree of satisfaction or dissatisfaction, is an influence on the search process.

Initial reactions of adoptive parents to adoptees' search activity primarily are negative (Pacheco & Eme, 1993; Sachdev, 1992); concern for the adoptee's well-being and fear of loss of the adoptee's love and loyalty are most prominent. Sachdev (1992) noted, however, that despite initial misgivings, adoptive parents support their children's search activity.

Reunion Themes. Extant research on reunions and their outcomes have addressed several critical questions: (a) the nature of the relationship between the adoptee and the birth family, (b) satisfaction of family members with the reunion, (c) the impact on the searcher's emotional functioning, and (d) the impact of the reunion on adoptive family relationships. Adoptees' reports of postreunion contact with their birth parents range from a close mother-child relationship with frequent contact, to a friendship with regular contact, to an acquaintance relationship with only occasional contact.

Satisfaction with the experiences of the search and the reunion typically is high among searchers (Campbell et al., 1991; Pacheco & Eme, 1993; Silverman et al., 1988). This pattern of satisfaction exists regardless of whether the new relationships meet the searcher's expectations; thus, it reflects a basic satisfaction with the ability to solve the genealogical puzzle (Pacheco & Eme, 1993; Sachdev, 1992).

The impact of the search on the searcher's emotional functioning consistently has been found to be positive (Campbell et al., 1991; Sachdev, 1992). Researchers have found that as a result of searching, adoptees who search generally report improved self-concept and interpersonal relationships.

Postreunion adoptive family relationships, although affected by the reunion, tend to show deterioration among only a small percentage of families. Pacheco and Eme (1993) noted that once adoptive families see that the adoptee can handle the outcome of the reunion, they often accept the newly established relationship.

Implications. Research on search and reunion has shown that two critical processes emerge as warranting further attention, both in research and in the delivery of mental health services. First, a salient element in the search process for adoptee and birth parent alike is the sense of control. Adoptees and birth parents who searched, therefore having greater control over the initiation of the reunion process, tended to feel more positive about the reunion experience. In contrast, adoptees who "were found" initially were confused and anxious (Sachdev, 1992). Nevertheless, postreunion comments of those who searched as well of those who were found indicate an overall positive experience. In fact, searchers and non-searchers alike noted they would search if they were to start over.

Searching adoptees and birth parents express concern about the reactions of their counterparts whom they seek to contact. Although worries about rejection are salient, most prominent are concerns about intruding into the other's life. As a result, searchers have noted that great deliberation precedes the actual contact (Campbell et al., 1991; Silverman et al., 1988). Some searchers have enlisted the aid of an intermediary (Sachdev, 1992; Silverman et al., 1988). Sachdev (1985, 1992) noted that adoptees support the voluntary use of intermediaries in the search process. Furthermore, he suggested that nonprofessionals, such as other adoptees or birth parents who have experienced a search and reunion, would be most sensitive and understanding of the searchers' needs.

A second critical process is that of adjustment and accommodation to the reality of reunion. Members of the triad who have experienced the search process, whether perceived as largely positive or negative, face the challenge of adjusting to the outcome. Current research findings indicate that following most reunions, all triad members readjust fairly well (Campbell et al., 1991; Pacheco & Eme, 1993; Sachdev, 1992; Silverman et al., 1988). Those reunions that are not perceived as successful by any triad member, however, nevertheless prompt a readjustment. Whatever the initial reaction to the reunion, a process of adjustment follows. Thus, just as adoption is viewed no longer as a one-time event but rather as a lifelong process, perhaps so should the search and reunion be seen as a process that, once initiated, will affect all triad members throughout their lives. Greater understanding about how normative this challenge is for those involved in the search and reunion process is needed.

Implications for Research and Delivery of Mental Health Services for Adoptive Families

Numerous questions remain about family functioning and openness, adoption appraisal, and the search for biological roots. Regarding openness, of interest is the impact of the degree of openness on family functioning throughout the child's life cycle, in particular, the family's ability to help the adoptee master critical developmental tasks. Also of interest is what role adoptive parents' perceived control over contact with birth parents has in family adjustment. To answer these and related questions, longitudinal studies of open adoptions, from placement through adulthood, are warranted. Such knowledge is important not only regarding infant adoptions but also regarding adoptions of older children. Given the probable history of abuse or neglect in adoptees' birth families (e.g., Pinderhughes, 1986) and the intervention of the child welfare and legal systems, understanding the impact of contact with members of birth families on adoptee and family functioning is critical. Inasmuch as the boundaries between adoptive families and birth parents get redefined and become blurred, understanding the impact of the open adoption on the older adoptee's adult development and subsequent family functioning is needed as well.

Longitudinal studies of appraisals of adoption would provide information on the association between appraisals, family life cycle challenges, and family functioning. Among families engaged in open adoptions, understanding how their appraisals are affected by the level of openness is needed. Finally, regarding the search and reunion, the role that adoptive families play in the search process as well as strategies these families use to adjust to their adopted child's reunion with birth parents needs further clarification.

The delivery of mental health services needs to be adapted in several ways. First, just as mental health professionals played a critical role in the closing of the adoption process, so should they have a role in facilitating family functioning with open adoptions. Services delivered to families engaged in open adoptions must take into account that these families are charting new territory, with few models on whom to rely (Nix, 1993). As a result, adoptive families face uncertainty about the management of boundaries and communication with birth parents and likely will feel isolated. Thus, for adoptive families engaged in open adoptions with birth families, appropriate services may include some joint intervention with birth parents. Mental health concerns include helping adoptive parents, adoptees, and birth parents function within their agreed-on definition of openness in the adoption process. When some type of openness is arranged, accomplishing the task of child rearing within the arrangement can be challenging. For families who choose an arrangement at the extreme pole of openness, regularly integrating the birth parent into family life may be difficult. Joint clinical work with adoptive families and birth parents is not only a service delivery issue but also a mental health coverage issue. Furthermore, support networks that are facilitated by sensitive mental health professionals for families involved in open adoptions may be useful.

A second needed adaptation is that services delivered to assist individuals with search and reunion activities should not be delivered following a deficit model, that is, with assumptions that low self-esteem and dissatisfaction with adoptive family functioning are the primary motivators. Mental health services need to be delivered in a way that promotes a sense of control for members of the adoption triad. Extant research on open adoptions as well as the adoption search consistently highlight the relationship between perceived control and satisfaction with these experiences. Regarding adoption searches, the role an intermediary serves needs to be explored, and the person considering initiating a search should be empowered to make the decision whether to rely on an intermediary.

Third, the role of appraisals about adoption and of birth mothers in presenting problems should be considered by mental professionals delivering services to adoptive families in closed adoptions (Campbell et al., 1991; Rosenberg, 1993). How families appraise the relation between their adoptive status and their problem may influence the effectiveness of mental health services. Similarly, fantasies or perceptions of birth parents, whether explicit or implicit, may affect adoptive family members' progress. The role of birth parents in adoptive family life should be explored, especially following adoption reunions. Finally, postreunion mental health services should be available to members of the adoption triad.

A challenge for mental health service providers is one of education and self-assessment regarding one's values about openness, search, and reunion in adoption. Unfortunately, the field lacks a strong base of empirical literature to guide clinical decision making about what is in the best interests of adopted children and adoptive families. Openness and adoption reunions, however, are developing phenomena that require sensitive and supportive delivery of mental health services. Mental health professionals must not undermine these arrangements but rather enable them to succeed.

Foster Families

Foster parenting is the second alternate path to family status addressed in this chapter. Foster families are estimated at fewer than 200,000 with a decrease in their number occurring since 1987 (Barden, 1991). Despite their few numbers, foster families provide an invaluable service to children and society; the role of foster families is to provide temporary care for infants and children whose birth parents are unable or unwilling to adequately care for them. Inasmuch as foster families directly care for children from troubled families, they are formally the caregiving component of the child welfare system. Foster families, however, have a complicated yet limited role in the child welfare system. Typically, foster families are not consulted in the decision making about children's placements (Fein, 1991). Thus, their challenge is to temporarily parent children from troubled biological families, knowing that they have no input into the children's future.

Research on foster families is limited (Fein, 1991; Fein, Maluccio, & Kluger, 1990). Researchers have addressed primarily children's characteristics (e.g., Fanshel, Finch, & Grundy, 1989; Festinger, 1983; McIntyre & Keesler, 1986) and the efficacy of services for reunification (e.g., Fein & Staff, 1993) and for permanency (e.g., Fein, Maluccio, Hamilton, & Ward, 1983). Furthermore, the social casework literature only briefly addresses foster family functioning (e.g., Carbino, 1991; Edelstein, 1981; Fein, 1991). Two critical areas deserving of discussion include the challenges that foster families face in incorporating children who have experienced dysfunctional family life and in adjusting to the removal of foster children from the home.

Postplacement Foster Family Adjustment

Foster family adjustment to the entry of a foster child has received little empirical attention. Using a 6-month longitudinal design with 120 families, Derr (1984) found that during the period following placement, families reported a decline in their average level of functioning. Factors positively related to family functioning included role flexibility, realistic expectations, family income, and prior foster experience. Families with less flexibility and unrealistic expectations were more likely to experience problems, as were families with lower incomes and no prior experience. These findings suggest that factors such as financial resources, parental expectations, and family flexibility influence how foster families adjust to the entry of a foster child. Other possible influences include external supports and the coping strategies of individual family members (McCubbin & Patterson, 1983).

For biological children of foster parents, foster care may be uniquely stressful. Kaplan (1988) studied a sample of 15 foster mothers and their latency-aged biological children who had experienced foster children's entry into and removal from their homes. She found high levels of separation anxiety among the children. For children under 9, the anxiety was noticeably pronounced, and they indicated fears of losing their own parents. Moreover, the children's fear of abandonment was heightened by incidents of their own misbehavior. Among children 9 and older, the anxiety was related to separation from the foster sibling, as well as empathy for the foster sibling. Older children also expressed guilt about having negative emotions toward their foster siblings. In addition, maternal awareness was found to be inversely related to children's concerns, indicating that mothers who were more sensitive to their children's worries had children who expressed fewer concerns. These findings suggest differential levels of maternal and child awareness about foster care and about difficulties for biological children. Unfortunately, because of limited sampling, these findings do not generalize to the population of foster families. The findings, however, do highlight aspects of foster family functioning that warrant further inquiry and attention. Moreover, inasmuch as the duration of foster placements is uncertain, understanding family adjustment to the entry as well as biological children's adjustment would facilitate more sensitive mental health service delivery.

Adjustment to the Removal of Foster Children

Although foster parents incorporate children into their family with the knowledge that the placement's duration is uncertain and that the placement will end, adjusting to the child's removal may be difficult. To date, no studies have reported on family adjustment following removal of foster children. In situations in which the removal is normative, that is, reunification with the biological family or adoption occurs, several factors may impede the foster family's resolution of the loss: (a) an ambivalent relationship with the foster child, (b) external assumptions about the ease with which foster parents can resolve losses of children, and (c) lack of external supports for foster parents (Edelstein, 1981). Furthermore, foster parents' inability to have input into the decision-making process involving the child's future may impede their resolution of the loss.

In addition to normative removals, foster children may be removed from foster families following allegations of abuse or neglect by the foster family. Data on the incidence of removal of foster children following abuse are extremely limited. Carbino (1992) has noted that although foster homes are involved in only 1% of all child removal situations nationally, the actual relative percentage of foster homes involved in removal following abuse allegations is higher. External factors such as greater monitoring of foster homes relative to biological family homes likely account for this discrepancy. Whatever the numbers, inasmuch as foster homes as critical resources for children are affected, an understanding of this phenomenon is warranted. In situations in which the removal is atypical, for example, precipitous removal following allegations of abuse or neglect by the foster family, the process of grieving is further complicated by investigations initiated by the child welfare system (Carbino, 1991, 1992). The role of the system as a support for the foster parent abruptly disappears, leaving foster families isolated and confused. Whether or not allegations are substantiated, foster parents in these situations often grieve not only the loss of the foster child but also the loss of their credibility with, and trust in, the child welfare system (Carbino, 1991).

Implications for Research and Delivery of Mental Health Services to Foster Families

Inasmuch as foster care is designed to provide children with a safer, more functional family, understanding in what way the child's entry into and removal from the home influence family functioning is important. Information is needed about the process of and influences on foster family readjustment following the placement of a child. Related questions involve (a) the factors that influence the process and (b) the temporal duration of readjustment. When children are removed, information is needed about those factors influencing foster family readjustment. Related topics include (a) the indicators of foster family readiness for another placement and (b) supports that are available for the processing of this experience. In cases of removal following abuse allegations, data are needed on frequency rates, the pattern of agency response to allegations, and the foster family's experiences. Families may need mental health services to facilitate their readjustment following the removal of a child. This is especially the case when removal follows allegations and the supports typically offered by the child welfare system vanish.

Knowledge about foster family functioning following placement can be used both to normalize the experience for current and potential foster families and to aid in planning the delivery of supportive mental health services for the family. Neophyte foster families may be especially vulnerable to developing problems in adjusting to the entry of foster children (Eastman, 1979). Supportive services include psychoeducational interventions to facilitate adjustment following placement and support groups for foster parents. Furthermore, understanding how biological children of foster families experience foster care will enable the delivery of sensitive mental health services to the entire foster family. The concern about biological children is not only for the role that they play in the foster care context but also for their own emotional development and well-being.

Finally, further inquiry also is warranted into two of the unique qualities of foster parenting. Information is needed about the impact of the uncertain placement duration and the foster family's inability to provide input on family functioning, on family adjustment to the removal of the child. With such information, mental health services can be directed at normalizing the experiences of foster families.

The decrease in the number of foster families noted at the beginning of this section has been connected not only to the challenges that foster families face but also to inadequate system supports, including training and respite care (Chamberlain, Moreland, & Reid, 1992). Recommendations abound for improvements in the child welfare system and delivery of foster care services (e.g., Allen, 1991; Carbino, 1991; Edelstein, 1981; Fein, 1991). In fact, some recommendations date more than 10 years (e.g., Maluccio & Sinanoglu, 1981). These recommendations include increasing financial compensation to foster families and providing increased respite services, training, supervision, and support. As with child welfare services, the delivery of mental health services can be improved. First, because foster children tend to exhibit more severe behavioral problems than a decade ago (Allen, 1991; Fein, 1991), training in child behavior management should be offered to all foster parents as a preventive measure. Second, foster families need access to mental health services, not only for the foster child but also for themselves. For example, support groups for foster parents may provide peer support in adjusting to children's entry into and removal from home. In addition, when children are removed from foster care following allegations of abuse, mental health services should be provided automatically to the family (Carbino, 1991). Finally, the provision of respite care, which uses experienced foster families for planned, short-term care, is viewed increasingly as a necessary wraparound service in the continuum of care available to foster families.

Implications for Mental Health Policies

An overarching goal of ensuring the healthy adaptation of adoptive and foster families should guide the formulation of mental health policies. Furthermore, implicit in such policies should be an understanding of the unique issues that challenge adoptive and foster families and that likely vary in salience across the family's life cycle as well as across families. Policies based on this understanding would enable services to be creatively designed or adapted to meet the needs of specific family types. Such services would be delivered at all levels of intervention: primary, secondary, and tertiary. For instance, in light of recent trends toward increasing openness in adoption practice, a more flexible definition of the family is appropriate. Moreover, for adoptive families who engage in highly open placements that are characterized not only by the exchange of identifying information but also by contact that includes the adopted child, a broader definition that includes the birth parent is appropriate. On the other hand, for adoptive families who engage in traditionally closed adoptions, a more narrow definition is in order. Greater flexibility in agencies' policy definitions regarding who can be served and in third-party payers' policies regarding the services that are covered would enable the delivery of more comprehensive services to adoptive families who face a myriad of issues. Such flexibility has further ramifications for families engaged in open adoptions when birth parents' own families—of origin and procreation—become involved.

For special needs adoptive and foster families, unique issues warrant policies regarding primary prevention services such as the delivery of preplacement training and continuing support. Policies need to ensure that adoptive and foster families who choose to parent older children receive extensive training to function as therapeutic families (Allen, 1991; Fein, 1991). In addition, policies should ensure the regular provision of postplacement respite services and the greater availability of sensitive and effective clinical services. The federal government has recognized this need and responded with specific funding for demonstration projects on training mental health professionals (e.g., Pinderhughes & Rosenberg, 1991).

Policies guiding service delivery at the primary prevention level should focus on a goal of enabling families to understand the normative issues challenging their respective family type. Furthermore, policies should call for the education of the public about the unique features of and contributions to society made by adoptive and foster families. Such a mental health education campaign might have a larger goal of generating an appreciation for similarities and differences among various family constellations and paths toward family status. Policies guiding service delivery at the secondary and tertiary levels of prevention should integrate relevant themes for clinical interventions designed for adoptive and foster families.

A final implication for mental health policies is the need to clarify and expand the role that mental health professionals have in the child welfare system. There should be increased collaboration between mental health and child welfare professionals so that services related to unification and placement are delivered more effectively. First, mental health professionals have an obligation to obtain training in adoption and foster care issues. Such training should be offered in graduate programs, as well as at professional development conferences from experts in foster care and adoption. Next, mental health professionals can work with state or local child welfare systems to improve direct and indirect delivery of mental health services to adoptive and foster families.

Conclusion

This discussion of salient issues for adoptive and foster families suggests that unique challenges confront these families: the degree of openness in adoptive-birth parent relationships; appraisals about adoptive family status, search, and reunion; and adjustment to children's entry into and removal from the foster home. Adoptive and foster families, however, also face the normative challenge confronting all families: the mastery of developmental tasks for individual family members. Flexibility in functioning and effective communication constitute key influences on families' abilities to meet this normative challenge. For adoptive and foster families, the unique challenges that derive from an alternate path to family status apparently interact with the normative challenge. Further complicating the understanding of this phenomenon is that the unique challenges vary in their salience throughout the family's life cycle and across families.

Adoptive and foster families, however, are but two types of families who achieve family status via an alternate path who need the delivery of sensitive and effective services from the mental health system. Other families potentially in need of sensitive and flexible services include stepfamilies and families headed by homosexual parents. Extant literature on these families suggests that they, too, face unique challenges deriving from their chosen paths (e.g., Giles-Sims & Crosbie-Burnett, 1989; Harris & Turner, 1986; Hetherington & Clingempeel, 1992; Patterson, 1992) that also seem to interact with the normative tasks confronting all families.

With the exception of stepfamilies, the literature on families who choose alternate paths to family status is in its infancy. So, too, is the understanding of the needs these families have for mental health services. As researchers generate greater knowledge about adoptive and foster families and families headed by homosexual parents, as well as other families who choose an alternate path to family status, the ability to design sensitive services that effectively promote their healthy adaptation will improve. That is the challenge for society: to ensure the healthy adaptation of all families, regardless of the constellation, ethnicity, or path to family status.

References

Allen, M. (1991). Crafting a federal legislative framework for child welfare reform. *American Journal of Orthopsychiatry, 61*(4), 610-617.

Baran, A., & Pannor, R. (1990). Open adoption. In D. M. Brodzinsky & M. D. Schechter (Eds.), *The psychology of adoption* (pp. 316-331). New York: Oxford University Press.

Barden, J. C. (1991, January 6). When foster care ends: Home is often the street. *New York Times*, p. 4E.

Barth, R. P., & Berry, M. (1988). *Adoption and disruption: Rates, risks, and responses.* New York: Aldine de Gruyter.

Beavers, W. R. (1977). *Psychotherapy and growth: A family systems perspective.* New York: Brunner/Mazel.

Belbas, N. F. (1986). *Staying in touch: Empathy in open adoptions.* Unpublished master's thesis, Smith College School for Social Work, Northampton, MA.

Benet, M. K. (1976). *The politics of adoption.* New York: Free Press.

Berry, M. (1991a). The effects of open adoption on biological and adoptive parents and the children: The arguments and the evidence. *Child Welfare, 70*(6), 637-651.

Berry, M. (1991b). The practice of open adoption: Findings from a study of 1396 adoptive families. *Children and Youth Service Review, 13*, 379-395.

Berry, M. (1993). Adoptive parents' perceptions of, and comfort with, open adoption. *Child Welfare, 72*(3), 231-253.

Blanton, T. L., & Deschner, J. (1990). Biological mothers' grief: The postadoptive experience in open versus confidential adoption. *Child Welfare, 69*(6), 525-535.

Bourguignon, J. P., & Watson, K. W. (1988). *After adoption: A manual for professionals working with adoptive families.* Springfield: Illinois Department of Children and Family Services.

Brodzinsky, D. M. (1987). Adjustment to adoption: A psychosocial perspective. *Clinical Psychology Review, 7,* 25-47.

Brodzinsky, D. M. (1990). A stress and coping model of adoption adjustment. In D. M. Brodzinsky & M. D. Schechter (Eds.), *The psychology of adoption* (pp. 3-24). New York: Oxford University Press.

Brodzinsky, D. M., Schechter, M. D., & Henig, R. M. (1992). *Being adopted: The lifelong search for self.* New York: Doubleday.

Campbell, L. H., Silverman, P. R., & Patti, P. B. (1991). Reunions between adoptees and birth parents: The adoptees' experience. *Social Work, 36*(4), 329-335.

Carbino, R. (1991). Child abuse and neglect reports in foster care: The issue for foster families of "false" allegations. *Child and Youth Services, 15*(2), 233-247.

Carbino, R. (1992). Policy and practice for response to foster families when child abuse or neglect is reported. *Child Welfare, 71*(6), 497-509.

Chamberlain, P., Moreland, S., & Reid, K. (1992). Enhanced services and stipends for foster parents: Effects on retention rates and outcomes for children. *Child Welfare, 71*(5), 387-401.

Clare, M. (1991). Family systems thinking and adoption practice. *Australian Social Work, 44*(3), 3-13.

Cohen, N. J., Coyne, J. C., & Duvall, J. D. (1995, April). Parents' sense of "entitlement" in adoptive and non-adoptive families. In E. E. Pinderhughes (Chair), *Cognitions and adjustment among children and families united through special needs adoption.* Symposium conducted at the biennial meeting of the Society for Research in Child Development, Indianapolis, IN.

Cole, E. S., & Donley, K. S. (1990). History, values, and placement policy issues in adoption. In D. M. Brodzinsky & M. D. Schechter (Eds.), *The psychology of adoption* (pp. 273-294). New York: Oxford University Press.

Demick, J., & Wapner, S. (1988). Open and closed adoption: A developmental conceptualization. *Family Process, 27,* 229-249.

Derr, D. F. (1984). The crisis of fostering for the foster family. *Dissertation Abstracts International,* vol. 44 (12a). (University Microfilms No. AAC 8406360, ProQuest)

Eastman, K. (1979). The foster family in a systems theory perspective. *Child Welfare, 58,* 564-570.

Edelstein, S. (1981). When foster children leave: Helping foster parents to grieve. *Child Welfare, 60*(7), 467-473.

Etter, J. (1993). Levels of cooperation and satisfaction in 56 open adoptions. *Child Welfare, 72*(3), 257-267.

Fanshel, D., Finch, S. J., & Grundy, J. F. (1989). Foster children in life-course perspective: The Casey family program experience. *Child Welfare, 62*(5), 467-478.

Fein, E. (1991). Issues in foster family care: Where do we stand? *American Journal of Orthopsychiatry, 61*(4), 578-583.

Fein, E., Maluccio, A. N., Hamilton, J., & Ward, D. (1983). After foster care: Outcomes of permanency planning for children. *Child Welfare, 62,* 485-562.

Fein, E., Maluccio, A. N., & Kluger, M. (1990). *No more partings: An examination of foster family care.* Washington, DC: Child Welfare League of America.

Fein, E., & Staff, I. (1993). Last best chance: Findings from a reunification services program. *Child Welfare, 72*(1), 25-40.

Festinger, T. (1983). *No one ever asked us: A postscript to foster care.* New York: Columbia University Press.

Fish, A., & Speirs, C. (1990). Biological parents choose adoptive parents: The use of profiles in adoption. *Child Welfare, 69*(2), 129-139.

Flango, V. E. (1990). Agency and private adoptions, by state. *Child Welfare, 69*(3), 263-275.

Flango, V. E., & Flango, C. R. (1993). Adoption statistics by state. *Child Welfare, 72*(3), 311-319.

Giles-Sims, J., & Crosbie-Burnett, M. (1989). Stepfamily research: Implications for policy, clinical interventions, and further research. *Family Relations, 38,* 19-23.

Gross, H. E. (1993). Open adoption: A research-based literature review and new data. *Child Welfare, 72*(3), 269-284.

Grotevant, H. D., McRoy, R. G., Elde, C. L., & Fravel, D. L. (1994). Adoptive family system dynamics: Variations by level of openness in the adoption. *Family Process, 33,* 125-146.

Groth, M., Bonnardel, D., Davis, D. A., Martin, J. C., & Vousden, H. E. (1987). An agency moves toward open adoption of infants. *Child Welfare, 66*(3), 247-257.

Harris, M. B., & Turner, P. H. (1986). Gay and lesbian parents. *Journal of Homosexuality, 12*(2), 101-113.

Hetherington, E. M., & Clingempeel, W. G. (1992). Coping with marital transitions: A family systems perspective. *Child Development, 57*(2-3), 1-35.

Hill, R. (1970). *Family development in three generations.* Cambridge, MA: Schenkman.

Hoffman-Riem, C. (1990). *The adopted child: Family life with double parenthood.* New Brunswick, NJ: Transaction Publishing.

Kaplan, C. P. (1988). The biological children of foster parents in the foster family. *Child and Adolescent Social Work, 5*(4), 281-299.

Kaye, K. (1990). Acknowledgement or rejection of differences? In D. M. Brodzinsky & M. D. Schechter (Eds.), *The psychology of adoption* (pp. 121-143). New York: Oxford University Press.

Kirk, H. D. (1964). *Shared fate.* New York: Free Press.

Lifton, B. J. (1975). *Twice born: Memoirs of an adopted daughter.* New York: McGraw-Hill.

Lifton, B. J. (1979). *Lost and found: The adoption experience.* New York: Dial.

Maluccio, A. N., & Sinanoglu, P. A. (Eds.). (1981). *The challenge of partnership.* New York: Child Welfare League of America.

McCubbin, H., & Patterson, J. (1983). Family transitions: Adaptation to stress. In H. I. McCubbin & C. Figley (Eds.), *Stress and the family: Coping with normative transitions* (Vol. 1). New York: Brunner/Mazel.

McIntyre, A., & Keesler, T. Y. (1986). Psychological disorders among foster children. *Journal of Clinical Child Psychology, 15*(4), 297-303.

McRoy, R. G., Grotevant, H. D., & White, K. L. (1988). *Openness in adoption: New practices, new issues.* New York: Praeger.

Nelson, K. A. (1985). *On the frontier of adoption: A study of special-needs adoptive families.* New York: Child Welfare League of America.

Nix, R. (1993, May). Empirical findings on open adoption. In E. E. Pinderhughes & K. F. Rosenberg (Chairs), *The impact of secrecy and openness adoption.* Symposium conducted at the annual meeting of the American Orthopsychiatric Association, San Francisco.

Norris, B. (1993, May). The advocacy and reform movement: Personal empowerment and social activism presentation. In E. E. Pinderhughes & K. F. Rosenberg (Chairs),

The impact of secrecy and openness adoption. Symposium conducted at the annual meeting of the American Orthopsychiatric Association, San Francisco.

Pacheco, F., & Eme, R. (1993). An outcome study of the reunion between adoptees and biological parents. *Child Welfare, 72*(1), 53-64.

Partridge, S., Hornby, H., & McDonald, T. (1986). *Learning from adoption disruption: Insights for practice.* Portland, ME: Human Services Development Institute.

Patterson, C. J. (1992). Children of lesbian and gay parents. *Child Development, 63,* 1025-1042.

Pinderhughes, E. E. (1986). *Characteristics of older adoptees and short term outcome of adoption.* Unpublished doctoral dissertation, Yale University, New Haven, CT.

Pinderhughes, E. E., & Rosenberg, K. F. (1991, March). The mental health/adoption training project: Development and effectiveness. In E. E. Pinderhughes & K. F. Rosenberg (Chairs), *Training programs that facilitate more effective service delivery for families adopting children with special needs.* Symposium conducted at the annual meeting of the American Orthopsychiatric Association, Toronto, Ontario, Canada.

Rhodes, S., & Wilson, J. (1981). *Surviving family life.* New York: Putnam.

Roe v. Wade, 410 U.S. 113 (1973).

Rosenberg, E. B. (1992). *The adoption life cycle: The children and their families through the years.* New York: Free Press.

Rosenberg, K. F. (1993, May). The impact of secrecy and denial in adoption: Clinical and treatment issues. In E. E. Pinderhughes & K. F. Rosenberg (Chairs), *The impact of secrecy and openness adoption.* Symposium conducted at the annual meeting of the American Orthopsychiatric Association, San Francisco.

Rosenthal, J. A., & Groze, V. K. (1992). *Special-needs adoption: A study of intact families.* New York: Praeger.

Sachdev, P. (1985). *Unlocking the adoption files.* Lexington, MA: Lexington.

Sachdev, P. (1992). Adoption reunion and after: A study of the search process and experience of adoptees. *Child Welfare, 71*(1), 53-68.

Schaffer, J., & Lindstrom, C. (1989). *How to raise an adopted child: A guide to help your child flourish from infancy through adolescence.* New York: Copestone.

Schechter, M. D., & Bertocci, D. (1990). The meaning of the search. In D. M. Brodzinsky & M. D. Schechter (Eds.), *The psychology of adoption* (pp. 62-90). New York: Oxford University Press.

Severson, R. (1993, May). Body not bruised to pleasure soul: The philosophy of open adoption. In E. E. Pinderhughes and K. F. Rosenberg (Chairs), *The impact of secrecy and openness adoption.* Symposium conducted at the annual meeting of the American Orthopsychiatric Association, San Francisco.

Siegel, D. H. (1993). Open adoption of infants: Adoptive parents' perceptions of advantages and disadvantages. *Social Work, 38*(1), 15-23.

Silber, K., & Dorner, P. M. (1990). *Children of open adoption.* San Antonio, TX: Corona.

Silverman, P. R., Campbell, L., Patti, P., & Style, C. B. (1988). Reunions between adoptees and birth parents: The birth parents' experience. *Social Work, 33,* 523-528.

Silverstein, D. R., & Demick, J. (1994). Toward an organization-relational model of open adoption. *Family Process, 33,* 111-124.

Sussman, M. B., & Steinmetz, S. K. (Eds.). (1987). *Handbook of marriage and the family.* New York: Plenum.

Triseliotis, J. (1984). Obtaining birth certificates. In P. Bean (Ed.), *Adoption.* London: Tavistock.

Mental Health Services for Rural Children, Youth, and Their Families

CAROLYN E. CUTRONA
MARCY B. J. HALVORSON
DANIEL W. RUSSELL

Almost one third of American youth live in rural areas. Nevertheless, rural youth have been virtually ignored by mental health service planners and providers (Petti & Leviton, 1986). Risk factors for poor mental health, such as poverty, parental alcohol abuse, and family instability, are common among rural children and adolescents and appear to be increasing (Petti & Leviton, 1986). Studies of rural adults have reported increases in suicide attempts, family violence, depression, and alcohol abuse (National Mental Health Association, 1988). Many of these increases appear to be tied to the economic farm crisis that began in the 1980s and continues in many areas today (Wagenfeld, 1990). It is well documented that the strains facing rural families have profound effects on the adjustment and mental health of rural youth (Conger, Elder, Lorenz, Simons, & Whitbeck, 1994).

Across the nation, children are one of the most neglected groups in mental health services. Large proportions of disturbed and disruptive children and adolescents do not receive adequate, comprehensive mental health services (Tuma, 1989). Epidemiologic data indicate that from 11% to 20% of the nation's approximately 63 million children and adolescents suffer from psychiatric disorders and/or behavior problems that warrant mental health treatment (Costello, 1989; Dougherty, 1988; Knitzer, 1982). Between 3% and 8% of these children are severely disturbed and require intensive care (Knitzer, 1982). Large numbers of children suffer from subclinical disorders and are exposed to many mental health risk factors (e.g., abuse, poverty, and parental divorce). Even if these latter children do not meet diagnostic criteria, they are at risk for later, and potentially more serious, problems and must be considered when addressing children's needs for mental health services (Tuma, 1989).

Taube and Barrett (1985) have estimated that 70% to 80% of the children who need mental health services do not receive them. Needed services are frequently not available. Often children are given overly restrictive care (e.g., inpatient hospital treatment) because less restrictive services, such as nonhospital residential treatment centers or day treatment centers, are not available (Tuma, 1989). Specialists trained to deal with children are in short supply. In 1982, only 10% of psychiatrists and 1% of psychologists reported that their practices were devoted primarily to serving children (Knitzer, 1982). In addition, there is a shortage of child psychiatrists, psychologists, child- and family-oriented social workers, and mental health nurses who specialize in children. Troubled children have a wide variety of needs, each of which is currently addressed by a different agency (e.g., school, juvenile justice system, human services, and community mental health centers). Coordination among agencies is typically poor. Seriously needed are case management and better communication among agencies that serve children and youth.

Problems with delivery of child and adolescent mental health care are especially severe in rural areas. Rural children, adolescents, and their families have much less access to mental health services than their metropolitan counterparts (Petti & Leviton, 1986). Rural mental health providers and families of youth with mental disorders face additional service barriers that result from geographic, economic, and cultural factors (Kelleher, Taylor, & Rickert, 1992). In sparsely populated areas, the costs of providing care are increased by travel and communication expenses. Support services are often lacking. It is difficult to recruit and retain child-trained specialists, who tend to concentrate in upper-income urban areas. Rural family members receive less formal education and have relatively fewer high-paying occupations than metropolitan families. As a result, rural families are less likely to have health insurance and more likely to fund their medical and mental health care through self-pay, Medicare, or Medicaid than metropolitan families (Norton & McManus, 1987). Even when services are available, families of troubled rural youth may be reluctant to pursue treatment from mental health professionals because of values and attitudes associated with self-reliance and mistrust of strangers.

Complexities of Studying Rural Mental Health Services for Youth

It is difficult to generalize across studies of rural mental health services. First, a variety of definitions are used to distinguish urban from rural areas. For example, the U.S. Bureau of the Census (1989) defines rural populations as those individuals living in places with fewer than 2,500 residents or in the open countryside. The urban population comprises (a) those who live in an urbanized area—a central city that including surrounding areas has a population of 50,000 or more and (b) those who live outside an urbanized area in a place with a population of 2,500 or more. A different metropolitan-nonmetropolitan distinction is used by the Office of Management and Budget. This distinction is based on metropolitan statistical areas (MSAs). An MSA includes a core city and adjacent communities that are economically and socially tied to it. Counties are the building blocks of MSAs in most areas. To qualify as an MSA, an area must have either a city with a population of at least 50,000 or an urbanized area of at least 50,000 people that is part of a county or counties that have at least 100,000 people. The concept of nonmetropolitan is residual: counties or aggregations of counties that are not metropolitan. The MSA concept has been used extensively by government agencies and business for planning and allocation decisions. Problems in MSA classification may occur when county boundaries do not conform closely to actual urban or suburban development. Also, rural enclaves can exist within metropolitan areas, and nonmetropolitan areas can contain small urban concentrations. According to the U.S. Congress (1989), 40% of the 1980 census rural population lived in MSAs and 14% of the MSA population lived in rural areas.

In addition to these two federal definitions, researchers have defined rurality in a number of ways. Nine different county-based typologies were identified by the U.S. Congress (1989) report, using the dimensions of population, size, density, urbanization, distance from an urban area, and type of economy. No approach to defining rurality is entirely satisfactory. Depending on which definition is chosen, some important characteristics will be overlooked (Wagenfeld, Murray, Mohatt, & DeBruyn, 1994).

Rural areas differ from each other dramatically. For example, poverty rates in the nonmetropolitan South (22.4%) are twice as high as those in the nonmetropolitan Northeast (11.2%; Porter, 1989). Much research ignores important regional differences among rural people by averaging across rural regions or by generalizing from specific rural samples (Kelleher & Rickert, 1991). Areas differ significantly in need, availability, and use of mental health services (Kelleher et al., 1992). Several typologies have been proposed to characterize differences among rural areas. For example, the Economic Research Service of the U.S. Department of Agriculture developed a classification of nonmetropolitan areas on the basis of economy, land use, and the socioeconomic character of the population. In this system, seven types of nonmetropolitan counties were identified: farming dependent, specialized government, manufacturing, mining dependent, federal land, persistent poverty, and retirement (Ross, 1987). The myth of rural homogeneity has been a barrier to the development of programs and policies that meet the specific needs of rural people, who face a wide variety of stressors and resources.

Problems Facing Rural Youth and Their Families

Risk Factors Facing Rural Youth

Some of the most serious risk factors associated with higher rates of mental health problems in children and adolescents are poverty, minority ethnic status, parental psychopathology, physical or other maltreatment, a teenage parent, premature birth and low birth weight, parental divorce, and serious childhood illness (Tuma, 1989). Rural youth face a number of these risk factors. Regarding economic disadvantage, rural areas have traditionally relied on the economic bases of agriculture, resource extraction (e.g., mining), and low-technology manufacturing. In recent years, these industries have declined. The growing importance of service industries and high-technology manufacturing has left rural areas increasingly disadvantaged economically. Foreign competition and unfavorable exchange rates have made the situation worse. The net effect has been to intensify the chronic economic instability of rural areas (Tickamyer & Duncan, 1990). Rural poverty is invisible because these areas are off the frequently traveled roadways. Grinding poverty of rural areas is often overlooked because of the great natural beauty and the myth of rural tranquility (Harrington, 1962). Communities outside metropolitan areas contain approximately 20% of the U.S. population and 50% of its poor (Tickamyer & Duncan, 1990). In 1987, the poverty rate in nonmetropolitan areas was 16.9%, compared with 12.5% in metropolitan areas. The nonmetropolitan poverty rate was almost as high as that for central-city areas (18.6%). Between 1978 and 1987, the rate of increase in poverty in nonmetropolitan areas (25%) was greater than that for central cities (21%; Porter, 1989). Many rural areas have high rates of unemployment, substandard housing, malnutrition, and maternal and infant mortality (Forrest, 1988).

With regard to the risk factor of parental psychopathology, two recent epidemiological studies showed that rates of psychopathology differ relatively little between urban and rural adults, suggesting that residing in a rural area does not provide protection against mental disorder. In the recent Epidemiologic Catchment Area Study, lifetime prevalence of disorder, percentage of active cases, and percentage of cases in remission were compared for rural versus urban respondents. When summarizing across disorders, rates were virtually identical for urban and rural areas (Robins, Locke, & Regier, 1991). When rates of specific disorders were compared for urban and rural areas, a small number of differences emerged. Rates of alcohol abuse and/or dependence and cognitive deficit were significantly higher in rural areas. Rates of major depression and drug abuse/dependence were significantly higher in urban areas (Blazer et al., 1985). A criticism of epidemiologic catchment area data is that the rural counties surveyed were relatively close to large urban centers and contained urban and suburban population centers. Efforts were made to obtain data from more distinctly rural areas in a second large-scale epidemiologic study, the National Comorbidity Study (Kessler et al., 1994). In this study, rates of disorder did not differ significantly for residents of urban and rural areas. A single significant difference was found. In rural areas, the rate of comorbidity (individuals with multiple diagnoses) was significantly lower. Thus, it appears that rural children and youth face the same risks from genetically based mental illness and from being reared by parents suffering from mental disorder as do urban children.

The interplay of physical and psychological health is undisputed. Rural adults report greater rates of chronic medical conditions and disabilities, which are likely to have an adverse impact on their children. The health status of rural children also differs from that of metropolitan children. Injuries, drownings, and some chronic illnesses or disabilities are more frequent in nonmetropolitan areas. Rural children are less likely to be immunized and more likely to be uninsured, which may lead parents to delay or avoid medical treatment for their children's physical ailments (Norton & McManus, 1987).

Traditionally, rural families have been close-knit; extended families have pulled together to aid those family members in need. The traditional close-knit structure of the rural family has been declining, however (Forrest, 1988). During times of economic, psychological, or social stress, rural families may not be able to rely as heavily on traditional support systems as they have in the past.

Prevalence of Mental Health Problems Among Rural Youth

Limited data for rural children and adolescents and the difficulty of measuring mental health status in children make it hard to reach conclusions about the mental health of youth in rural areas (McManus, Newacheck, & Weader, 1990). Offord et al. (1987) compared published prevalence rates for psychiatric disorder among urban versus rural children and adolescents. They found a single significant difference, a higher rate of hyperactivity in urban children. A national survey of mental health among 4- to 16-year-olds was conducted by Achenbach, Howell, Quay, and Conners (1991). Half of the children were assessed at intake into mental health services and half were demographically matched nonreferred children ($N = 5{,}000$). Although significant sex, age, and social class differences were found, urban-rural differences in prevalence of problems and referral rates were minimal. Data based on parent and teacher symptom reports from an epidemiologic survey of children residing in Connecticut revealed a small number of urban-rural differences (Zahner, Jacobs, Freeman, & Trainor, in press). Among girls, higher rates of social withdrawal and behavioral disturbance were found among urban residents. Among boys, higher rates of emotional disturbance were found in urban areas. These differences were largely associated with economic and cultural differences rather than urbanization per se. Handal and Hopper (1985) examined the prevalence of aggression, moodiness, and learning problems among preschoolers. When the researchers controlled for socioeconomic status, no significant differences between urban and rural children emerged. Two epidemiologic studies of conduct disorder also showed no difference in prevalence rates for urban versus rural children and adolescents (Offord, Alder, & Boyle, 1986; Richards, Bear, Stewart, & Norman, 1992).

Recent research also documents an increasing prevalence of substance use among rural youth and their parents. In 1980, lifetime substance use in rural areas was two thirds that in urban areas. By 1990, however, rates of rural substance use had risen to match urban rates (U.S. General Accounting Office, 1990). The National Household Survey on Drug Abuse (U.S. Department of Health and Human Services, 1994) confirms that 12- to 17-year-olds from metropolitan and nonmetropolitan areas show similar rates of alcohol use during the past month (17.8% and 18.3%, respectively). National data show little difference between urban and rural use of alcohol and marijuana. Use of most other illegal drugs is greater in urban areas, although the differences between areas are narrowing (Kelleher et al., 1992).

The prevalence of problem drinking among rural adolescents from some regions is much greater than national averages (Alexander & Klassen, 1988; Sarvela & McClendon, 1987). Tremendous variation exists across rural areas in substance use and abuse, and some rural areas display evidence of serious problems with excessive use of alcohol by youth (Kelleher et al., 1992).

Loneliness appears to be a problem for rural youth, who are often geographically isolated from friends and opportunities to socialize. Woodward and Frank (1988) found high rates of loneliness among rural Nebraska youth and noted a significant negative correlation between loneliness and self-esteem. There is evidence that suicide rates are higher than national averages among rural youth. In a sample of more than 2,000 adolescents in rural Minnesota, suicide attempts were several times higher than the national average (Rosenberg, 1986).

Studies of behavior problems among rural youth indicate that the use of smokeless tobacco is particularly high. Rates of smokeless tobacco use are two to four times higher among rural than among urban male adolescents (Botvin, Baker, Tortu, Dusenbury, & Gessula, 1989; Lisnerski, McClary, Brown, Martin, & Jones, 1991). Another problem behavior, precocious sexual activity, is found at comparable rates among rural and urban youth (McCormick, 1986; National Center for Health Statistics, 1988; Yawn & Yawn, 1993). Twenty percent of adolescent pregnancies occur among rural teens (Yawn & Yawn, 1993).

Barriers to Accessing Mental Health Services in Rural Areas

Rural children, adolescents, and their families have poorer access to mental health services than their metropolitan peers (Petti & Leviton, 1986). In 1988, the U.S. Department of Health and Human Services estimated that 61% of the total rural population lived in designated psychiatric shortage areas (U.S. Congress, 1988). A survey of community mental health centers (CMHCs) revealed that only 4% provided programs and treatment specific to rural children and adolescents (Curry, Anderson, & Munn, 1980). Nonmetropolitan areas have difficulty placing specialists in their communities, and, once placed, turnover is high (Copans & Racusin, 1983). Contributing to the problems of recruitment and retention in rural areas are professional isolation, limited financial resources, lack of opportunity for continuing education and training experiences, lower income, and misconceptions about or lack of familiarity with rural life (Murray &

Keller, 1991). In nonmetropolitan public mental health facilities, psychiatrists make up a smaller percentage of total staff than their metropolitan counterparts (Jerrell & DiPasquale, 1984). Child psychiatrists are rarely found in rural areas. Less than 7% of child psychiatrists practice in communities of 10,000 to 50,000 population, and fewer than 0.1% are in private practice in communities of less than 10,000 (Roeske, 1984). Some states, especially those in the South, have severe shortages of child psychiatrists. Mississippi and Arkansas have fewer than 0.1 child psychiatrists per 100,000 children in nonmetropolitan areas (American Medical Association, 1990). Psychology, too, remains primarily an urban profession. Despite an increase in psychologists in nonmetropolitan areas, rural areas remain underserved in all regions of the country. Furthermore, psychologists in rural areas are less likely to be licensed and have less experience than psychologists in more urban locations (Sladen & Mozdzierz, 1989).

Barriers exist to delivery of mental health services within schools in rural areas. In a study of 50 rural school psychologists in five states, respondents reported that they were required to travel long distances between multiple schools in distant areas, often over hazardous terrain. Time spent traveling often resulted in limited time for professional contact with students (McLeskey, Waldron, Cummings, & Huebner, 1988). Because of the low tax base in rural communities, resources were frequently insufficient to fund school psychologists. School psychologists expressed frustration about trying to meet the emotional needs of students whose basic needs for food, shelter, supervision, and guidance were not being met at home. Rural school psychologists are often faced with strong resistance to change from rural students and their families. They must overcome attitudes of suspiciousness toward outsiders held by rural students, families, and, sometimes, school staff (McLeskey et al., 1988).

When psychiatric hospitalization resources are considered, rural residents are again at a marked disadvantage. In 1988, more than 95% of the most urbanized counties in major or medium-sized metropolitan areas had inpatient psychiatric services, in contrast to only 13% of rural counties (U.S. Congress, 1988). Rural areas are more dependent on psychiatric beds in general hospitals than are metropolitan areas. The closure of many rural community hospitals during the last decade has further restricted the number of psychiatric beds available to these communities (Werner, Knarr, & Stack, 1977). Nonmetropolitan communities, which encompass 28% of the nation's population, contain only 0.1% of the psychiatric beds. Rural populations have significantly less access to inpatient resources, and most rural residents must receive inpatient psychiatric care outside their community (Wagenfeld, Goldsmith, Stiles, & Manderscheid, 1988).

Attitudes Toward Service Use

Even in those few rural areas in which adequate providers, facilities, and resources are available, many children and adolescents do not receive appropriate mental health services because of the stigma attached to mental illness and mental health care (Kelleher et al., 1992). Controversy exists about whether rural residents have attitudes and values that distinguish them in important ways from those residing in urban areas. Although rural-urban differences in attitudes are not as great as once thought, several authors have suggested that rural values emphasize self-reliance, conservatism, a distrust of outsiders, religion, family loyalty, and fatalism (Flax, Wagenfeld, Ivens, & Weiss, 1979; Wagenfeld & Wagenfeld, 1981). Flax et al. have suggested that these attitudes are inimical to seeking help from formal caregivers for mental health problems. At special hearings conducted by the National Institute of Mental Health (NIMH) in 1989, the stigma surrounding mental illness was viewed as the greatest barrier to effective mental health care for rural people with mental illness (Kelleher et al., 1992). Rural families and youth are less likely to seek treatment than those who reside in urban areas, even when rates of psychopathology are similar (Cohen & Hesselbart, 1993; Linn & Husaini, 1987). When they do seek help, rural residents are more likely to seek help from clergy or general medical practitioners. Rural residents, especially farmers and those working in agriculture, are likely to delay seeking help for long periods and to turn to religion rather than to mental health professionals for assistance with emotional problems (Linn & Husaini, 1987). Many rural residents do not perceive a need for greater availability of mental health services, even when mental health resources are inadequate in their community (Flaskerud & Kuiz, 1984).

Service Delivery and Coordination Problems

The mental health needs of rural children continue to be met through a patchwork of programs and agencies (Petti & Leviton, 1986). Studies frequently have noted a lack of integration and coordination of services for rural youth. Cases in which a school counselor deals with school-related behavior problems, a community mental health center provides outpatient counseling, a court worker deals with abuse issues, and a social service worker manages family-related issues, all with little collaboration or integration, are the rule rather than the exception in rural America (Mohatt & Sharer-Mohatt, 1990). Several programs to improve integration have been initiated, such as the NIMH's Child and Adolescent Service System Program (CASSP), but few data on applications to rural populations have been published (Kelleher et al., 1992).

Federal Funding Policies as Contributors to Rural Access Problems

Rural mental health facilities are heavily dependent on public sector funds because of a relative deficit of third-party payers in rural areas (Jerrell, 1984). The Omnibus Budget Reconciliation Act of 1981 (OBRA) initiated a major shift in the funding environment for mental health services. OBRA authorized the Alcohol, Drug Abuse, and Mental Health Services Block Grant Program, which shifted the responsibility for deciding how to distribute federal mental health dollars to state mental health authorities. This initial shift to block grant funding resulted in a 25% reduction in federal support for mental health services (Andrulis & Mazade, 1983). Between 1980 and 1987, the amount of federal revenues directed toward mental health services declined by nearly 50% (Bergland, 1988).

The shift in control of federal mental health dollars to individual states has led CMHCs to focus their efforts on programs mandated by state mental health authorities and away from needs defined by their local communities. These changes placed increasing strain on rural CMHCs. CMHCs are often the sole source of mental health care in rural areas. Federal and state restructuring of mental health funding appears to have led to a shift in programmatic focus of CMHCs toward an emphasis on services to persons with serious mental illnesses and on fee-generating services (Andrulis & Mazade, 1983). As the block grant and fee-for-service shifts took place, rural mental health centers were forced to step away from their role as a multiservice agency accessible for general community use and into a narrower role of provider of services to persons who are seriously impaired or those able to pay (Hargrave & Melton, 1987). Focus on services to persons who are most seriously impaired, plus the lack of private caregiving alternatives, has created a situation in which many rural persons with less than chronic mental illness go unserved (Wagenfeld et al., 1994). Critics have argued that dependence on third-party payers rendered rural CMHCs unable to react proactively to the mental health needs engendered by the economic farm crisis of the 1980s (Bergland, 1988).

Rural CMHCs receive a majority of their funding from Medicaid fee-for-service programming (Mohatt, 1992). The Medicaid system operates on a medical model of specialized care, which is not appropriate for many rural areas (Mohatt, 1992). Because rural providers face chronic shortages of mental health professionals, they have great difficulty meeting the standards of the Medicaid program for mental health service providers. For example, to be reimbursed under Medicaid, all care delivered must be ordered by a physician. As a result, valuable physician time is used to authorize mental health providers to perform procedures (Wagenfeld et al., 1994). Innovative models of service delivery that use satellite clinics, mobile clinics, and limited inpatient facilities are often handicapped by certification or licensure requirements (Agency for Health Care Policy and Research, 1991). Medicaid regulations forbid reimbursement for treatment provided in churches, in homes, in some school settings, and by telephone, thus blocking effective delivery of care to children and adolescents with psychiatric and behavioral problems in rural areas (Petti & Leviton, 1986). In addition, Medicaid makes reimbursement of midlevel mental health practitioners difficult. This is particularly unfortunate for rural areas, in which master's-prepared professionals (psychologists, counselors, and social workers) provide a large proportion of mental health services (National Advisory Committee on Rural Health, 1991).

Many states have moved away from the model of freestanding CMHCs and toward systems of privatization and managed care.

Some state mental health authorities have implemented systems of managed care or capitated funding. The implications of these moves for rural areas have yet to be determined. It seems, however, that all of these systems require economies of scale that are not possible in rural areas with their sparse populations and paucity of providers (Wagenfeld et al., 1994). Rural America, where mental health and general health services are already in short supply due to poor accessibility and lack of human and fiscal resources, will require special attention in implementing any managed care system (Wagenfeld et al., 1994).

Examples of Innovative Mental Health Programs for Rural Youth

What are some ways to bypass barriers so that those in need of mental health services in rural areas can receive care? A number of intervention programs have been developed during the last decade, three of which are discussed here. Benswanger, Faust, and Brinker (1986) described the development and evaluation of a program for rural adolescents. This was a 2-year project that targeted 13,000 youth between the ages of 10 and 17 in one rural county. To plan and carry out the project, agency directors in the county (e.g., the chief juvenile probation officer) collaborated with a multidisciplinary team from an urban university. All aspects of the project were monitored by an ad hoc advisory committee consisting of 40 representatives and leaders from the rural community. The project involved five phases. The first of these was a school survey that generated involvement from the school, parents, and students in the identification of behavior problems. As part of the survey, community members were encouraged to suggest constructive solutions to the problems they identified. Recommendations were made regarding screening procedures and referrals, the types of services needed, and the availability of supplemental resources from the community.

The second phase of the project was a service use study. An inventory of existing community services and their use by adolescents and their families was conducted. The third phase of the project involved case reviews. Three of the community services (juvenile justice, mental health, and child welfare) worked together to review a sample of the most complex multiproblem cases in the study. Fourth, systems-oriented staffings (SOS) were conducted. These were monthly case conferences on the nine most complex cases in the sample. These SOSs included the adolescent client, the family, and the network of human service workers listed above. The purpose of these SOSs was to facilitate the sharing of information and to increase the coordination of services. The final phase in the Benswanger et al. (1986) project was to develop an advocacy plan that addressed future needs. This was a 5-year plan that focused each year on a different problem or need that had significant impact on the community. The goal for each year was to increase the services for families with a designated problem and to strengthen the capabilities of children, adolescents, and parents to advocate on their own. This project emphasized the cooperation of several community agencies as well as the adolescents and their families and was viewed as highly successful. Since the project has been completed, active community involvement has been sustained, and there has been an increase in commitment to youth in the county.

King and Kirschenbaum (1990) conducted an experimental evaluation of the Wisconsin Early Intervention (WEI) program. The program was brief and designed to assist rural elementary school children with social adjustment problems. The WEI included professional consultation between parents, teachers, and trained paraprofessionals leading social skills groups. In this study, 135 kindergartners through 4th graders from two rural elementary schools were randomly assigned to one of three conditions for 4 months. The full-service group included collaboration between parents and teachers, as well as a social skills group. The partial-service group included consultation between parents and teachers but no social skills group. The no-service group had no consultation or group activities. In both the full- and partial-service groups, the children showed increased competencies and decreased behavioral problems. Children in the full-service group, however, also showed a decrease in depressed mood, an increase in initiative and participation, and an increase in self-confidence, relative to the partial- and no-service groups. Thus, the combination of consultation and social skills training appeared to be the most effective.

The above programs were initiated through the school system, an important element of mental health services for children and adolescents. Several other programs, however, focus on the home environment. Such home-based programs emphasize maintaining the family structure and serve as an alternative to removing a troubled adolescent from the home.

Werrbach (1992) described such a rural home-based program for troubled adolescents who are at risk for removal from the home. He outlined five major assumptions underlying this program. First, family members were active participants in problem definition and goal setting. Second, the primary site for provision of services was in the home. Third, the whole family—not just the identified adolescent—was the primary unit of intervention. Fourth, the program emphasized the involvement of the nuclear family, the extended family, the neighborhood, and community resources. Last, the intervention was designed to address a wide range of problems facing the family, including problems in the domains of parenting, marital relations, school performance, employment, and relations with other agencies.

Those who participated in the program were compared with a demographically matched sample of adolescents who experienced an out-of-home placement. At the time of follow-up, those adolescents who remained in the home had fewer emotional and behavioral difficulties, had lower rates of hospitalization, and participated more successfully in substance use treatments than those adolescents who were removed from their homes. Werrbach (1992) suggested that family-centered home-based programs need to be refined to work with more difficult family situations, for example, families in which substance abuse is prevalent, blended families, and families in which sexual abuse has occurred.

All the intervention programs for rural families described above emphasize the involvement of the child or adolescent, the family, and community service sectors such as child welfare, mental health, public health, education, and the juvenile justice system (Beachler, 1990; England & Cole, 1992). New interventions for rural families are being designed and evaluated with promising results. The majority of these interventions are focused on the family system. It is assumed that the family, with the collaboration of a variety of community agencies, is the best place for the child or adolescent to be treated.

Directions for the Future

A number of barriers prevent rural youth and their families from receiving prompt and appropriate mental health care. These barriers must be approached at multiple levels. At the legislative level, efforts should be made to approve waivers or change mandates about the appropriate location of rural mental health care delivery, so that sites other than hospitals may bill for mental health services. For example, cooperative billing of Medicaid by hospitals for mental health services provided in rural school districts has improved access for rural youth (Feild, Kirby, & Hudson, 1990). Policies regarding health care providers who may bill Medicaid for services rendered should also be reexamined to allow midlevel professionals to provide needed mental health services in rural areas (e.g., master's-prepared psychologists, social workers, and counselors). Appropriate consultation with child psychiatrists and Ph.D. psychologists could be made available through teleconferencing or periodic in-person consultations.

Improving access to affordable health insurance is critical in improving access to mental health prevention and treatment services. A variety of strategies for expanding access to health insurance have been discussed, including high-risk pools, school-based grouping, and Medicaid expansions (Castle, 1991; Cunningham & Monheit, 1990).

Special efforts should be made to recruit and retain mental health professionals in rural communities. Some communities offer special bonuses or loan forgiveness programs to encourage physicians to locate in their community. The same incentives should be directed at recruitment of mental health professionals. Retention of professionals in rural communities may be enhanced using various strategies. For example, funds could be provided by the community for continuing education experiences (Petti & Leviton, 1986). Efforts should be made to introduce new mental health providers to key members of the community and to integrate them into the life of the community (e.g., see Telesford, Chapter 4 in this volume). Links to existing community resources should be established early to foster acceptance of the professional into the community. For example, informational presentations to service clubs, 4-H members, and Future Farmers of America groups, as well as meetings with county extension agents and school principals, may all be useful in easing the entry of a mental health professional into a rural community.

General medical settings are often relied on by rural families for assistance with mental health problems. The quality of mental health services in such settings needs to be improved through educational and training opportunities (Wagenfeld, 1990). Improved training in early detection, diagnosis, referral options, and appropriate psychopharmacological treatment should be provided to rural practitioners. Consultation with psychiatrists and psychologists should be available for rural physicians through regional hospitals, mental health centers, and/or universities, perhaps through teleconferencing.

Greater use should be made of paraprofessionals to extend the range of rural mental health services (Kelleher et al., 1992). With adequate supervision, peer counselors provide an inexpensive and cost-effective way to decrease high-risk behaviors and reduce stress in adolescents. Such a program of paraprofessional outreach was recently implemented through primary medical care settings in rural Mississippi (Lower Mississippi Delta Development Commission, 1990).

Conclusion

No single solution will solve the problems facing disturbed children and adolescents in rural America. Innovative financing; recruitment and retention of mental health professionals in rural communities; greater integration and coordination of mental health agencies, general medical settings, schools, juvenile courts, and social services; and use of midlevel professionals and paraprofessionals should all be vigorously pursued to meet the mental health needs of this nation's rural youth.

References

Achenbach, T., Howell, C. T., Quay, H. C., & Conners, H. C. (1991). National survey of problems and competencies among 4-16 year olds: Parents' reports for normative and clinical samples. *Monographs of the Society for Research in Child Development, 56*(3, Serial No. 225).

Agency for Health Care Policy and Research. (1991). *Delivering essential health care services in rural areas: An analysis of alternative models* (AHCPR No. 91-0017). Rockville, MD: U.S. Department of Health and Human Services.

Alexander, C. S., & Klassen, A. C. (1988). Drug use and illnesses among eighth grade students in rural schools. *Public Health Reports, 103,* 394-399.

American Medical Association. (1990). *AMA Physicians Masterfile, Community Hospital File, U.S. Dept. of Commerce, Bureau of Economic Analyses, U.S. Bureau of the Census.* Unpublished manuscript.

Andrulis, D. P., & Mazade, N. A. (1983). American mental health policy: Changing directions in the 80s. *Hospital and Community Psychiatry, 34,* 601-606.

Beachler, M. (1990). The mental health services program for youth. *Journal of Mental Health Administration, 17*(1), 115-121.

Benswanger, E. G., Faust, M. J., & Brinker, W. B. (1986). Human services for adolescents in a rural community: A systems perspective. *Journal of Rural Community Psychology, 7*(1), 3-24.

Bergland, B. (1988). Rural mental health: Report of the National Action Commission of the mental health of rural Americans. *Journal of Rural Community Psychology, 9*(2), 29-39.

Blazer, D., George, L. K., Landerman, R., Pennybacker, M., Melville, M. L., Woodbury, M., Manton, K. G., Jordan, K., & Locke, B. Z. (1985). Psychiatric disorders: A rural/urban comparison. *Archives of General Psychiatry, 42,* 653-656.

Botvin, G. J., Baker, E., Tortu, S., Dusenbury, L., & Gessula, J. (1989). Smokeless tobacco use among adolescents: Correlates and concurrent predictors. *Journal of Developmental and Behavioral Pediatrics, 10*(4), 181-186.

Castle, M. (1991). *Hearing on health care system reform.* Washington, DC: National Governors' Association.

Cohen, P., & Hesselbart, C. S. (1993). Demographic factors in the use of children's mental health services. *American Journal of Public Health, 83,* 49-52.

Conger, R. D., Elder, G. H., Jr., Lorenz, F. O., Simons, R. L., & Whitbeck, L. B. (1994). *Families in troubled times: Adapting to change in rural America.* Hawthorne, NY: Aldine.

Copans, S., & Racusin, R. (1983). Child psychiatry perspective: Rural child psychiatry. *Journal of the American Academy of Child Psychiatry, 22,* 184-190.

Costello, E. J. (1989). Developments in child psychiatric epidemiology. *Journal of the American Academy of Child and Adolescent Psychiatry, 28,* 836-841.

Cunningham, P. J., & Monheit, A. C. (1990, Winter). Insuring the children: A decade of change. *Health Affairs, 9,* 76-89.

Curry, J. F., Anderson, D. R., & Munn, D. E. (1980). Psychological consultation to rural development centers. *Journal of Rural Community Psychology, 1*(2), 24-33.

Dougherty, D. (1988). Children's mental health problems and services: Current federal efforts and policy implications. *American Psychologist, 43,* 808-812.

England, M. J., & Cole, R. F. (1992). Building systems of care for youth with serious mental illness: Special section: Treatment and service systems for adolescents. *Hospital and Community Psychiatry, 43*(6), 630-633.

Feild, C., Kirby, R., & Hudson, H. (1990). Medicaid and medically related special education in a rural state. *Clinical Research, 38,* 944A.

Flaskerud, J. H., & Kuiz, F. J. (1984). Determining the need for mental health services in rural areas. *American Journal of Community Psychology, 12,* 497-510.

Flax, J. W., Wagenfeld, M. O., Ivens, R. E., & Weiss, R. J. (1979). *Mental health and rural America: An overview and annotated bibliography* (DHEW Publication No. ADM 78-753). Rockville, MD: National Institute of Mental Health.

Forrest, S. (1988). Suicide and the rural adolescent. *Adolescence, 23*(90), 341-347.

Handal, P. J., & Hopper, S. (1985). Relationship of sex, social class and rural/urban locale to preschoolers' AML scores. *Psychological Reports, 57*(3), 707-713.

Hargrave, D. S., & Melton, G. B. (1987). Block grants and rural mental health services. *Journal of Rural Community Psychology, 8*(1), 4-11.

Harrington, M. (1962). *The other America.* New York: Penguin.

Jerrell, J. M. (1984). The effects of service policy and funding shifts on rural community-based mental health services. *Journal of Rural Community Psychology, 5*(2), 3-17.

Jerrell, J. M., & DiPasquale, S. A. (1984). Staffing patterns in rural health services for children and adolescents. *Community Mental Health Journal, 20,* 212-222.

Kelleher, K. J., & Rickert, V. I. (1991). Rural adolescent alcohol use: An overview. *Journal of Rural Health, 7,* 293-299.

Kelleher, K. J., Taylor, J. L., & Rickert, V. I. (1992). Mental health services for rural children and adolescents. *Clinical Psychology Review, 12*(8), 841-852. (Special issue: Child and adolescent mental health)

Kessler, R. C., McGonagle, K. A., Zhoa, S., Nelson, C. B., Hughes, M., Eshleman, S., Wittchen, H., & Kendler, K. S. (1994). Lifetime and 12-month prevalence of DSM-III-R psychiatric disorders in the United States. *Archives of General Psychiatry, 51,* 8-19.

King, C. A., & Kirschenbaum, D. S. (1990). An experimental evaluation of a school-based program for children at risk: Wisconsin Early Intervention. *Journal of Community Psychology, 18*(2), 167-177.

Knitzer, J. (1982). *Unclaimed children: The failure of public responsibility to children and adolescents in need of mental health services.* Washington, DC: Children's Defense Fund.

Linn, J. G., & Husaini, B. A. (1987). Determinants of psychological depression and coping behaviors of Tennessee farm residents. *Journal of Community Psychology, 15,* 503-512.

Lisnerski, D. D., McClary, C. L., Brown, T. L., Martin, J. P., & Jones, D. R. (1991). Demographic and predictive correlates of smokeless tobacco use in elementary school children. *American Journal of Health Promotion, 5*(6), 426-431.

Lower Mississippi Delta Development Commission. (1990). *Final report: The delta initiative.* Memphis, TN: Author.

McCormick, N. B. (1986). Encouraging rural youth to be sexually responsible. *Journal of Sex Education and Therapy, 12*(1), 28-31.

McLeskey, J., Waldron, N. L., Cummings, J. A., & Huebner, E. S. (1988). A descriptive study of psychological service delivery in selected rural school settings. *School Psychology International, 9*(2), 91-97.

McManus, M. A., Newacheck, P. W., & Weader, R. A. (1990). Metropolitan and nonmetropolitan adolescents: Differences in demographics and health characteristics. *Journal of Rural Health, 6,* 39-51.

Mohatt, D. F. (1992, June). *Rural mental health today.* Testimony given to the National Advisory Committee on Rural Health, Kalamazoo, MI.

Mohatt, D. F., & Sharer-Mohatt, K. (1990). *At risk rural youth: A community psychology approach to identification and intervention.* Paper presented at the Second International Rural Mental Health and Addictions Conference, North Bay, Ontario, Canada.

Murray, J. D., & Keller, P. A. (1991). Psychology and rural America. *American Psychologist, 46*(3), 220-231.

National Advisory Committee on Rural Health. (1991). *Fourth annual report to the secretary of health and human services.* Rockville, MD: Office of Rural Health Policy.

National Center for Health Statistics. (1988). *National survey of family growth.* Hyattsville, MD: U.S. Department of Health and Human Services.

National Mental Health Association. (1988). *Report of the National Action Commission on the mental health of rural Americans.* Washington, DC: Author.

Norton, C. H., & McManus, M. A. (1987). Background tables on demographic characteristics, health status, and health services utilization. *Health Services Research, 23,* 725-864.

Offord, D. R., Alder, R. J., Boyle, M. H. (1986). Prevalence and sociodemographic correlates of conduct disorder. *American Journal of Social Psychiatry, 6*(4), 272-278. (Special issue: Psychiatric epidemiology)

Offord, D. R., Boyle, M. H., Szatmari, P., Rae-Grant, N. I., Links, P. S., Cadman, D. T., Byles, J. A., Crawford, J. W., Blum, H. M., Byrne, C., Thomas, H., & Woodward, C. A. (1987). Ontario child health study. *Archives of General Psychiatry, 44,* 832-855.

Omnibus Budget Reconciliation Act of 1981 (OBRA), Pub. L. No. 97-35, 95 Stat. 357.

Petti, T. A., & Leviton, L. C. (1986). Re-thinking rural mental health services for children and adolescents. *Journal of Public Health Policy, 7*(1), 58-77.

Porter, K. H. (1989). *Poverty in rural America: A national overview.* Washington, DC: Center on Budget and Public Priorities.

Richards, H. C., Bear, G. G., Stewart, A. L., & Norman, A. D. (1992). Moral reasoning and classroom conduct: Evidence of a curvilinear relationship. *Merrill Palmer Quarterly, 38*(2), 176-190.

Robins, L., Locke, B. Z., & Regier, D. A. (1991). An overview of psychiatric disorders in America. In L. N. Robins & D. A. Regier (Eds.), *Psychiatric disorders in America* (pp. 328-366). New York: Free Press.

Roeske, N. C. A. (1984). *National survey of child psychiatrists: Their location, patient population, and sources of income.* Washington, DC: American Academy of Child and Adolescent Psychiatry.

Rosenberg, J. (1986). *Policy forum: The personal stress problems of farmers and rural Americans.* Rockville, MD: National Institute of Mental Health.

Ross, P. J. (1987). Remarks on the development of a policy-oriented classification of non-metropolitan counties. In A. E. Luloff (Ed.), *Rural people and places: A symposium on typologies* (Publication No. 47, pp. 177-180). University Park, PA: Northeast Regional Center for Rural Development.

Sarvela, P. D., & McClendon, E. J. (1987). Early adolescent alcohol abuse in rural northern Michigan. *Community of Mental Health Journal, 23,* 183-191.

Sladen, B. J., & Mozdzierz, G. J. (1989). Distribution of psychologists in underserved areas: Changes over time, 1970-1981. *Professional Psychology Research and Practice, 20,* 244-247.

Taube, C. A., & Barrett, S. A. (Eds.). (1985). *Mental health: United States, 1985* (DHHS Publication No. ADM 85-1378). Washington, DC: U.S. Department of Health and Human Services.

Tickamyer, A. R., & Duncan, C. M. (1990). Poverty and opportunity structure in rural America. *Annual Review of Sociology, 16,* 67-86.

Tuma, J. M. (1989). Mental health services for children. *American Psychologist, 44,* 188-199.

U.S. Bureau of the Census. (1989). *Statistical abstract of the United States: 1989* (104th ed.). Washington, DC: Government Printing Office.

U.S. Congress. (1988). *A report to Congress: Health Professions Reauthorization Act of 1988* [Title VI of Pub. L. No. 100-607, 102 Stat. 3048]. Washington, DC: Author.

U.S. Congress, Office of Technology Transfer, Health Program. (1989). *Defining "rural" areas: Impact on health care policy and research.* Washington, DC: Government Printing Office.

U.S. Department of Health and Human Services. (1994). *Preliminary estimates from the 1993 National Household Survey on Drug Abuse* (Advance Rep. No. 7). Washington, DC: Author.

U.S. General Accounting Office. (1990). *Rural drug abuse: Prevalence, relation to crime, and programs*. Washington, DC: Author.

Wagenfeld, M. O. (1990). Mental health and rural America: A decade review. *Journal of Rural Health, 6*, 507-522.

Wagenfeld, M. O., Goldsmith, H. F., Stiles, D., & Manderscheid, R. W. (1988). Inpatient mental health services in metropolitan and non-metropolitan counties. *Journal of Rural Community Psychology, 9*(2), 13-23.

Wagenfeld, M. O., Murray, J. D., Mohatt, D. F., & DeBruyn, J. C. (1994). *Mental health and rural America: 1980-1993: An overview and annotated bibliography* (NIH Publication No. 94-3500). Washington, DC: Government Printing Office.

Wagenfeld, M. O., & Wagenfeld, J. K. (1981). Values, culture, and the delivery of mental health services in rural areas. In M. O. Wagenfeld (Ed.), *Perspectives on rural mental health* (New Directions for Mental Health Services Series, Vol. 9). San Francisco: Jossey-Bass.

Werner, A., Knarr, F. A., & Stack, J. M. (1977). Psychiatric services in a rural general hospital. *International Journal of Psychiatry in Medicine, 8*, 25-34.

Werrbach, G. B. (1992). A study of home-based services for families of adolescents. *Child and Adolescent Social Work Journal, 9*(6), 505-523.

Woodward, J. C., & Frank, B. D. (1988). Rural adolescent loneliness and coping strategies. *Adolescence, 23*(91), 559-565.

Yawn, B. P., & Yawn, R. A. (1993). Adolescent pregnancies in rural America: A review of the literature and strategies for primary prevention. *Family and Community Health, 16*(1), 36-45.

Zahner, G. E. P., Jacobs, J. H., Freeman, D. H., & Trainor, K. F. (in press). Rural-urban child psychopathology in a northeastern U.S. state: 1986-1989. *Journal of the American Academy of Child and Adolescent Psychiatry*.

Index

ABCX Model of family stress, 79-88
  application of, 80
  categories of variables, 80
  family adaptation category of, 81
  family appraisal category of, 81, 86-87
  family life events category of, 80-82
  family resources category of, 80-85
  heuristic value of for research, 79-80
  implications of for intervention with families, 79
  limitations of, 79
Adoptees:
  as percentage of U.S. population, 193
  older children as, 198, 200
Adoption:
  family appraisal of, 198-200, 205
  family communication about, 198-200
  reunions, 202-203
  searching, 200-204
  searching precipitants, 201-202
  See also Adoptive families; Adopted individuals
Adoptive families, 43, 192-206, 212
  choice of facilitating agent by, 193, 197
  degree of openness between birth and adoptive parents, 193-198
  diversity among, 192-193
  mental health delivery services to, 204-206
  mental health issues concerning, 193-204
  mental health policies and, 210-212
  mental health research concerning, 204-206
  See also Adoption; Adoptees
Advocacy movement, 105
African Americans:
  and fictive kin as family, 119
  increase in U.S. population of, 167
  view of illness and health, 169
Alcohol, Drug Abuse, and Mental Health Services Block Grant Program, 227
Alcoholics Anonymous, 68
Annie E. Casey Foundation, 63
Asian Americans/Pacific Islanders:
  increase in U.S. population of, 167
  view of illness and health, 169
Assessment approaches, 31-32
  culturally appropriate, 31
  individualized services and, 31

Beavers Interactional Style Scale, 130
Blended families, 43

Card Sort Procedure, 128
Carnegie Corporation of New York, 52

Case management/service coordination:
- comprehensive model of, 30
- definition of, 29
- future of, 30
- minimal model of, 20
- variety of, 30

Catastrophic stressors, 79

Center for Mental Health Services, 97

Child and Adolescent Service System Program (CASSP), 10, 24, 76, 85, 165, 227
- principles, 97
- program objectives, 76-77
- services, 77
- support, 102
- *See also* Child and Adolescent Service System Program (CASSP) cultural competence model

Child and Adolescent Service System Program (CASSP) cultural competence model, 166-167, 173-178
- adapting to diversity in, 175
- attitude in, 175-176
- conducting cultural self-assessment in, 174
- cultural competence values of, 173-175
- elements of, 175-177
- implications of, 187
- incorporating cultural knowledge in, 174-175
- organizational implications of, 183-186
- policy in, 176
- practice in, 176
- structure in, 176-177
- understanding dynamics of difference in, 174
- valuing diversity in, 173-174
- *See also* Cultural competence continuum

Child and Youth Mental Health Program, Robert Wood Johnson Foundation, 11, 32

Child care centers:
- need for publicly supported, 55
- unenforced uniform standards for, 55

Child care professionals, improvement in training of, 55

Children/adolescents with mental/emotional disorders:
- child-focused treatment for, 18
- community-based services for, 18, 96
- denial of in, 1
- excessive hospitalization of, 3, 18
- families' role in treatment of, 18
- family-focused treatment for, 18
- family-professional relationship in treating, 76
- inappropriate hospitalization of, 3
- inappropriateness of mental health services for, 1
- institutionalized care of, 18, 96, 218
- lack of adequate insurance coverage for, 1
- lack of early identification of, 1
- lack of early intervention efforts for, 1
- mental health system failure and, 75
- percentage using mental health services, 1
- prevalence of, 1, 75, 218
- scarcity of mental health services for, 1, 218
- scarcity of specialists for, 218
- stigma of, 1
- use rate of mental health services for, 1
- *See also* Mental health services for children; Rural children and youth

Clinical Rating Scale, 130

Colorado Family Assessment (CFA), 128, 147, 148, 150-160
- advantages of, 158-160
- as diagnostic instrument, 159
- as insider assessment, 147
- as new instrument, 150
- child rearing assessment, 155
- first-person self-report measures, 152-154
- levels of analysis, 152-158
- procedure, 152
- relational data in, 152
- software program for, 152

third-person self-report measures, 154-156
transactional family measures, 152, 156-158
Community mental health programs, implementing, 63-74. *See also* Mental Health Initiative for Urban Children
Competence paradigm, 91
advantages to, 77-78
as professional practice framework, 79, 91
as research framework, 79, 91
benefits of, 78
empirical support for, 78
versus pathology paradigm, 77-78
Component-based system, 25
Contextual Model of Family Stress, 135
Coping behaviors, 82. *See also* Coping responses; Coping strategies
Coping effectiveness:
self-efficacy and, 83
self-esteem and, 83
wellness and, 83
Coping Health Inventory for Parents (CHIP), 127
Coping resources, 82
Coping responses, 83
Coping strategies:
behavioral, 84
cognitive, 84
emotional, 84
social, 84-85
Corporal punishment, 54, 55
Cultural competence continuum, 177-178
cultural blindness on, 177
cultural competence on, 177
cultural destructiveness on, 177
cultural incapacity on, 177
cultural precompetence on, 177
cultural proficiency on, 177
developmental process of, 177
goal of, 177
usefulness of, 178
Cultural competence model. *See* Child and Adolescent Service System Program (CASSP) cultural competence model
Cultural diversity:
and barriers to cultural pluralism, 171-173
changing U.S. demographics and, 167
cultural paranoia and, 170
didactic approaches for learning about, 182
experiential techniques for learning about, 182
health and human service delivery systems and, 165
health professionals and, 165
interactive approaches for learning about, 182
paranorm and, 170
values and belief systems of people of color, 168-171
Culturally appropriate service delivery, rationale for, 166-173
Cultural pluralism, barriers to, 171-173

Denial:
of children's emotional disorders, 1
Dual career families, 43

Educational services, family:
as part of comprehensive support programs, 29
purpose of, 27
types of, 27
Education and Human Services Consortium, 24
Education of All Handicapped Children Act of 1975, 23, 89, 100
Emotional disorders:
prevalence of in children, 1
Epidemiologic Catchment Area Study, 221

Family:
adoptive, 43
blended, 43
cultural variability and, 118
definition of "normal," 43
definitions, 118-119, 146
dual career, 43
ethnic variability and, 118
implications of prevalent definitions of for clinical intervention, 46

implications of prevalent definitions of for prevention, 46
implications of prevalent definitions of for research, 46
implications of prevalent definitions of for social policy, 46
in North American psychology, 42-46
nuclear, 43, 44, 191-192
parental-relatives with children, 43
problems with prevalent definitions of, 44-45
single-parent, 43
Family, happy:
traits of, 149-150
Family, paths to becoming, 191, 192
adopting children, 192
artificial insemination, 192
foster parenting, 192
surrogate parenting, 192
See also Adoptive families; Foster families
Family Adaptability and Cohesion Evaluation Scales (FACES), 130, 136, 152
Family adaptation, 87-88
changes characterizing, 88
criteria of, 87-88
definition of coping in, 137
Family Adjustment and Adaptation Response (FAAR) Model, 135
major constructs of, 135
resources in, 136
Family and health research, theoretical frameworks for, 129-138
research questions, 129
Family appraisal, 86-87
family coherence and, 87
family meaning and, 87
family paradigm and, 86
models of serious emotional disturbance and, 87
variables influencing, 86
Family assessment:
and understanding individual behavior, 146
complexity of, 146
family functioning and, 145-146
individual level of, 147
relational level of, 147
transactional level of, 147
See also Family assessment procedures
Family Assessment Device, 152
Family Assessment Measure, 152
Family assessment procedures:
analysis of physiological data, 147
family member self-reports, 147
insider, 146, 147
laboratory studies, 147
outsider, 146
See also Colorado Family Assessment (CFA)
Family boundaries:
definition of, 132
external, 132-133
internal, 132
Family-Centered Intensive Case Management, 29, 32
Family centeredness, 35
Family-centered service:
addressing family needs in, 21-22
barriers to development of, 85
broad conception of possible interventions and, 25
characteristics of, 19-24
cognitive coping strategies and, 21-22
defining principles of, 20
definition of, 20
developing, 19
family choice and, 25
family context and, 20-21
family-defined needs and, 25
family participation in planning/evaluation, 23-24
family strengths and, 25
family support in, 22
family systems theory and, 20
flexibility and, 26
individualized care and, 24-26, 31
putting into practice, 24-26
See also Family-centered system
Family-centered service approach, implications of:
assessment approaches, 31-32
choosing relevant/acceptable dependent variables, 34-35

for program planning/practice, 31-34
for research, 31, 34-36
range of services, 32-33
service and program flexibility, 34
studying partially implemented concept, 35-36
training and human resource issues, 33
Family-centered system, 26-30
case-management/service coordination, 29-30
educational services, 27
family-focused therapeutic services, 26-27
family support services, 28-29
Family coherence, 87
Family cohesion:
as curvilinear, 130
as resource, 136-137
assessing, 130
definition of, 130
health outcomes and, 130
problems with too much, 130
Family communication theory, 129, 133-134
affective aspects of, 134
communication deviance, 133
description of, 133
expressed emotion, 133
instrumental aspects of, 134
quality of and health outcomes, 133-134
Family competencies:
affective, 84
behavioral, 84
cognitive, 84
social, 84
Family data classification typology, 125-128
level I data, 125
level III data, 127-128, 130, 131, 132, 133, 134, 137, 138, 139
level II data, 125-127, 130, 135, 136, 137, 139
Family empowerment:
as goal of parental-professional partnership models, 104
choice as critical to, 106-107
competence, 105, 106, 112
descriptions of, 104-105
model of, 107-111
resources, 105, 106, 112
self-efficacy, 105, 106, 112
Family Environment Scale (FES), 130, 136, 152
Family Evaluation Scales, 152
Family flexibility, 154
as family competence, 131
curvilinear view of, 131
definition of, 130-131
family functioning and, 131
linear view of, 131
Family-focused therapeutic services:
as part of comprehensive support program, 29
benefits of, 26
goal of, 26
home-based, 26-27
negative consequences of, 26
therapeutic foster care, 27
Family functioning, adequate:
criteria for, 149
Family functioning, healthy:
characteristics of, 148-150
comparative approaches to conceptualization of, 151
flexibility and change, 148, 154, 157
identity processes, 148, 154
information processing, 148, 154, 155
potential uses of, 158-160
role structuring, 148-149, 154, 157
Family health:
conceptualizing as familial health, 120
conceptualizing as family functioning patterns, 120
differing perspectives on, 120-121
dysfunctional, 120
optimal, 120-121
systems perspective linking individual health and, 121-123
transactional, 121
Family Inventory of Life Events and Changes, 126
Family life events, 81-82
examples of, 81
Family meaning, 86

Family paradigm, 86
Family patterns:
defined by ethnicity, 191
defined by path to becoming family, 191, 192
defined by structure, 191
See also Adoptive families; Foster families
Family reality:
versus family Reality, 128
Family research:
and measurement of family-level constructs, 125-128
and need for longitudinal studies, 124
and need for studies of ethnically diverse families, 124
biopsychosocial paradigm, 117-118
clinical reports, 123
empirical literature, 123-124
experimental, 124
issues concerning, 123-128
personal descriptive accounts, 123
recommendations for future, 138-140
Family resources, 82-85
coping behaviors, 82
coping resources, 82
coping responses, 83
coping strategies, 84-85
for coping with serious emotional disturbances of child, 83-85
functional family coping, 82
levels of, 82-83
Family stress theory, 129, 134-138
coping behaviors, 135, 137
family adaptation, 135
family behaviors, 135
family meanings, 135
parental coping, 137
pileup of demands, 135, 137-138
resources, 135, 136-137
Family support services:
as part of comprehensive support programs, 29
cash assistance, 28-29
clusters of, 29
family advocacy groups/organizations, 28
family self-help groups/organizations, 28
family support groups/organizations, 28
food, 28
home maintenance, 28
purpose of, 28
respite care, 28
transportation, 28
Family system:
definition of, 118
family functioning in, 118, 119
family structure in, 118
purpose of, 97
Family systems theory, 129-133
boundaries, 132-133
cohesion, 130
flexibility, 130-131
Family violence, 51-52
against children, 51
against teenagers, 51
children against parents, 51
children against siblings, 51
husband against wife, 51
in poor families, 52
Federation of Families, 89
Fetal alcohol syndrome, 53
Foster care, needs for improvement in, 55, 210. *See also* Foster families
Foster care, therapeutic, 27
Foster children, adjustment to removal of, 208-209
Foster families, 206-210, 212
adoption placement decisions and, 206
as path to family status, 192, 206
biological children of, 207-208, 209
mental health policies and, 210-212
mental health research and, 209-210
mental health service delivery to, 209-210
number of in United States, 206
provision of respite care for, 210
research on, 206-207
role of, 206
supportive services for, 209
See also Foster family adjustment, postplacement

Foster family adjustment, postplacement, 207-208
Foster parenting, unique qualities of, 210
Functional family coping, characteristics of, 82

Genetic/prenatal risks:
in disadvantaged ethnic groups, 54

Head Start, 68, 70
Health:
definitions of, 119-121
dimensions of adult, 120
multidimensional nature of, 119
See also Family health
Health care reform implementation challenges, 13-14
collaboration among sectors and systems, 13
consumer advocacy, 12
lack of infrastructure, 13
Medicaid's future and, 14
monitoring mechanisms and, 14
needed public/private sector investments, 13
organized systems of care, 14
quality assurance mechanisms and, 14
risk adjustment mechanisms and, 14
Health care reform issues for children, 2-6
exclusionary insurance coverage, 4
family context, 3
fragmented mental health delivery system, 5-6
high consumer cost sharing, 4
insurance benefit problems, 3-4
uniqueness of population, 2
Health care reform principles for children, 6-13
broad range of services coverage, 7-10
organized systems of care, 10-11
Health needs, unmet:
foster children and, 53
infant mortality and, 53
institutionalized children and, 53-54
maternal deaths and, 53
poor childhood health and, 53
prenatal care and, 53
teenage pregnancies and, 53
Health Security Act of 1993, Clinton Administration's, 11-13
comprehensive coverage, 12
elimination of exclusions, 12
expanded coverage for mental health services, 12
range of services expansion, 12
universal coverage in, 12
Healthy family functioning. *See* Family functioning, healthy
Hispanics:
increase in U.S. population of, 167
view of illness and health, 169
Homebuilders, 26, 27
Home visitor programs, 55

Identification of emotional disorders, early:
lack of among children, 1
Illinois Department of Mental Health, 29
Impact on Family Scales, 135
Individualized care, 31
definition of, 25
family-centered service and, 24-26
wraparound services and, 25
Individuals With Disabilities Education Act of 1990 (IDEA), 23, 89
Insurance coverage, adequate:
lack of for children, 1
International Year of the Child, 53
Intervention efforts, early:
lack of among children, 1
Intervention strategies, effective, 88-91
clinical, 90-91
educational programs, 88-89, 90
nonclinical, 88-90
support groups, 88, 89

Latchkey children, 55

MATESIM, 159
Medicaid, 32, 232
future of in reformed health care system, 14
used by rural families, 219

Medicare:
used by rural families, 219
Mental disorders:
biological model of, 51
social learning model of, 51
Mental Health and Substance Abuse Working Group, Clinton Task Force on Health Care Reform, 6, 7, 10
Mental Health Initiative for Urban Children:
experience gained from, 74
female-headed households and, 66
goal of, 63
in Boston, 63
in Houston, 63
in Miami, 63
in Richmond, VA, 63
long-range vision of, 63
parental involvement in, 71
sites, 69
See also Mental Health Initiative for Urban Children, comprehensive outreach strategy of; Mental Health Initiative for Urban Children, recognition of community strengths in; Mental Health Initiative for Urban Children, recognition of individual strengths in
Mental Health Initiative for Urban Children, comprehensive outreach strategy of, 64, 68-74
appropriate logistical planning for meeting, 68-70
community leader identification, 68
incentives, 70
intensive follow-up, 68, 71
meeting site selection, 69
meeting time and date, 69
parent involvement in collaborative process, 72
parents' role in context of empowerment process, 73-74
presentation of family-friendly initiative, 68, 70-71
publicizing meeting, 70
respecting geographical boundaries, 68-69
support group development, 71-72
Mental Health Initiative for Urban Children, recognition of community strengths in, 64-66, 74
churches, 65
community-based organizations, 65
schools, 65-66
Mental Health Initiative for Urban Children, recognition of individual strengths of women in, 64, 65, 66-68, 74
community involvement, 67
employment possibilities, 67
sobriety, 67-68
spiritual, 66
support systems, 66
valuing of education, 66-67
Mental health services for children:
and collateral services, 9
case management, 9
changes in conceptualization of, 18
changes in development of technologies in, 18
child-focused treatment, 18
community-based, 18
family-focused treatment, 18
fiscal barriers to, 19
fragmentation among various service systems and, 19
home-based, 8, 9
inaccessibility of to community-based programs, 19
inappropriateness of, 1
inpatient/residential, 7, 9, 18
intensive nonresidential, 7-8, 9
lack of community-based programs and, 19
lack of coordination among various service systems and, 19
outpatient, 7
policy barriers to, 19
role of family in, 18
scarcity of, 1
therapeutic family homes, 9
use of behavioral aides, 8-9
use rates, 1
See also Family-centered services; Rural mental health services for youth

Minority youth and families, mental health service delivery for:
  assessing environmental stressors in, 180
  culturally blind approach to, 179-180
  culturally competent professional in, 180-182
  culturally sensitive individualized services and, 180
  identifying barriers to, 178-179
  program development suggestions for, 185-186
  service provision and, 179-183
Multilevel family evaluation, computer-based procedure for. *See* Colorado Family Assessment

Narcotics Anonymous, 68
National Alliance for the Mentally Ill Children and Adolescents Network (NAMI-CAN), 89
National Comorbidity Study, 222
National Governor's Association, 24
National Household Survey on Drug Abuse, 223
National Institute of Mental Health (NIMH), 10
  1989 hearings, 226
  study funded by, 108
Native Americans/Alaskan Natives:
  culture as right-brain functioning, 170
  increase in U.S. population of, 167
  view of illness and health, 169
North Idaho CASSP Rural System of Care, 27
Nuclear families, 43, 44
  as minorities, 44
  costs to wife in, 45
  gender arrangements of, 44
  maternal employment in, 45
  maternal unemployment in, 45
  men's satisfaction versus women's satisfaction in, 45

Omnibus Budget Reconciliation Act of 1981 (OBRA), 227
Organized systems of care, 10-11
  improvements in cost efficiency from, 11
  improvements in outcomes from, 11

Parental Coping Scale, 83
Parental leave policies, 55
Parental mandates, policy and, 97-98
Parental-relatives with children families, 43
Parental relinquishment, 5-6
Parental rights, 100
Parent-focused intervention, limitations of, 111-112
Parent-professional partnership, 97-98
  barriers to, 103-104
  client and family rights and, 99-100
  concepts supporting, 98-100
  needs-based framework for, 98-99
  transactionalism and, 99
  See also Parent-professional partnership models
Parent-professional partnership models, 100-103, 112
  consumer/partnership model, 101-102
  enablement model of helping, 102
  Families as Allies Project, 102
  family consultation model, 100-101
  reflection in action model, 100, 101
  technical rationality model, 100, 101, 103
  See also Parent-professional partnership
Parent training programs, NIMH-funded, 108-109
Poverty:
  children living in, 52
  ethnic minority status and, 52
  problems associated with, 52
  working-class status and, 52
Prevention of mental/emotional disorders:
  future of, 48
  identifying and reducing noxious agents, 47
  macro approach to, 48-49
  micro approach to, 48, 50-51
  preventing transmission of noxious agents to host, 47

public health methods of, 47-56
social justice approach, 49-51
strengthening resistance of host, 47
See also Primary prevention of mental/emotional disorders
Primary prevention of mental/emotional disorders:
amniocentesis and, 60
as worldwide problem, 58-59
breast feeding and, 60
child spacing and, 60
economic security and, 60
exploitation and, 57
family-focused programs and, 57-58
good day care and, 60
home-based programs and, 58
macro programs, 56-57, 58
micro programs, 56, 57, 58
model for, 56-58
organic factors and, 56-57
prenatal care and, 60
recommendations for, 59-60
self-esteem and, 57
social competence and, 57
stress and, 57
support networks and, 57-58

Referral information centers, 55
Research and Training Center on Family Support and Children's Mental Health, 102
Resiliency Model of Family Stress, 135
Revealed differences experiment (RDE), 156-157, 160
Rosalynn Carter Institute for Human Development, 50
Rural access problems, federal funding policies as contributors to, 227-229
Rural areas:
access to mental health services in, 224-226
attitudes toward mental health service use in, 226
differences in, 220
Rural children and youth:
adjustment of, 217
alchohol abuse among, 221, 223-224
cognitive deficit among, 221
health status of, 222
increasing substance abuse among, 223
lack of health insurance among, 219
lack of mental health specialists for, 225
lack of mental health support services for, 218
loneliness among, 224
mental health of, 217
mental health services coordination problems for, 227
mental health services delivery problems and, 218, 227
percentage of in United States, 217
poverty among, 221
prevalence of mental health problems among, 222-224
problems facing, 220-229
risk factors facing, 217, 220-222
suicide rates among, 224
use of Medicaid by, 219
use of Medicare by, 219
See also Rural mental health services for youth
Rurality, various definitions of, 220
Rural mental health services for youth:
complexities of studying, 219-220
examples of innovative, 229-231
future of, 232-233
Wisconsin Early Intervention (WEI) program, 230

Schools, need for improvements in, 55
Self-efficacy:
definition of, 109
theory, 109-110
Self-Report Family Inventory, 130
Single-parent families, 43
Social learning model of mental disorders:
family violence, 51-52
genetic/prenatal risks, 54
poverty, 51, 52
stress on children and families, 54-56
substance abuse, 51, 52-53
unmet health needs, 53-54
Social support:
as resource against stress, 136

risk of losing, 136
Society:
and preventing child emotional disorders, 41
and strengthening family, 41
Stigma:
of children's emotional disorders, 1
of mental health disorders in rural areas, 226
Substance Abuse and Mental Health Services Administration, 97
Substance abuse during pregnancy:
alcohol use, 52-53
narcotics use, 53
smoking, 53
See also Fetal alcohol syndrome
Support groups, 28, 88, 89
examples of, 89
meeting family needs, 89
See also specific support groups
Support networks:
as family resources, 85

U.S. Census Bureau, 167
definition of family, 118-119
U.S. Department of Agriculture, Economic Research Service of, 220
U.S. Department of Health and Human Services, 97, 224
U.S. Office of Management and Budget, 219
U.S. Public Health Service, 97
United Nations Children's Fund (UNICEF), 42
Urban Mental Health Initiative for Children, 11

Wisconsin Early Intervention (WEI) program, 230
"Wives' family sociology," 147

About the Editors

Craig Anne Heflinger, Ph.D., is a Senior Research Associate at the Center for Mental Health Policy in the Vanderbilt Institute for Public Policy Studies and a Research Assistant Professor in the Policy Development and Program Evaluation Program at Vanderbilt University. Since receiving her Ph.D. in 1989, she has been Project Manager and Implementation Study Coordinator of the Fort Bragg Evaluation Project, a large-scale evaluation of an innovative continuum of care for delivering mental health services to children and adolescents of military personnel. A clinical psychologist by training, her expertise and research interests lie in measuring family functioning and in the implementation of policies for children's services. She is Principal Investigator on a National Institute of Mental Health-funded grant to study the use of residential treatment for children with serious emotional disturbances. She has several research and consultation projects with Tennessee state agencies serving children.

Carol T. Nixon, M.A., is a Graduate Research Assistant at the Center for Mental Health Policy, Vanderbilt Institute for Public Policy Studies. She is finishing her doctoral studies as a trainee on the National Institute of Mental Health-funded Child and Adolescent Mental Health Services Research Training Grant. Her research interests include program and services evaluation and measurement, with her current efforts directed at the measurement of quality in mental health services for children and their families while addressing the perspectives of multiple stakeholders. Her additional research efforts include investigating the factors related to parental agreement on ratings of child behavior as well as issues of confidentiality and disclosure in research settings.

About the Contributors

George W. Albee is Professor Emeritus at the University of Vermont (Burlington) and Courtesy Professor at the Florida Mental Health Institute. After 16 years at Case Western Reserve University, he spent 25 years at the University of Vermont, where in 1975 he established the Vermont Conference on the Primary Prevention of Psychopathology. He is past President of the American Psychological Association and 1993 recipient of an American Psychological Foundation Gold Medal Award for Public Service. He directed the Task Force on Manpower for President Eisenhower's Joint Commission on Mental Illness and Health and the Task Panel on Prevention for President Carter's Commission on Mental Health. He and his colleagues have edited 17 volumes on primary prevention, based on annual conferences at the University of Vermont. He is a longtime advocate of a social-cultural model of mental disorders and finds causation in class exploitation, sexism, and racism.

Marva P. Benjamin, M.S.W., is Director of the Maternal and Child Health National Center for Cultural Competence at the Center for Child Health and Mental Health Policy, Georgetown University Child Development Center. She is also Assistant Professor at Georgetown University Medical Center and Director of the Cultural Competence Initiative at the National Technical Assistance Center for Children's Mental Health, Georgetown University Child Development Center. Previously, she was Executive Director of the Elahan Center for Mental Health and Family Living in Vancouver, Washington, and Demonstration Program Director of the DC Community Support

Systems Program, Mental Health Services Administration, in Washington, D.C. In addition to authoring or coauthoring numerous articles and chapters on cultural competence, she has written *Effective Collaboration as the Key to Understanding and Reducing Youth Violence* (in press). She is on the advisory councils of the National Child Day Care Association, the Transitioning Young Culturally Diverse Children With Disabilities Into the General Education Setting Project, and the Research and Training Center on Family Support and Children's Mental Health (Portland State University, Oregon). She has also served on the board of directors of the Federation of Families for Children's Mental Health.

Leonard Bickman, Ph.D., is Director of the Center for Mental Health Policy at Vanderbilt University and is Professor of Psychology, Psychiatry, and Public Policy. He is a nationally recognized leader in mental health services research on children and adolescents and has just completed the evaluation of the largest mental health services demonstration project ever conducted on children and adolescents. The evaluation of the Fort Bragg demonstration was funded by both the U.S. Army and the National Institute of Mental Health (NIMH) to study the effects of a full continuum of care provided by a civilian clinic on military dependents. NIMH is also funding an additional 3-year study of 800 participants. He is collaborating with state and local officials in Ohio in a multiyear randomized experiment that focuses on an innovative mental health system for children and adolescents in the public sector. He is co-Principal Investigator on the recently funded national UNO-CCAP study (Use, Need, Outcomes, and Costs in Child and Adolescent Populations). This $45-million project involves a consortium of universities and survey organizations to conduct the first national household survey of children and adolescents to determine need and use of mental health services. His expertise in services research training was acknowledged by the award of the first training grant in child and adolescent mental health services research. He also coedited the first monograph on methodological issues in the evaluation of child and adolescent mental health services. His standing in this field has been recognized by Secretary of Health and Human Services Donna Shalala with his appointment as the only services researcher to the nation's highest advisory council on mental health and substance abuse services. He is President-Elect of the American Evaluation Association.

Bernard L. Bloom is Professor Emeritus in the Department of Psychology at the University of Colorado. Prior to his arrival there in 1965, he served on the staff of the National Institute of Mental Health (1962-1965), was Director of Psychological Training and Research at the Hawaii State Hospital (1956-1961), and was on the staff of the Veterans Administration Outpatient Clinic in Boston (1952-1956). He received his Ph.D. from the University of Connecticut in 1952 and an M.S. in Hygiene from Harvard School of Public Health in 1962. His early research was in the field of psychological assessment. Since 1962, his work has been related to community psychology. He has published in the field of psychiatric epidemiology and preventive intervention and since 1980 has been active in the field of planned short-term psychotherapy. One aspect of that work explores the use of computers for purposes of assessment and intervention. His chapter in this volume represents a specific component of that interest.

Silvia Sara Canetto, Ph.D., is Assistant Professor of Psychology at Colorado State University. She has doctoral degrees from the University of Padova, Italy, and Northwestern University Medical School, Chicago, and a master's degree from the Hebrew University of Jerusalem. Her major research interests include gender, family, adult development and aging, and suicidal behaviors. She edited (with David Lester) *Women and Suicidal Behavior* (1995). She serves on the editorial boards of *Suicide and Life-Threatening Behavior, Omega,* and *Death Studies.* She is Director of the Research Division of the American Association of Suicidology and a member of the American Psychological Association, the National Council on Family Relations, the Gerontological Society of America, the Association of Women in Psychology, and the International Council of Psychologists.

Carolyn E. Cutrona, Ph.D., is Professor of Psychology at Iowa State University in Ames, where she recently moved after 12 years at the University of Iowa. She splits her time between the Department of Psychology and the Center for Family Research in Rural Mental Health. She received her Ph.D. in clinical psychology at UCLA in 1981. Her interests are in the areas of social support and depression. She has conducted research on the protective effects of social support in a variety of stressed populations, including pregnant adolescents, caregivers of Alzheimer's patients, and spouses of cancer patients. She has published a number of papers and chapters on determinants of perceived social support, using a range of methods (daily diary, observation, and informant reports). With Julie Suhr, she has developed an observational method for assessing social support behaviors in dyadic interactions. Her most recent work focuses on social support in the context of marriage, on which she is writing a book. She is a previous Associate Editor for the *Journal of Personality and Social Psychology.*

Barbara J. Friesen, Ph.D., is Director of the Research and Training Center on Family Support and Children's Mental Health and is Professor in the Graduate School of Social Work at Portland State University, Oregon. Her research and publications cover family perspectives on the service delivery system, family participation at the service delivery and policy levels, evaluation of system of care concepts and approaches, empowerment, and family-centered services.

Marcy B. J. Halvorson, M.S., is a doctoral candidate in counseling psychology at Iowa State University. She graduated from the University of Iowa with honors in psychology in 1990, where she conducted her honors thesis under the guidance of Carolyn Cutrona. During the first 3 years of her graduate career, she was involved in the Study of Mathematically Precocious Youth, working with Camilla P. Benbow and David Lubinski. After her projected doctoral graduation in 1997, she plans on pursuing an academic career in counseling psychology. She is currently investigating the coping processes employed by children with cancer and their families and is studying the similarities and differences in coping strategies between college students and their parents. Other research interests include how individuals cope with stressors and how family members of the chronic mentally ill cope with the illness.

Richard W. Hunter, M.S.W., is Coordinator of the Partnership for Children Graduate Education Program and is Assistant Professor in the Graduate School of Social Work, Portland State University,

Oregon. He is past Director of Training at the Research and Training Center on Family Support and Children's Mental Health at Portland State University, where he developed national training programs and curricula on issues of family support and parent-professional collaboration. He is the author of numerous training materials on children's mental health. His major research interests include children's mental health and family support services, family and professional collaboration processes, and child welfare training and education.

Sarah A. Lewis has been a Research Intern and an Assistant Program Development Specialist for the Multnomah County (Portland, Oregon) Office of Child and Adolescent Mental Health. She was the Project Manager for the Multicultural Initiative Project for the Research and Training Center on Family Support and Children's Mental Health at Portland State University. She received her B.S. in psychology with an emphasis on child development and is currently pursuing a graduate degree in psychology. She has held membership in the Portland Chapter of the National Council of Negro Women, the Alpha Kappa Alpha sorority, and the Portland Metropolitan Human Rights Commission. She has conducted antiracism and cultural diversity workshops among widely diverse audiences.

Diane T. Marsh, Ph.D., is Professor of Psychology at the University of Pittsburgh at Greensburg. She specializes in professional practice with people who have serious mental illness and with their families and is the author of numerous publications and five books, including *Families and Mental Illness: New Directions in Professional Practice* (1992), *Families and Mental Retardation: New Directions in Professional Practice* (1992), *New Directions in the Psychological Treatment of Serious Mental Illness* (1994), *Troubled Journey: If You Have a Sibling or Parent With Mental Illness* (forthcoming), and *Ethical and Legal Issues in Working With Families* (forthcoming). Active nationally as a psychologist, an advocate, and a workshop presenter, she has many years of experience as a psychotherapist and consultant.

James L. Mason is Director of Training for the Research and Training Center on Family Support and Children's Mental Health at Portland State University, Oregon. He is also Principal Investigator for the

Center's Increasing Multicultural Parent Involvement Project. A Ph.D. candidate in the Urban Studies Program at Portland State University, he is writing his dissertation on cultural competence characteristics in human service professionals. He has worked in administrative and direct service positions in programs serving culturally diverse children and youth throughout the country. In addition to serving on many state and local government task forces regarding the delivery of human and social services, he has conducted workshops and other training activities for the RTC for the last 9 years and is a nationally recognized expert in the assessment of cultural competence in agencies and organizations. He has served on the advisory board to the Oregon Children Services Division, on the Minority Resource Committee of the Georgetown University CASSP Technical Assistance Center, on the University of Wisconsin, Stoutt National Advisory Body on the Minority Over-Representation in Special Education Project, and on the board of the Oregon Black United Fund, in addition to serving as Vice President of the Oregon Chapter to Prevent Child Abuse.

Joan M. Patterson, Ph.D., is Associate Professor and Chair of the Maternal and Child Health Program in the School of Public Health, Director of Research for the Center for Children With Chronic Illness and Disability, and Adjunct Associate Professor of Family Social Science, all at the University of Minnesota. Her research focuses on children with special health care needs and their families. She is Co-Principal Investigator of Project Resilience, a longitudinal study of children with chronic conditions, which focuses on the condition, child, family, and community factors and processes associated with psychosocial competence in the children and in their families. She is also involved in intervention research for this population with the goal of identifying which families need which types of programs at which times to support their successful adaptation to living with chronic conditions. She has published extensively on family stress and adaptation theory and has developed questionnaires for assessing stress and coping concepts.

Ellen E. Pinderhughes, Ph.D., is Assistant Professor in the Department of Psychology and Human Development at Peabody College,

Vanderbilt University, Nashville, Tennessee, where she has interests in familial influences on the development of children at varying risk for dysfunctional behavioral outcomes. Her primary research focuses on child and family adjustment associated with older child adoption and foster care. She currently studies processes of family readjustment following placement of children older than 5 years. A secondary research interest concerns contextual influences on parenting beliefs and practices among families whose biological children are at risk for maladjustment.

Sheila A. Pires is a Partner in the Human Service Collaborative of Washington, D.C., a policy and consulting group specializing in child and family service systems. She has more than 20 years of experience in national, state, and local government and nonprofit organizations serving children and families at risk. She has held senior positions in the U.S. House of Representatives; the U.S. Department of Health, Education, and Welfare; and the White House during the Carter administration. Recently, she served on the Mental Health and Substance Abuse Working Group of President Clinton's Task Force on Health Care Reform. At the state and local levels, she served as Deputy Commissioner of Social Services for the District of Columbia and led a major reorganization of the city's child mental health system as Acting Child/Youth Services Administrator in the Commission on Mental Health Services. She has consulted with numerous states, counties, and cities and has authored several publications on systems change. She received her B.A. from Boston University and a master's in Public Administration from Harvard.

Daniel W. Russell, Ph.D., is Professor of Psychology and Statistics at Iowa State University. He also has an appointment at the Center for Family Research in Rural Mental Health at ISU. His research interests include the role of interpersonal relationships and social support in health and well-being among stressed populations; the influence of social networks on use of health services; and psychometrics, as evidenced by his role (with Carolyn Cutrona) in developing widely used measures such as the UCLA Loneliness Scale and the Social Provisions Scale. He has employed such techniques as confirmatory factor analysis and structural equation analysis with latent variables to pursue important conceptual issues in these areas of research, developing new methods of applying these multivariate techniques.

Beth A. Stroul, M.Ed., is Vice President and Cofounder of Management and Training Innovations, Inc., a consulting firm in McLean, Virginia. For more than 15 years, she has served as a consultant to the federal government on mental health policy. She has completed numerous research, analysis, and technical assistance projects related to service systems for children and adolescents with emotional disorders and their families, many through her affiliation with the National Technical Assistance Center for Children's Mental Health at Georgetown University. These projects include coauthoring a widely circulated monograph that presents a conceptual framework and philosophy for a system of care for this population titled *A System of Care for Children and Adolescents With Severe Emotional Disturbances.* She has authored monographs on home-based services, therapeutic foster care, and profiles of well-developed comprehensive systems of care. She also published a monograph reviewing the outcomes achieved by systems of care and is serving as coeditor of a book series titled Systems of Care for Children's Mental Health. In addition, she has served on the Mental Health and Substance Abuse Working Group of President Clinton's Task Force on Health Care Reform. Her current projects include a major focus on the implementation of managed care in behavioral health services and its effect on children's mental health services and systems of care.

Mary C. Telesford is a staff member of the Federation of Families for Children's Mental Health. Her primary responsibility is advising families and state and local officials on how best to work together in the Mental Health Initiative for Urban Children. This initiative, funded by the Annie E. Casey Foundation, is designed to facilitate system reform by promoting mental health and mental well-being for families and children of four urban areas located in Boston, Miami, Houston, and Richmond (Virginia). A graduate of Howard University, she has served as a faculty member at Georgetown University's Child and Adolescent Service System Program (CASSP) Center, reviewed state mental health block grants, and presented at research conferences on methods to get families involved in system reform. As a consultant or staff member, she has worked for organizations addressing the needs of specialized populations, including Melwood Horticultural Training Center, the Washington Lawyers' Committee for Civil Rights Under Law, Healthcare for the Homeless, the Developmental State Planning Council of the District of Columbia, I Have a Dream Foundation, and the Senior Citizens Counseling and Delivery Service.